The Ascent of Mount Hum

First published in 2008 by
Signal Books Limited
36 Minster Road
Oxford
OX4 1LY
www.signalbooks.co.uk

A catalogue record for this book is available from the British Library

ISBN 978-1-904955-48-1 Cloth

Production: Devdan Sen
Cover Design: Baseline Arts
Cover Images: Steven Haslemere; Pete Twitchett; Jon Dawson; Richard
Naisby; Liz Haslemere; istockphoto.com
Photographs: all photographs © Steven Haslemere, except p.46
© Frances Jones; p.108 © Jon Dawson; p.124 © Pete Twitchett; p.178
Caroline Saywell; p.208 © Craig Wear
Printed in India

The Ascent of Mount Hum

A Croatian Cricketing Odyssey

Steven Haslemere

To Eyebrows
My deepest thanks
for your input

Steve
x

Signal Books
Oxford

...ἀνέμισγε δὲ σίτῳ
φάρμακα λύγρ᾿, ἵνα πάγχυ λαθοίατο πατρίδος αἴης.
αὐτὰρ ἐπεὶ δῶκέν τε καὶ ἔκπιον, αὐτίκ᾿ ἔπειτα
ῥάβδῳ πεπληγυῖα κατὰ συφεοῖσιν ἐέργνυ.
οἱ δὲ συῶν μὲν ἔχον κεφαλὰς φωνήν τε τρίχας τε
καὶ δέμας, αὐτὰρ νοῦς ἦν ἔμπεδος, ὡς τὸ πάρος περ.

Homer, *The Odyssey*. Book X, ll 235–240

"The history book on the shelf
Is always repeating itself."
Abba, *Waterloo*

Contents

For "the old man", with love and gratitude

Prologue
The Rokis

The island's high central plain, which nestled between the ridges of the hills.

"Arsehole!"

Terry Kavanagh emerged unsteadily from a dense thicket hot, sweaty and pricked by thorns and continued down the steep hillside. The curse he had just muttered was in no way directed at the owner of the garden into which he had inadvertently stumbled, but simply at his own poor choice of short cuts. The old woman looked up at the ruddy-faced Englishman from the bed where she was busy gathering vegetables. Terry offered a brisk "Good afternoon!" by way of apology and was quickly on his way, not waiting long enough to find out if he had been understood.

His ill-chosen route had, nevertheless, offered him a stunning panorama of the broad harbour, whose deep blue waters shimmered in the sunlight and which was surrounded by steep hills of broken down terracing and thick scrub. As he penetrated deeper into the town, the monotonous drone of the work going on to rebuild the ferry dock grew louder. In short time he descended narrow stone steps between imposing Venetian-era townhouses and arrived at his destination, the town's main hotel, the Tamaris. At least, he thought, his general sense of direction had not let him down.

Soon he had booked a room for the night, and was sitting at an outside table on the town's bustling harbour front, enjoying a Rothmans, and waiting for the sun to disappear behind the hills across the bay. Now in his mid-sixties and grown rather stout, he shifted heavily in his seat as the waiter brought him a bottle of beer before settling back to idly watch the people coming and going. Beyond the yachts ranged along the quay-side, directly opposite him, was a small peninsula called Prirovo on which stood a Franciscan priory and church. The bell tower chimed six o'clock.

He flicked through his guidebook to Croatia, searching again for a passage which, when he first came across it, had tantalised: "Vis spent a brief period of time during the early 19th century under the British, who saw it as an ideal base from which to confront Napoleon's Adriatic hold, and also introduced the game of cricket, a peculiarity which has remained until this day."[i]

Terry had known of the island's historical association with the British for a number of years: the Royal Navy had fought one of the last major naval battles of the Napoleonic Wars off Vis' – then known as Lissa – north coast. The revelation that cricket had once been played on the island had, by contrast, been news to him. Having more than a passing interest in the game, he had begun to doubt what he read. He well knew that cricket is played on Corfu, indeed had himself played there some twenty years earlier for a Commonwealth XI against the only cricket club in the Ionian Sea. But on Vis? In Croatia, or communist Yugoslavia as it once had been? How could that be on an island closed to outsiders for over forty years? So vague and unresolved had the entry in the guidebook been that it appeared almost an afterthought, and although he had arrived on Vis the day before with other priorities uppermost in his mind he had managed, through a huge slice of good fortune, to solve the mystery quite satisfactorily.

▲

The day before, he had taken an afternoon ferry from Split. Even for early May, the temperature had been comfortably warm, the day lucid in that Mediterranean way. Vis lay thirty miles south-west of Split in the Adriatic Sea, and the ferry would navigate between some of southern Dalmatia's more picturesque islands before reaching its destination two and a half hours later. Terry felt his sense of anticipation rising. He had long held a desire to go to Vis and, at long last, was about to realise it.

The last time he had been in this part of the world was nearly forty years before in the 1960s, when Croatia was one part of the Socialist Federal Republic of Yugoslavia. He had been working in odd jobs in Scandinavia since the previous year and was on a trip through central Europe with three friends. In Split, Terry found out that passage to Vis was impossible on the grounds that the island was a base of the Yugoslav military, open only to close relatives of its inhabitants and off limits to foreigners. A measure of tourism had been allowed on the Dalmatian coast as part of a programme of economic liberalisation instigated by President Tito, but such largesse did not extend to foreigners taking snapshots of sensitive military installations. Terry understood, grudgingly. He had other places to visit.

Along with his three friends he was on his way overland to India. They were consciously following in the footsteps of Tim Slessor and colleagues of the Oxford & Cambridge Far Eastern Expedition,[ii] who had driven all the way from Britain to Singapore in seven months in 1955. Like that earlier Combined Universities' venture, the McNastie World Tour (named after the Horace Silver classic *Filthy McNasty*, and an obscure character from the Hancock's Half Hour radio programme) undertaken by Terry and company had been inspired by notions of adventure and cultural exchange, but unlike the Oxbridge boys who, thanks to some cannily won sponsorship, travelled in two well-equipped Land Rovers, the McNastie party had made the trip by the somewhat more limited means of a single 1959 Volkswagen Combi. Amazingly, after having travelled more than 4,000 miles over some of the roughest terrain on Earth, the VW was still working by the time they reached Delhi, and managed to make it as far as Kathmandu. There they had managed to sell it on (at over 100 per cent profit) to an eager citizen scant minutes before its engine gave up the ghost, prompting angry scenes and a hasty retreat by Terry and the others.

The Vis ferry started its slow progress out of the harbour, dwarfing the yachts and sailing boats that crowded the small marina nearby. Seen from the stern of the boat, Split sat hugging the coast under the gaze of forbidding mountains, a ridge of craggy rock broken by scrub that marked the beginnings of the interior. As the city receded, he tired of the view and wandered round to the port side. Presently the boat threaded its way through the narrow strait between Šolta and Brač, islands of gently sloping wooden hills with a ribbon of rocky beaches at the foreshore.

From there the boat had passed the western extremity of the island of Hvar before heading out into the Viški kanal, where its destination soon became visible, though Terry struggled to see it at first beyond the mass of the boat's bridge. As they neared, though, he got more of an idea of Vis' size and shape as it sat there squat and unlovely on the open sea. The remotest of Croatia's permanently inhabited islands, covering an area of some fifty square miles, it made for a marked contrast with the other, larger islands the boat had passed, their undulating hills replaced by a rugged, sea-girt rock covered in scrubby vegetation.

The ferry made for the inlet – guarded by an islet on which sat a lighthouse and ruined stone buildings – on the north of the island. The huge natural harbour ran for about a mile long and half a mile wide. The small town which hugged its parabola was shaded by stony hills on which lay strewn scree from the dilapidated terraces of abandoned vineyards. Small stone houses with terracotta roofs ringed the harbour-side. Below the level of the road, fishing boats were tied up against tiny jetties.

The boat did not penetrate deep into the harbour but turned to starboard to make landfall in a bay off the western shore, below a couple of hills atop of which were ruined fortifications. To the south he could see a Venetian church on a peninsula jutting out into the bay. The boat had landed some way out of town. As he disembarked he was told by a steward that the landing stage was only temporary while the original ferry dock in the main part of town was being dredged and rebuilt. Though half a mile away, the noise from the reconstruction was clearly audible. A small, old-fashioned looking bus was parked nearby to take the ferry passengers into town before travelling on to the other side of the island. On a whim Terry decided to reverse his original plan and first visit the town of Komiža, on the west coast.

The bus trundled up a small hill past an imposing, but ugly, concrete hotel from the 1960s, and into Vis town. A large number of yachts were moored up, a sign that a certain well-heeled type of tourism was flourishing on the island. As the bus reached the centre of the port and a triangular area of parkland lined with palm trees, it turned right and chugged up a steep incline out of town to the south. Presently it made a short descent to a crossroads beyond a run-down industrial site before beginning a steady climb across the top of the island. After nearly five miles of vineyards – some worked, others not – isolated farmhouses and the occasional ruined church, the bus turned a corner between two substantial peaks to reveal the town of Komiža below.

The bus descended to sea level via a number of hairpin turns and came to rest not far from the town's main square. Dominating the town was another large church, and the hillsides were again studded with abandoned terraces. Komiža sat in an impressive natural harbour four times the width of Vis town's and bound by two horns of headland. The harbour arced from north to south, its graceful sweep broken only by the addition of a long concrete breakwater. Terry took a walk along it. Beyond, some five miles distant to the south-west, he could make out the island of Biševo, about whose wondrous blue grotto he had heard so much.

Halfway along the mole he stopped to look at a stone plaque mounted on the inner wall. It was written in both Croatian and English: "IN MEMORY OF THE BRITISH SEAMEN WHO SAILED FROM THIS HARBOUR IN SUPPORT OF THE LIBERATING FORCES AND WHOSE RESTING PLACE IS THE SEA." Above the inscription was the seal of the British Veterans' Association, and below it the dates

1943-1945. He knew of the British wartime association with the island, when it was an Allied base supporting Tito's *Partižani* movement, and was glad to see the contribution of the British armed forces still recognised.

Walking back into town, which seemed much smaller and more compact than Vis, he noticed more yachts ranged along the mole and fishermen attending their boats and mending nets. Komiža, it was clear, was still a working fishing town.

He settled at a table outside a bar called Speedy. Given the pace of life he was witnessing, it seemed optimistic to expect speedy service, so he sat and watched the comings and goings with amused detachment. It seemed a quiet sort of place. Then, just after five o'clock, everything began to change. The pace quickened as the harbour-side started to fill with people stopping by to chat and pass the time. This would be the Dalmatian equivalent of the Italian *passeggiata,* or perhaps it was the more universal currency of the after-work drink, with which he was all too familiar. He watched as young men and women larked and flirted and waited for the sun to go down. He had other plans, chiefly finding a bed for the night.

A tourist bureau was close to the bus stop, and he thought he would enquire there. The dark-haired woman behind the counter had a relaxed air, but was efficient enough in securing him an en suite first-floor double room in a nearby apartment – impressive view of the whole harbour included – at a very reasonable rate.

Leaving the young of Komiža to their fun, Terry made his way from the main square through some narrow alleyways to a fish restaurant called Bako that overlooked the bay. Seated in the shade of a robust vine, he soon found himself choosing a lobster from an aquarium tank inside the restaurant before tucking into some local squid, washed down with a glass of the local white wine, the Vugava. The wines of the island had a good reputation, viniculture having been practised on the island – which the ancient Greeks called Issa – for thousands of years, and this one did not disappoint. It was full and rich with a honeyed sweetness, closer to a dessert wine than anything else.

Deciding it was time to turn in for the evening, he left to watch the sunset from the balcony of his apartment. Out to sea he could see the last few boats returning from their fishing trips. Or were they boats coming back from an excursion to Biševo and the *modra špilja* or Blue Cave? He had wanted to go there, but the lady at the tourist bureau had informed him that the grotto is seen at its best either side of midday when the sun is in a certain position. Perhaps tomorrow, he thought, though the lady had told him the weather outlook was not too promising. Once the sun had dissipated itself into the vast expanse of the sea and he had written his diary entry for the day, he turned in for the night.

The following morning Terry awoke feeling well-slept and refreshed, but ravenous. Ordinarily never a huge eater first thing in the morning – he preferred a good lunch and an equally fortifying dinner – he took this as a sure sign that his body knew it was on holiday. There was a price to pay, however, for staying in an apartment – and that was the necessity of foraging for breakfast. However, he had no sooner stepped out of the door and walked a hundred yards than he found a small bakery nestled between a good-looking café and a grocer's shop. A few minutes later, and armed with fresh bread, *pršut* or prosciutto ham, cheese and a bottle of peach nectar he was sitting at an outdoor cafe table helping his breakfast down with a couple of strong *espressi*.

The forecast winds he had been warned about at the tourist bureau the day before had indeed arrived, so there would be no boat trips out to the Blue Cave today. This was a disappointment. For all its charm, Komiža was too quiet a place out of season, and with the Bako and other restaurants only open in the evenings, he felt it was time to move on and explore some more of the island.

He had first read about Vis' connection with the Allied war effort in Fitzroy Maclean's account of his part in military operations in the Western Desert and the Balkans.[iii] Towards the end of the Second World War British commandos had made sea-borne raids on the German-held mainland from Vis town and an airfield had been set up in the hinterland for refuelling Allied bombers on their sorties into the Yugoslav interior. There was also a cave halfway up the island's highest peak in which Tito had made his temporary headquarters in 1944. It would be worth, he thought, spending the morning discovering what remained of the island's wartime activity before moving on to Vis town.

The woman who had been so helpful the day before was again on duty behind the counter of the tourist bureau. Terry explained his interest. The woman listened, nodded, and told him that her son Antonio would drive him up to the cave in the bureau's minibus, for a nominal sum. This seemed generous. Antonio told Terry that there wasn't that much to see at the cave, so first drove him up to the former Benedictine monastery and church of St Nicholas – the large church he had seen on arriving in Komiža – above the town. Although of little interest to him, he quickly realised it was a "must see" for any tourist, and thus a "must show" for any tour guide. Set on the hill of Muster above the town to the south-east, the monastery's bell tower dominated the surrounding landscape, rising up above the wine terraces. Croatia had been Christianised from the islands inwards, starting at Biševo and Palagruža in the 9th century. The Benedictines had built their abbey in the 16th century by which time the Dalmatian coast and islands had become a part of the Venetian Republic. Terry bit his tongue out of politeness while Antonio did his tour-guide thing.

Up from the monastery was the "old" coastal road to Vis town that rose nearly a thousand feet before dropping through the villages of Podhumlje and Podšpilje, a loose aggregation of farmhouses in the south of the island, where the wine growers lived and worked. At Podšpilje the minibus took a left turn towards the village of Borovik, climbed a further 300 feet and stopped by a sharp bend. They got out and walked up a flight of stone steps on the side of Mount Hum, the island's highest point. About halfway up was the cave.

Antonio had been right: there was little to see. The cave, still known as *Titova špilja* (Tito's Cave), was boarded up and surrounded by barbed wire. Terry asked why the islanders didn't do more to exploit the late marshal's presence on the island. Wouldn't some bright spark be interested in opening the site up as a commercial proposition? Antonio didn't have an answer, but Terry found that intriguing in itself. Were memories of communism still too recent? He thought twice about bombarding Antonio with too many questions.

They walked back down to the minibus. Antonio asked if there was anything else that Terry would like to see. He answered that he wouldn't mind seeing what was left of the Second World War airfield. This suited Antonio well as the site was farther along the road, in Plisko Polje. As they drove along they soon dropped into the island's high central plain, which nestled between the ridges of the hills. Vineyards stretched from east to west.

Antonio stopped the minibus outside a restaurant and winery and indicated that the airfield was on the owner's land. Terry thanked Antonio for his chauffeuring, paid him the agreed sum and a gratuity, and said goodbye. Hauling his travel bag over his shoulder he made his way down a concrete ramp into a small field, past a sign that indicated the restaurant was called Konoba Roki's, and carried on towards a modest farmhouse with shuttered windows, set in luscious vineyards.

There was movement from one of the farmhouse's small outbuildings. A man not many years Terry's junior was pottering about inside. Close by were outdoor tables and chairs, and in a corner a large heap of dried out vines. Several cats played skittishly around the outbuildings and fences. The man was tall, well-built and tanned. A crop of silver hair sat atop his head, his face was fringed with a short white beard. He was dressed for work in the hot midday: an open collared shirt and jeans. Terry caught his attention.

"Mister Roki?" he asked. The silver-haired gentleman acknowledged him in perfect English, in an accent that sounded familiar. Terry explained his purpose.

"I've been told that the airfield is on your land." The man smiled a smile that suggested Terry was not the first to come this way and make the same enquiry.

"Come up to the house," he said in an accent with an Australian twang. As they walked up to the farmhouse the man introduced himself as Niko. They went into the courtyard, which also doubled as the outdoor dining area of the restaurant. Niko called to his wife, Valerie, and further introductions were made.

"We were just about to have some lunch. Would you join us?" Valerie asked. Terry said he would be delighted, and soon the three of them were ensconced under a leafy vine that formed a natural canopy over the courtyard, sharing a farmhouse stew and a bottle of his hosts' homemade wine, and swapping stories.

Valerie was, it turned out, born in Hackney, in East London. Her father was from Islington, her mother from Malta. Nik, as she referred to her husband, was born on the island, though they met each other in Perth, Australia, where both were living at the time.

Niko asked about Terry's interest in the airfields. Had he served in the Royal Air Force himself? He had, in the late 1950s, as part of National Service. Niko was just old enough to remember the British airmen on the island, and the bombers taking off and landing nearby, during the war. The airfield Terry wanted to see was visible from the entrance to the property. After lunch they could take a little walk and have a look at it. This suited Terry well.

After the war ended and the island had become a Yugoslav naval base, Niko left for Australia, where there was demand for workers. The island suffered in the time it was closed. The population fell as people took their chance of a better life elsewhere. A number of inhabitants made their escape illicitly, by boat across to southern Italy. Later, after the restrictions were relaxed, entire families upped and left for the United States, Canada and Australia. The staple industries of the island, such as wine growing, suffered greatly.

Had Terry ever been to Australia? He lit a Rothmans and told them the story of what happened after he and his three friends had left India. From Delhi they went on through Burma, then Thailand and on to Singapore.

"I was staying in a youth hostel in Bangkok. I was just about to take to my bed for the night, when I heard this voice from a corner of the room: 'Not only is the place full of Nips, we have the Hun as well!' My hair was a lot fairer than it is now, and this bloke had mistaken me for a Kraut.

"'Bloody hell! A Londoner!' he said, when he found out where I was from. The man's name was Ted Bates, and we got on like a house on fire. I told him my plans and we agreed to meet at the Sydney Cricket Ground during the third test in 1966. What a game that was! Boycott and Bob Barber put on over 200 for the first wicket, Edrich got a century as well. Australia were all out for 221 in the first innings.

"When I met Ted on The Hill, the Aussies had one wicket left to avoid an innings defeat. I went to get some drinks. When I got there the barman had a mouth on him like a steel trap. I said: 'Two beers, please.' Silence, so I decided to have a little fun. 'What do you think of the game then, Aussie?' Quick as a flash he said: 'I think if you put us in again you'd still beat us by an innings. Now take your beers and fuck off!'"

Terry found the Rokis convivial company. They listened with interest as he told them about his other travels, which included some time in Bali, running a pub on the Falkland Islands and a number of years as a journalist in Athens. At some point the conversation steered back to the subject of cricket. Though Niko had watched the game when he and Valerie moved to Melbourne, he himself had not played it since he was a schoolboy. They returned to Yugoslavia in the early 1970s when their son Oliver was four years old. At first they lived in Split but soon moved back to take over the farmhouse at Plisko Polje, which had been in the family since the time of Niko's great-grandfather.

"Did you know," asked Valerie, "that cricket was played on this island?"

"So it said in my guidebook," said Terry. "What's the story?"

Valerie spoke at length of a neighbour of the Rokis who worked in the town museum in Vis and had very recently shown them a copy of a biography of a 19th-century Royal Navy captain stationed on the island during the Napoleonic Wars. It contained a reference, taken from a letter home to his family in England, to the British seamen playing cricket by the harbour to pass the time between engagements with the French. The Rokis' neighbour, though not exactly familiar with the game, knew enough to think that they would be interested in its small place in the island's history. They were. Terry's curiosity was aroused:

"In my guidebook it suggests that cricket is still alive on the island. Is that true?"

"Ah, that may have been down to me," Niko sighed. "A few months ago a young lady came to the restaurant. She was writing a travel book on Croatia and as we talked about the British and the cricket I let slip that we were thinking of starting up a cricket club here. She must have thought it interesting enough to put in the book."

"And are you," Terry asked, "starting up a cricket club?"

"You really need to speak to Oliver," Niko replied, "but I don't know when he's due back. You might have to wait."

It was gone four o'clock by the time Terry left the Rokis' farmhouse. Mellowed by the excellent wine, he enjoyed a lift in the back of a flatbed truck drawn by tractor as one of the Rokis' employees, a young man with a friendly smile by the name of Stanko, drove him the few miles from the village and on to the road that snaked around the hills above Vis town. Halfway around the steep, winding road Terry told Stanko he did not mind getting out and finding his own way.

"Are you sure?" Stanko asked. It was no problem to take Terry all the way into town. Terry was adamant that he did not want to put Stanko to any trouble, so the two parted company. Terry said goodbye and walked down a path that went off at an angle to the main road. The route into town was somewhat circuitous. The sun beat down quite fiercely, and three-quarters along the way he decided to take the quickest available way down and shortcut across fields and then somebody's back garden.

▲

The bell tower chimed six o'clock. Outside the Tamaris, Terry lit another Rothmans and put away his guidebook. It was behind the Franciscan priory on the Prirovo peninsula, Valerie had told him, that the British had played their cricket games in the early 19th century. Terry wondered what a spectacle that would have made to the islanders at the time. Did any of them try to learn the game?

He decided to go for a walk and find something to eat. Turning right from the Tamaris he followed the road north until it rose to disappear behind harbour-front houses on the way to the suburb of Kut. After a few minutes' walk the road reappeared twenty feet above the bay, and he passed a small stone church and a large defensive battery set in expansive grounds with huge palms, where a pair of ancient cannon kept ominous watch over the bay. Farther along it he found a high-walled garden with a wooden sign that indicated a restaurant called the Villa Kaliopa.

Terry entered the garden and saw tables and chairs set out among bamboos, palms, pines and statuary, all decoratively connected by a series of stone paths. The setting was romantic, but there were no other diners and the evening air was beginning to chill so he opted for a table indoors, up half a dozen steps at the top of the garden. The interior was dimly lit. Huge plate-glass windows looked onto the garden itself. The waiter, who dressed casually, was in attendance in a flash, his manner courteous and efficient.

Terry asked for the menu. The waiter told him he wouldn't need one. This set alarm bells ringing, but Terry soon realised he was actually talking to the restaurant's owner:

"All I need to know is if you want meat or fish for the main course."

Terry replied that he would prefer fish but didn't want a huge meal. The owner then proceeded to reel off a number of starters that were available: fish soup, cheese and *pršut*, monkfish carpaccio. It was all a bit too much to take in. At the owner's suggestion Terry settled on some fresh prawns prepared in a special sauce.

"If you don't like it then you don't have to pay," the owner assured him. Terry was already warming to the restaurant and its charismatic owner with the prominent nose, and deep set, sad-looking eyes. He was absolutely right about the prawns and their special sauce. They were succulent, the sauce rich, and delicately spicy with an underlying hint of curry. A half carafe of chilled Vugava was an admirable balance to the prawns. Terry complimented the owner on a superb meal and invited him to join him at table.

Goran Pečarević, as he introduced himself, did so and asked Terry what brought him to Vis on his own. Terry relayed his long-time interest in the island, and mentioned his visit to the Rokis.

"Oliver is a good friend of mine. He runs a good restaurant, works hard." They chatted for an hour or more. Goran was forthright on what he saw as the island's future, after a long period of neglect. A benefit – one of the few – of the island being closed for so long was that his generation now had an opportunity to develop a kind of tourism in harmony with the island's traditions. Of course they had fallen behind the other nearby islands in the intervening years. Hvar, Brač, and Korčula had all prospered while Vis had been held back, but they didn't want an island overrun by tourists, like some kind of Adriatic Majorca. Besides, Goran continued, the town's infrastructure couldn't handle it in its present state. New roads and sewers cost money, and Croatia was not a rich country. The yachts and sailboats brought regular money in, and they had been coming here since the end of the 19th century, and would continue to do so. Only the concrete Hotel Issa across the bay catered for the package-holiday trade, and that was minimal. Here was, Goran said, the perfect chance to do things on their own terms.

Over a glass of herb-flavoured brandy Terry listened, fascinated and impressed by Goran's vision. He was clearly something of an entrepreneur. The Villa Kaliopa was considered to be in the top ten restaurants in Croatia, and Goran was also renovating a Venetian merchant's house just around the corner and turning it into a bar. The islanders of his, and Oliver Roki's, generation were the ones making things happen. Terry concluded that Goran, at the very least, didn't want for energy. Presently he decided it was time to go back to the hotel, so Goran presented the bill. For a restaurant with such a high reputation and food of such quality, it was surprisingly moderate in price. As he walked back through the darkened streets of Kut, Terry reflected that he had enjoyed himself so much that he didn't care what the meal cost.

The drilling of the ferry dock appeared to go on round the clock, so there was little need for an alarm call the following morning. Terry took a breakfast of espresso and a Rothmans on the terrace of the Tamaris before heading off to explore more of Kut.

His guidebook told him the island's main museum was not far away, behind the grounds of the battery he had passed the previous evening. It being Sunday, though, the museum was shut. He would have liked to see the prize exhibit, a 3rd-century BCE bust of the Greek goddess Artemis – unfortunately a copy, the real one being safely locked away in a vault somewhere.

He strolled on past the Villa Kaliopa and into the main square of Kut, where builders were hard at work on Goran's new bar. Everywhere he went in the neighbourhood he saw people unloading stone or fixing new roof tiles, working on their houses to get everything ready for the holiday season. Beyond the square, to the north, the road rejoined the harbour-side and, once past the last houses, dwindled into nothing more than a dirt track leading to a peninsula by the harbour mouth. It was now quiet. The scent of orange blossom filled the air. Small lizards scurried across his path looking for darkened corners. On the peninsula, which boasted an unmatched prospect of the town, stood a grand detached residence, once the mansion of a wealthy merchant family from Hvar but now, criminally it seemed, unoccupied.

Farther on through some trees, beyond a small chapel, lay a rectangular walled cemetery. The graves were those of British servicemen from either the Napoleonic wars or the Second World War. Terry paid his respects at a memorial plaque hung on one of the walls. Written in both English and Croatian, it bore the words: "IN MEMORY OF THE BRITISH FORCES WHO FROM THIS ISLAND OF VIS GAVE THEIR LIVES IN COMRADESHIP, SUPPORTING TITO's ARMY OF LIBERATION, 1943-1945. FROM BRITISH WAR VETERANS 6 SEPTEMBER 1999."

The cemetery was close to the northern shore of the island where Terry, discovering a small, secluded bay and a shingle beach, decided on an impromptu dip in the clear waters. Walking back into Kut he passed some high-walled, vine-covered arbours. Reached from the road by steep stone steps, they concealed some attractive looking two- and three-storey apartment houses. Farther on, off the main square and not far from Goran's restaurant, he discovered another garden restaurant, smaller and in less grand a setting than the Kaliopa, but still charming enough.

He sat outside, shaded by lemon and lime trees, and toyed with a superb squid risotto. Yet again the owner–proprietor was on duty and was only too eager to strike up a conversation with his guest. Zoran Brajčić was of medium height and brawny. He was born on the island but had spent forty years away in Zagreb, and had been drawn back through homesickness and a desire to help build the island up again. The island had only been re-opened to foreign tourists since 1988 but already there were warning signs of undesirable change. Property on the island was becoming sought after by foreign investors looking for second homes, and some islanders were already selling out. A lot of people's incomes were dependent on letting their apartments out to visitors during the summer months. If more of that property fell into foreign hands there was a danger of the island losing its identity. It was a question of balance, and Zoran hoped there was enough island to keep everyone happy.

Terry pondered this as he walked back to the Tamaris for gin and tonics on the terrace. The next day he would be leaving. The islanders he had met were proud people, and he had been struck by a sense of them trying to make up for lost time. From his brief glimpse they seemed determined to try to shape the future of this small island community in a way that few people anywhere bother to any more. They lived in a magical place that in some ways belonged to another time, and whose forty years of near-isolation had bred something like a sense of injustice. Their aversion to exploitation by outsiders struck a chord and appealed to Terry's sense of fair play, though looking at it realistically he knew they had a fight on their hands to preserve what they had. Perhaps he could help them in some way?

He recalled the day before at the Rokis' farmhouse when, after lunch had been cleared away, Niko's son had turned up and, over another glass of wine, they had talked about cricket. Oliver was in his early thirties, tall and well-built like his father, olive-skinned, with a thick mop of dark curls on his head and a beard trimmed in a straight line across his chin. He spoke rapidly and was quick-witted. He had never played cricket in his life, but that didn't seem to bother him. He talked enthusiastically, and Terry found the enthusiasm infectious.

"We have a climate here that's good for ten months out of twelve," Oliver said. "We could get English cricket teams coming to play in the winter. That would really give business a boost in the low season." Terry smiled at the fact that Oliver had, with entrepreneurial zeal, immediately leapt on the economic benefits before considering the practicalities.

"But do you think you could raise a team on the island?" Terry asked.

"For sure, why not?" Oliver replied, and Terry found it hard to disbelieve him. They drained their glasses. It was time to have a look at the airfield. The three of them – Terry, Oliver and Niko – wandered down past the outbuildings to the edge of the vineyards. Niko pointed out how flat the ground was there.

"They pulled up some of the best vineyards and olive trees on the island and levelled the earth. Look, you can still see the posts that marked the edge of the runway."

Terry looked, and saw a series of twenty-feet high poles set at intervals of about fifty yards on either side of the vineyard. They were painted with alternating red and white stripes, not unlike a traditional barber's pole. At the airfield's – or vineyard's – nearest edge was a rectangular area of land not under cultivation, overgrown with tall grass.

"It has potential, don't you think?" Niko asked.

Terry agreed. He could see what Niko was driving at. The land was flat enough and the area could be made into something with a bit of work.

"It would take a lot of effort," Niko continued, "And I'd have to talk to some of the other villagers about the land. Who knows? Given time, then why not a pavilion as well?"

It was an ambitious plan, Terry told them, to convert this end of the vineyard into a fully functioning cricket pitch, but the ambition was ad mirable.

"Do you think it's too small to play on?" Oliver asked. Although it was difficult to tell the exact dimensions, Terry was upbeat:

"Certainly not. It looks a perfect size."

"Of course, if we get a team together there's the problem of who we would play," Oliver said. Terry's eyes twinkled.

"My pub in Cambridge has a cricket team."

It was quickly settled. Next year. July and August were high season, so some time either before or after that would be ideal. Even if the pitch at Plisko Polje was not ready in time they would find a place to play on the island come what may, Oliver was certain. They shook hands on it and Niko, smiling, said: "I don't think you'll have a problem coming over and getting a game."

NOTES:

i   Foster, Jane. *Croatia Handbook*. Bath, Footprint Handbooks, 2001, p 233
ii   Slessor, Tim, *First Overland. The Story of the Oxford and Cambridge Far Eastern Exhibition*. London, The Companion Book Club, 1957. Reprinted in 2005 by Signal Books, Oxford
iii Maclean, Fitzroy. *Eastern Approaches*. London, Jonathan Cape, 1949

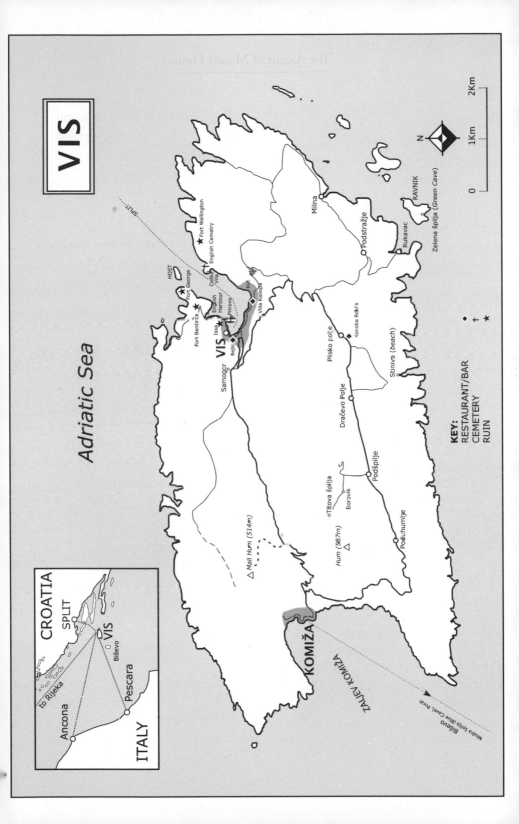

VIS

Adriatic Sea

CROATIA
SPLIT
to Rijeka
VIS
Biševo
Ancona
Pescara
ITALY

SPLIT

HOST

Fort Wellington
English Cemetery
Fort George
Češko Vila
Fort Bentinck
English Harbour
Issa
Prirovo
Kut
Villa Kaliopa
VIS
Beglu
Samogr

Mali Hum (514m)

Titova špilja
Borovik
Hum (587m)

Plisko polje
Koniba Raki's
Dračevo Polje
Podšpilje
Poduhumlje
Stiniva (beach)

Milna
Podstražje
Rukavac
RAVNIK
Zelena špilja (Green Cave)

KOMIŽA
ZALJEV KOMIŽA
Biševo
Modra špilja (Blue Cave), Porat

KEY:
RESTAURANT/BAR
CEMETERY
RUIN

N

0   1Km   2Km

1

The Rad

The weight of accumulated bric-a-brac, affording the solitary drinker many a distraction.

King Street in Cambridge, previously known as Walls Lane by virtue of its position between the boundaries of Christ's and Sidney Sussex Colleges, runs east towards Four Lamps roundabout and the wide expanse of Midsummer Common and marked, until the development of a modern shopping centre in the formerly residential Kite area, the north-eastern extent of the city centre. Until the early 1970s, when those two colleges and nearby Jesus College developed huge new residential blocks and completely changed the look of the street, its 1,000-feet stretch was home to a mixture of residential dwellings, almshouses and artisans' workplaces, where watchmakers, furnishers, confectioners, grocers, fishmongers, coffee merchants and dressmakers rubbed shoulders and plied their trades in service to the colleges and their undergraduates.

The street was also home to a number of pubs. On the south side of the street, from west to east these were named – at various times between the late-19th until the middle of the 20th century – the Cambridge Arms, the Earl Grey, Champion of the Thames, the Horse and Groom, and on the north side the Glazier's Arms, Two Swans, the Boot, the Carpenter's Arms, the Harp Tavern, the Sebastopol and the Garrick.

To the present-day visitor to Cambridge, King Street boasts a collection of independent restaurants, coffee shops, hairdressers and chic boutiques, and though the nature of these businesses reflects a degree of gentrification and the rise in prosperity of the modern city, the character of the street, with its mixture of the residential and the commercial, still thrives. Its reputation for entrepreneurial small business flair and the neighbourliness of its inhabitants gives it something of the air of a village high street, unusual given its proximity to the city centre.

In the wider world the street is known, anecdotally at least, for the King Street Run. This has been celebrated at various times over the last fifty years as an initiation into manhood, a glorified pub crawl, or a bit of both depending on one's age and point of view. The journalist and polemicist Christopher Hitchens recalled an adolescence of occasional truancy in Cambridge in a review of a pair of books about smoking and drinking: "Round a corner or two in Petty Cury was King Street, where stood a rank of pubs. A rite of passage in those days was to inhale a pint of suds in each within the space of an hour… without puking, or without puking until the end… and it was an induction no less potent than the heated gropings in the Arts Cinema that was ready to hand." [i]

3

It is pretty much a given that any concentration of alehouses in a small area is likely to act as a temptation to recklessness, and so it has certainly proved down the years, but what is less well known outside of the street itself is that the King Street Run started out as a physiological experiment, of sorts.

One evening in Michaelmas term of 1955 in the now defunct Criterion bar in Market Passage a discussion took place between three undergraduates of St John's College, all either Royal Navy or Royal Marines, and a group of medical students of unknown college affiliation. Over a few ales a lively scientific enquiry began about the drinking capacity of the human male. One of the medical students asserted with authority that the male bladder could hold no more than four pints before it would need emptying. The John's boys disagreed in principle and the group agreed to settle the argument empirically by having a drink in every pub on King Street.

On an appointed evening the students from St John's met in the Criterion before starting their experiment at the eastern end of the street. They tasted their first pint in the Duke of Cambridge in Short Street, then made their way westwards via the six existing pubs in King Street, before ending up at the Prince of Wales in Hobson Street. For some reason the medical students failed to show, which was a shame because the John's boys happened to pick up a friend (again with naval connections) who had already been on his second or third pint in the Criterion bar and invited him to join them. This intrepid toper managed a further ten pints before he needed to relieve himself – settling the argument to one party's satisfaction at least – and a good night out was had by all. Better still, the evening gave birth to what soon became a Cambridge University institution.

The King Street Pint to Pint Club, as it was soon formally constituted, had a basic objective that was pretty much as Hitchens describes it: to take a pint of ale in seven of the street's pubs before returning for an eighth in the pub you started in. The club set a number of rules to be observed for the duration of drinking, among them the award of a penalty pint for the commission of either of the two Ps, "peeing or puking". Given the number of pubs along the route, to complete a run without doing either showed, by anybody's standards, impressive stamina.

The club's members wore a special tie. It was plain navy blue, decorated with the image of a tankard and surmounted by a crown (its design taken from the Royal Navy's own emblem), both of which were machine-stitched in light blue.[ii] A tie that bore an embroidered letter 'P' (in either pee yellow or puke green) indicated that the bearer had incurred a penalty pint in the course of completing the run. The tie soon became a highly sought after item of apparel and by the mid-1960s the original aims of the club had become somewhat obscured by the desire to gain the coveted dress accessory, and the King Street Run (as it had become popularly known) itself was viewed more as an initiation or rite of passage than an end in itself.

The tolerance of the university proctors (the club was an official university society) and the patience of King Street's publicans and residents eventually ran thin and the Pint to Pint Club was banned by the University authorities some eleven years after it was founded. The King Street Run, however, persisted as an ad hoc activity – enjoyed by both town and gown – during the 1970s, though stripped of the rules that bound the original club together. By the end of the decade only five of the run's original pubs remained in King Street, and the King Street Run had become an informal shadow of its past glory.

▲

In 1978 a small ad appeared in the local newspaper inviting interested parties to attend the inaugural meeting of the Cambridge Hash House Harriers: "HASH HOUSE HARRIERS. Isn't it time there was a hash in Cambridge? Interested runners please call Taylor – Comberton 3636." [iii]

A variety of the game Hares and Hounds, the hash was founded by British ex-pats in Kuala Lumpur before the Second World War. Howard Taylor, who placed the ad (with, it should be said, some difficulty, having had first to convince the paper that the ad was nothing to do with drug running), had been one of the foursome on the McNastie World Tour, but stayed behind in Bangkok for fourteen years, during which time he ran regularly with the Bangkok Hash. So it was that a small but enthusiastic group of respondents met at the Fort St George pub on the banks of the River Cam a couple of weeks later, among them Howard's old friend Terry Kavanagh, now installed as a barman at the Fort.

The Cambridge HHH, a self-styled club for "drinkers with a running problem", was established along traditional lines. Runners, or "hashers", would meet once a week to follow a circuitous and often deliberately misleading trail marked in flour by a "hare". The hashers would find their way to the finish (usually the same place as the starting point, a local pub) where they would drink beer in "down downs" – friendly drinking races conducted for the particular benefit of newcomers or short-cutters – and sing raucously and rudely from the Hash's book of drinking songs.

Although the first run attracted only thirteen participants, the Cambridge Hash soon flourished, and to mark its 200th run in 1982 it was decided to revive the King Street Run. Some of the Hash's members recalled the run in its heyday, and so it was deemed only right that the penalty pints for peeing or puking be reintroduced, but, in keeping with the spirit of the Hash, in its new incarnation it would have a pseudo-serious competitive aspect. The main objective henceforward was to down eight pints of a different variety of beer (which meant "doubling up" in three of the five remaining King Street pubs) within a one-hour time limit.

In 1992 Terry Kavanagh, now universally known by his hash handle of "Bunter", became landlord of the Rhadegund Free House, formerly the Garrick, the second port of call on the original King Street Run, and the smallest hostelry in Cambridge. In a nod to tradition he immediately renamed it the St Radegund,[iv] thus making explicit the nominal association between the pub and the Benedictine nunnery built in the 12th century on part of the site where now stands Jesus College.

Radegund was born in 518, the daughter of one of three brothers who together ruled Thuringia, in modern-day Germany. Her early life was turbulent, as she was deprived, first, of her father, killed by one of her uncles, and then, at the age of twelve, of her homeland, when she and her brother were carried off as booty by the Frankish king Clothaire following a successful invasion. When she reached the age of eighteen, Clothaire had Radegund marry him, and had her taken to his court at Soissons to be his queen. Radegund's consent was hard won, and even after her marriage she continued to lead a simple Christian life marked by spiritual devotion. This enraged Clothaire, but somehow Radegund was able to assuage him, all the while diverting large portions of her husband's fortune to charitable work.

Some years after the marriage, Clothaire, sensing in Radegund's now mature brother a political rival as the male heir of the Thuringian royal family, had him murdered. This appalled Radegund and she fled to Noyon where she took the veil and was consecrated as a deaconess. Clothaire's attempts to return the prodigal to his court proved fruitless, the power of the Church being considerable in those days, and after Germanus of Paris exerted some episcopal muscle the king eventually relented. Radegund was released from any further obligations by the king's death in 561.

In the meantime, Radegund had founded what was to become a renowned nunnery at Poitiers under a strict rule: the nuns were permanently confined to the convent, and encouraged to undertake daily scripture classes and manuscript copying. Thanks to the nunnery's acquisition, at Radegund's initiative, of the holiest of relics a fragment of the cross on which Jesus was crucified – the Convent of the Holy Cross, as the house became known, became an important site of pilgrimage, famed for its miraculous cures.

As Radegund grew older, she devoted more and more time to prayer, to the point where she withdrew entirely from the day-to-day life of the order and had herself walled up. Following her death in 587 and her canonization in the 9th century, her reputation for piety and charity gained her a cult following and her influence grew steadily. In England several parish churches were named after her, while in the 12th century an abbey was founded in her name near Dover as well as the nunnery of St Mary and St Radegund on fields near the River Cam in Cambridge.

When Bunter took over the Rhadegund, a stone's throw from the site of the old nunnery, he was quick to put his stamp on the place. A new pub sign was commissioned, to be based on St Radegund's coat of arms. Unfortunately Bunter could find no record of the appropriate blazon so he had the sign painted in the style of the coat of arms of an Austrian town named after her.

The pub stands at the eastern end of King Street opposite (both geographically and temperamentally) a Methodist church. Essentially a wedge-shaped, single-room saloon bar, one enters at the thin end of the wedge and passes, to the right, a series of framed prints depicting the Age of Steam, and the long bench where regulars gather to engage in the cut and thrust, and make the hard decisions. In the years since Bunter's incumbency, the pub's crowded nicotine-brown interior has fairly begun to groan under the weight of accumulated bric-a-brac, affording the solitary drinker many a distraction. Above the bar is a sign proclaiming, starkly, NO

GOOSES SAUSAGED. This baffles visitors without a working knowledge of cockney rhyming slang, but there is usually someone around the bar willing to oblige with a translation.[v]

To the right-hand side is the Wall of Shame, upon which people lingering too long with their pints after closing time have the misfortune of being immortalised. As Bunter passes through the bar encouraging punters to drink up he offers them one of three choices, delivered with his trademark bluster:

"Either you drink it, I drink it, or you sign!"

Should the hapless dawdler choose the last option he is immediately invited to autograph a chitty declaring "This is to certify that Terry's beer is too strong for me", and said chitty is then pinned to the Wall. The Raincheck Tree, actually the central support of the bar, bears receipts for drinks paid for by people unlucky enough to have missed a friend's visit, or in thanks for a favour called in, and so forth. The ceiling around the central quatrefoil fan is covered with the names, burned onto the surface with a black candle, of various pub worthies who have made a distinguished contribution to the pub or swelled the coffers of Bunter's retirement plan by simply having drunk in there for a long time.

Above the long bench hangs a huge map of Eurasia, extending from the eastern Mediterranean as far as Delhi, and showing the various routes taken by those intrepid souls who have gone overland to India. Either side of the map is a framed list of those strangers, friends and customers known to have made the journey (including, of course, the 1954 Oxford and Cambridge Far Eastern Expedition, and the 1964 McNastie World Tour); the mode of transport employed in each case is specified and the list itself divided between those who favoured the "Elite Northern Route" and those who took the "Southern Trash Route".

Above the main entrance to the bar, visible properly only as one leaves, is a notice that reads: "Thank you for flying St Radegund Beer-Lines. Have a nice hangover."

Presiding over what Bunter himself styles "The Temple of Low Debauchery" and regulars refer to as "The Rad" is the man himself, his bluff front-of-house showmanship drawing students and townspeople across the threshold in roughly equal measure. His management style takes the form of a sort of benevolent dictatorship, with Bunter conferring upon himself a kind of infallibility to the point where, if anything goes wrong, it is inevitably the fault of "some arsehole" or "some prat". Nobody who enters the pub is ever in any doubt who is its lord and master.

Within, the mobile phone is prohibited and transgressions of this rule punished ruthlessly. Anybody foolish enough to ignore the numerous signs around the place and allow their phone to ring is immediately invited to make a charitable contribution, whilst being serenaded with the following ditty, sung to the tune of Guide Me, O Thou Great Redeemer:

Who's the arsehole?
Who's the arsehole?
Who's the arsehole with the mobile phone?
Who's the arsehole with the mobile phone?

Such is Bunter's manner behind the bar that he can be a tad off-putting to the neophyte drinker, and often appears little more than a badly executed cartoon of the rude pub landlord. He is liable to turn at will from graceless to charming and back again, one minute berating a customer for paying for a single drink with a £20 note, the next insisting they sign one of the pub's many visitors' books. Hang about the bar long enough, though, and you soon realise that a lot of this is just an act, a series of verbal tics that he uses as a shorthand intended to make unwanted conversation less of a chore to him after keeping long hours behind the bar. This goes beyond the mere repetition of some joke from the day's newspaper to every customer (though Bunter does that too) and into the realms of the surreal.

These "Bunterisms", as they are known, range over most of life's eventualities with an at times arcane inscrutability that the uninitiated often struggle with. Tell Bunter that the beer is good, and he will reply "It should be, I piss in the barrel every morning!" Fail to offer him a cigarette, and it's "Did mine roll off the bar?" Forgotten your pen? "Social cripple!" Lingering too long over a pint? "Brush the flies off it!" Need to present bad news in a favourable light, he will advise "Back up the hearse and let them smell the flowers". There are many more. You would expect at least some of these pronouncements to have a counter-productive effect on his business but, oddly enough, takings remain buoyant and the customers, in the main, happy.

Occasionally, if the hour is late and the mood takes him, Bunter will perform his party piece. With a bar towel draped across his head (why, for God's sake?) he will hold court with a rendition of *Lili Marlene* that would clear the bar if it weren't so damned funny. He starts, when he can remember it correctly, with the first verse in the English translation. Thereafter his powers of recall start to go, and by the third or fourth verse he has begun to slur together several verses of the German and English versions, and is improvising wildly:

Orders reif der Posten,
Blasen over there
Wohlen auf den billets
Ich komme mein lieb'herr
We said good bye, Auf Wiedersehen
I heard your feet und mit dir geh'n
Mit dir Lili Marlene
Wie heiß Lili Marlene.

By this point, if the crowd is getting restless, he starts goose-stepping around the bar. With such antics in his repertoire it is no surprise that the St Radegund draws in many a student, as the walls of the pub bear witness. Interspersed among the framed photographs of college sporting clubs (admittedly *de rigueur* in most Cambridge pubs) are treasured invitations from various drinking and dining societies, and behind the bar hang the official ties of those very same clubs, collected by Bunter along with honorary memberships over the years. A television set hides behind the panelling above to be revealed and switched on only for Rugby Union internationals, with the Six (originally Five) Nations being the obvious highlight, and in the summer months England's cricket tests.

In 1993 a Cambridge University or, formally, Cantabrigensis Hash was instituted with the initial aim of running once a week only during the university term. The Cantabrigensis HHH would use the St Radegund as the meeting point for their regular Monday night run, with a small area at the end of the bar marked off for their use, complete with a notice board on which to display announcements and other "Hash Trash". So it was that the latter-day King Street Run found its spiritual home under the rafters of the St Radegund, to be run every time the hash notched up a hundred of its weekly meetings, and Bunter became its unlikely custodian. Further modifications have been made to the original rules since, in so far as penalty pints have been replaced by instant disqualification for peeing or puking, but the King Street Run tie – to the same design as the original – is still awarded to anybody who completes the course within the one-hour time limit. The competitive aspect of the run does have the effect of attracting every gunslinging pisspot for miles around with an eye on a record time, but it is a fool who underestimates the rigours of the run and its sheer difficulty. Start too quickly and you risk blowing up by the sixth pint; drink too slowly and you could end up out of time.[vi]

The third stop on the modern run, half-way down King Street, is the Champion of The Thames, the oldest surviving pub on the street, and named after a successful 19th-century rowing coach and sculler.[vii] The Champ, as it is popularly known, is only slightly bigger than the St Radegund by virtue of a second bar, but its low ceilings make it look smaller than it actually is. Bunter, who was all for being part of the close-knit King Street community, would often drop by for a lunchtime drink on a Sunday, when his own pub was closed, to chat with the landlord.

On such an occasion in the summer of 1992, Bunter learned that the Champ had acquired a cricket team, made up from a bunch of regulars. Gathered together under the name of Psatirists[viii] CC, they had played a couple of convivial beer matches against local hostelries and were interested in playing more. Would Bunter like to field a team to represent his pub? Seizing on the invitation with typical enthusiasm, Bunter promised to recruit the semblance of a side from, as he put it, the St Radegund's "old codgers and bar-room sweepings". He decided that an old friend from his teenage years in North London, Ron "Eyebrows" Taylor, should be captain as he had played in the odd Gentlemen versus Players match at Fenner's organised by the Cambridge Hash. Howard Taylor from the McNastie World Tour, and the man who had bowled Bunter for a duck on Corfu, was another obvious choice, as was Ted Bates, who was now back living in London, and some of the more cricketing minded Hashers like Roger "Crabbo" Crabb and his thirteen-year-old son. The Jesus College grounds-man of the time was an occasional drinker in the St Radegund and his intercession secured a pitch at The Close, within Jesus College's picturesque grounds, with a date a few Sundays thence set for the match.

During a routine clearing out of the pub's cellar Bunter came across a brass claret jug that at one point in the past had doubtless adorned the walls as an "authentic" pub fitting. So wretched was the thing to look at that Bunter's immediate impulse was to consign it to the rubbish bin. However, never one to turn down the opportunity for a bit of ceremonial, he soon realised that it would make a fittingly ugly trophy for the imminent, and no doubt equally ugly, contest between the two pub teams.

Sunday 27 July 1992 saw an expectant and good-humoured crowd gather by the thatched pavilion of Jesus College to witness, when they could be bothered to look up from their picnic hampers and glasses of wine, this titanic clash of cricketing has-beens and never-weres. The claret jug – now renamed and inscribed The King Street Trophy, and duly given pride of place on the pavilion balcony – was universally agreed to be such a tawdry piece of tat that no self-respecting cricket captain in his right mind would ever put himself in the position of competing seriously for the honour of winning it. So the two teams took to the lush lawns of The Close with cries of "Let the worst team win!"[ix] ringing in their ears, as they bravely tried their best not to claim the poor quality ewer.

The St Radegund's captain, Eyebrows, immediately seized what he believed to be a palpable advantage in this regard by declining to take to the field at all, and contented himself with barking the occasional orders to his troops from beyond the boundary rope, in so far as the wine and canapés allowed. To everyone's surprise the St Radegund, batting first, managed not only to survive their forty overs but to put on a respectable, if pedestrian, score of 142 for nine with the team's youngest player, Crabbo Junior, one of those remaining unbeaten. The score would have been considerably lower without the effort of one keen batsman who, with a personal tally of 65, was the leading run-maker and gave the impression of wanting to win the game. Indeed, such was his enthusiasm that he was sacked by Eyebrows not long after for taking proceedings far too seriously. As did, it must be said, the Champion of the Thames who, in reply to the St Radegund's total took little more than 27 overs to knock off the required runs. Only a late flurry of wickets gave the impression of a closer match than it actually was.

This rather unsporting gesture on the Champ's part was forgotten as the two teams repaired to King Street to discuss the day's events over a few beers. There it was agreed that the day had been such an unqualified success as a social occasion that the game should henceforth be played every year. Bunter dutifully handed the unwanted King Street Trophy to his opposite number with a sense of relief so it could take pride of place behind the bar of the Champion of the Thames, where it has – the occasional aberration aside – remained ever since.

Having been born by chance, the St Radegund cricket team (Eyebrows could not bring himself to call it a club: "It sounds too serious, dear boy") was happy enough to play its solitary annual fixture with not a whit of enthusiasm for anything more strenuous. Eyebrows, for his part, failed to take the field of play in the three subsequent matches (all lost by the St Radegund), and then decided that being a spectator was a far more enjoyable way to involve oneself anyway. Scouting around for a successor he hit upon the brilliant idea of offering it to the genial, burly Rad barman Jon Dawson, whose major cricketing credentials were to have turned out against the St Radegund for the previous three King Street Trophy matches. This was a masterstroke, Eyebrows having reasoned by some tortuous private logic that the team probably stood more chance of maintaining their losing streak with a captain who had formerly turned out for the opposition actively involved in the play. Whatever the justification, it proved an inspired choice. An accomplished racquets player, JD brought to the game a keen eye, good co-ordination and an unfailing reluctance to take the simplest of runs. The handover was made with no ceremony, the initiation carried out with no fuss. The only things that needed passing on from captain to captain were a general commitment to playing the game *in the right spirit,* and that under no circumstances should the King Street Trophy be allowed to darken the portals of the St Radegund again. In this last the Rad were ably abetted by their rivals down King Street who, following a change of landlord and the introduction of a number of midweek league cricketers into the team rather than regular drinkers, possessed a team quite capable of beating the St Radegund on any given day hands down and with both of them tied behind their backs.

If the style and ethos of St Radegund cricket were forged in those early Rad versus Champ encounters, then JD honoured both impeccably. He was a popular figure behind the bar, which continued to attract a steady stream of new blood be it town, gown, or ex-gown-now-town. His principles as captain were those he maintained as a batsman, and best described as economy of effort. As the decade wore on and the majority of the original team's stalwarts had begun to move on to more sedentary pursuits to be replaced by a new generation of cricketing incompetents, so JD decided to hand over the captaincy. He did not have far to look to find a willing idiot.

Highball first came into the pub to sink a few ales after mid-week games of rounders played on nearby Jesus Green. He and his companions would occupy the big table on the left by the pub's entrance and sup until closing time. Eventually Highball worked up the nerve to sit at the bar, where he could often be found of a Saturday lunchtime pitting his wits, so to speak, against The Guardian crossword. Asked by JD on one such occasion if he played cricket, Highball responded with an enthusiastic affirmative. A six-feet-plus-tall bespectacled Lancastrian, he proudly admitted that the only noteworthy cricketing things on his CV were a failed trial at his local town club as a teenager and the occasional game for the second XI side at university. Impeccable credentials for the St Radegund, surely, but more importantly he possessed that key prerequisite for the athletically challenged: enthusiasm over ability.

Highball did distinguish himself by scoring in double figures in his first Rad versus Champ game but his bowling, whence he eventually attained his nickname, was comfortingly wayward. Any facing batsman who lived in fear of the bouncer could rest easy when Highball bowled, as the ball was more than likely to loop over the batsman's head and land in the welcoming gloves of the wicket-keeper. Clearly, JD thought he had picked a worthy successor.

In response to interest from the new generation of drinkers now frequenting the pub, Highball's first act as captain was to sanction as many games of cricket over the summer as the majority of the rest of the team wanted, with no potential opposition ruled out provided that they were of a broadly equal standard to the Rad, played for enjoyment rather than seriousness, and enjoyed a drink and a natter after the match. He also stipulated that the captaincy should, henceforth, change hands on an annual basis.

The unintended consequence of the extra games was that the St Radegund's cricket actually started to improve, to the point where the team became semi-serious in a semi-established sort of way, and revolved around a core of borderline-competent players who would represent it year in and year out for the next decade. By the turn of the millennium the team was playing four or five games a season, and became so well practised that it actually won the King Street Trophy match after eight years of Champion of the Thames domination.

In spite of this the team retained its semi-established character. No membership fees were collected save for the occasional whip-round to cover the cost of hiring local pitches, and anything carrying with it the associations of committee politics, infighting and backstabbing was strenuously avoided. So while Bunter was the team's main benefactor, nominal president and final arbiter of policy, and former captains such as Eyebrows and JD enjoyed a respectable eminence, this was about as serious as things got, and the Rad's cheerful spirit of Corinthian amateurism was maintained. Highball, meanwhile, moved into a behind-the-scenes, administrative capacity, becoming unofficial fixture organiser and general dogsbody, though did still play in most games, where his wayward bowling featured prominently. Naturally mistakes were occasionally made, particularly in the selection of opposition, for no matter how good the word of the opposing captain, you never really know if you're out of your depth until you've been on the end of a 10-wicket or 100-run drubbing. In general, though, there were enough like-minded pub teams within the Cambridge area to ensure a number of games of a mildly competitive nature with an emphasis on enjoyment.

It soon became apparent to Highball that the number of fixtures played made it possible to produce a list of cricket averages for the year. These, when pinned to the pub's notice board, induced many a chuckle as players pored over the details of this statistical record of their individual shortcomings, and the true depth of the St Radegund's collective incompetence was disclosed for the first time. The joke was lost on no one, but Highball began to believe it could be taken further and, not long after, he joined Bunter at the bar for a lunchtime pint to put a proposition to the landlord.

"I'd like to do a cricket magazine," he announced boldly. "Match reports, averages, that sort of thing." Bunter's eyes lit up as he seized with relish upon the idea, and began to appropriate it.

"Good idea! We'll need a poem, a quiz, and a cartoon. I will be the editor." Whereupon he pulled down a copy of a magazine he had published to celebrate ten years of the Cambridge Hash. It contained sundry articles on the history of the running club, along with photographs, advertisements from local businesses and, unsurprisingly, a poem, a quiz, and a cartoon. If Highball's idea of the magazine's contents was slightly at variance with Bunter's, both were in no doubt that the tone of the magazine should be resolutely mock-heroic. Brilliantly, Bunter suggested that the cover should parody the traditional chocolate brown and gold frontispiece to *Wisden Cricketers' Almanack*. Bunter's name would appear on the cover as editor, and Highball would do the work putting it together. The printing would be handled by a local printing firm, with costs offset by advertising revenue and a nominal cover price, with the excess to go towards the St Radegund cricket team's expenses for the coming season. Bunter and Highball satisfied themselves it would be a worthwhile endeavour. But what to call it? Bunter suggested punning on *Wisden* to leave nobody in any doubt they were picking up a magazine that celebrated the St Radegund's less than artful contribution to the noble game. When *Witless Cricketers' Almanack* – the bible of the witless cricketer? – appeared in late 2001, what had been intended as a modestly sized, well-intentioned in-joke, was just that. The cover aped that of the more celebrated annual tome in every detail, right down to lifting its contents previews word for word and adapting them – more often than not labouredly – to the various personalities in and around the pub and cricket team.

Inside the magazine's covers, on the third page, Bunter contributed a preface and overview of the cricket season in which he thanked all those around the club whose efforts would otherwise go unacknowledged. It was called *Foreword Defensive*. No attempt was made to justify or explain the new-born publishing venture and there was nothing as pompous as a mission statement. The magazine appeared to have sprung, fully armed from the heads of its co-creators, and rightly so.

On the following page the captain for the year, known to all as The Yorkshire Sipper – a nickname coined, in questionable taste, by Bunter but which nevertheless had stuck – gave his reflections on the season just passed, and came closest to summing up the tacitly agreed ethos of the magazine: "'Never read print, it spoils the eyes.' Since WG's habitual advice to his players assumes a measure of proficiency in the first place, there seems no harm in recording the St Radegund's exploits on the square. This extraordinary tradition of underachievement is now 10 years old, but not surprisingly it has taken until now for anyone to suggest that these deeds of derring-do be set down for posterity." [x]

The Sipper had got the point with no prompting whatsoever. A handsome, six-foot-tall Bradford lad with short blond hair waxed into a Tintin quiff, and elegantly sideburned, The Sipper was a regular either side of the bar of the Rad and so knew his subject well. A graduate of St John's College, his major claim to fame and the subject of numerous jokes at his expense, was his PhD in applied mathematics that, still awaiting completion, had been embarked upon so long ago that its existence was beginning to assume legendary proportions. His other contribution to the first issue of *Witless* was a report on the year's match against the Champion of the Thames, one of five fixtures the St Radegund played that season. The record shows that The Sipper's incumbency produced three wins to two losses (including the Champ match), which he wrote about over a couple of pages with panache, with any reference to his own exploits reported, matter of factly, in the third person – a stylistic quirk Highball insisted upon. The lion's share of the rest of the match reports, chronicling the team's various triumphant failures and dismal victories, were written by Highball himself. Bunter, as threatened, contributed a full-page poem in tribute to the team's scorer of long standing, executed as a parody of Keats' *Ode to A Nightingale*:

His Heart aches, and a drowsy numbness pains
His senses, as though of Raki he had drunk,
Or emptied some Real Ale to his brains
One minute past closing time had sunk.

Or a beaker full of the cold Celt,
Malt of Balvenie, Founders Reserve,
That I may drink, and then fade and melt
Into that drunken stupor I deserve.

Away! Away! To the Rad I will scamp,
Not charioted by Bacchus and his pards,
But down the well worn path to the Champ
Though the dull brain perplexes and retards...[xi]

And so on and so forth. The subject, or victim, of this doggerel managed to compose himself for long enough to dash off a barely coherent piece on the origins of the Rad versus Champ fixture that Highball published under the title *Memory Lame*. The season's averages were included on the final page of the magazine, and Bunter's insistence on including a quiz and a cartoon was met. An accommodation had been reached between the two would-be publishers, who soon realised that the only real editorial consideration for such a modest 28-page enterprise was finding something vaguely humorous to fit between the magazine's yellow card covers. A particularly serviceable idea of Bunter's was to include cricketing quotations in small print at the foot of every other page. These ranged from the sublime to the coarse, from CLR James' "What do they know of cricket who only cricket know?" which appeared – appropriately enough – below the quiz, to Fred Trueman's "You've got more edges than a broken piss pot."

Bunter's rationale was simple: "At least that way you're guaranteed a laugh a page," he said.

To everyone's surprise and its publishers' delight, it sold out its modest print run almost immediately. This was thanks in no small part to Bunter's bullying of anybody who stepped over the threshold into buying it, and in doing so he added a new phrase to the long list of Bunterisms:

"If you don't laugh within five minutes of reading it, I'll give you your money back."

The salesmanship was consummate. *Witless* was judged an unqualified success. Somewhat embarrassingly, copies of the magazine were deposited in the University library and in the city council library's Cambridge Collection, a repository for publications of local, historic interest. The magazine was adjudged to be an indispensable item for the gentleman cricketer at stool, and took pride of place in many a local jakes. Bunter and Highball, flush with success, agreed to improve on the first issue by producing another one the following, and subsequent years.

▲

When he returned from his trip to Vis at the end of May, Bunter was brimful with enthusiasm.

"I know where we're going for our next cricket tour!" he said, bending the ear of anyone and everyone. Those players within earshot as he recounted his travels could have been forgiven for thinking that Bunter had taken leave of his senses. The team had yet to finalise, let alone undertake, its first ever domestic cricket tour – a projected four-day jaunt over the late August bank holiday to Gloucestershire taking in a beer festival, a 30-

over cricket match and a six-a-side competition – and here was the old man already suggesting something that seemed, by St Radegund's modest standards, hugely ambitious. Certainly all agreed, as they pored over Bunter's maps and brochures, that the place looked idyllic, but the more they heard about it the more sceptical they became. The players listened patiently to Bunter as he repeated the story for the second and third times, and nodded politely that it sounded like a good idea. In Bunter's mind, there was no doubt, even at this early stage, it would go ahead.

"What people have got to appreciate," he opined, "is the craic!" and opined again and again, in versions that he took pleasure in drilling into the players on any and every occasion. Most laughed off the plan as nothing more than the latest bee in the landlord's bonnet, to be soon forgotten and replaced by a more novel and interesting bee. Bunter, however, was convinced that only a surfeit of ambition would see the venture succeed, and coined what appeared to be a brand new Bunterism in the process: "You don't understand. You have to aim for the moon to reach Mount Everest."

The exoticism of this particular phrase was startling, but most people agreed that it was, in fact, a variation on "aiming for the sun to reach the moon", or something similar. That is, however, often the way with a Bunterism: at first apparently recondite, only through constant repetition does the phrase's meaning reveal itself, as its metaphorical ribbons and wrapping paper become tattered and torn from overuse.

A number of players kept their counsel out of politeness and respect, in the hope that Bunter would lose interest in the idea. In secret they thought that the St Radegund team was taking on too much: less Mount Everest, more piling Mount Pelion on Mount Ossa. Sensing indifference in the ranks, Bunter decided to sell the team the Vis trip through the pages of Witless, and asked Highball to make space for a double-page article on his recent trip in the forthcoming second edition of the magazine. In it Bunter described a little of the island's history and his meeting with Roki: "Most of our conversation was about cricket, and I was shown over the old airfield. It would be perfect for a pitch, if a bit on the small side. Preparing the wicket could also prove a problem, but not an insoluble one." [xii]

If anything it was the prospect of having to travel all that way without the guarantee of a pitch to play on that made most people reluctant. Bunter was aware of the drawbacks but decided to back up the hearse and let the players smell the flowers: "Vis is unique. Until recently it has remained a closed military base with few tourists visiting since world war two. One of the benefits has been that pesticides have never been introduced there, and so all of the island's produce is organic. Having been locked in a time warp for so long, Vis is now very much ahead of its time."

And then, inevitably, the gauntlet was thrown down: "Guess whom I have in mind to play in this revival game? Yes YOU, playmates! Just think about it: a beautiful, sunny Adriatic island and a pitch next to a vineyard and restaurant: the perfect place for a future St Radegund summer cricket tour."

The article, as it appeared, was as much a dare as it was a recruitment ad. Accompanied by a photograph of Niko Roki in the farmhouse courtyard, and another of the former airfield at Plisko Polje, it intrigued but did not cause a huge rush to enlist. Next to the eight-page coverage of the Gloucestershire tour's ribaldry it seemed too downright exotic to be anything other than a fanciful proposition, and many of the players remained unconvinced. As a demonstration of his earnest intention that the St Radegund travel to Vis, Bunter made a show of sending a number of copies of the magazine to the Rokis.

As the new year rolled around and *Witless* began to sell out its second issue, a meeting was called by the elders of the club – The Sipper, Highball, JD, Eyebrows and Bunter among them – to discuss plans for the season, kit, fixtures, and potential tours. They gathered round the long bench like cardinals in solemn conclave one Sunday lunchtime in January. All passed off peacefully until it came to the question of whether to go on tour again that year. A repeat of the previous season's Gloucestershire tour was mooted, it having been agreed to have been a thoroughly successful and enjoyable jaunt. On this Bunter was sage, with another of his well-worn saws: "Never put your foot in the same puddle twice."

Highball raised the small matter of the trip to Vis, pointing out that January was when people normally started thinking about their holidays, and players would need to think about booking time off work and starting to save money, et cetera, but Bunter said he could offer nothing firm at this stage and told the assembled company he would not be able to confirm the tour until May at the earliest, when he planned to stop over in Vis on his way back from Montenegro. As far as Bunter was concerned the subject was closed, therefore, until he went back to the island.

The cardinals having failed to send up white smoke rather put the tin hat on it as far as a number of players were concerned. The tour would never go ahead. Best make your own holiday plans. Bunter's act of deferment gave the whole enterprise a gloss of futility. Bunter, though, had no doubt in his mind that the tour would happen and whenever he got the chance would remind them of the challenge that lay ahead, in a phrase becoming so familiar that it sounded like a mantra: "You don't understand. You have to aim for the moon to reach Mount Everest!"

NOTES

i   Hitchens, Christopher. "Booze and Fags", in *London Review of Books*, March 1992

ii   Local legend has it that the tie was designed by one ER Dexter of Jesus College, later captain of Sussex County Cricket Club and England, but this is typical of the tall tales that have accumulated around the run in the intervening years

iii   *Cambridge Evening News*, 11 September 1978

iv   The variant spellings, "Rhadegund" or "Radegund" are interchangeable

v   "No" is self-explanatory. "Gooses" = goose's neck = cheque. "Sausaged" = sausage and mash = cashed

vi   The record for the course is held by five-time winner and St Radegund regular John Phillips, who downed his eight pints in, a frankly astonishing, 14 minutes and 50 seconds. He is, sensibly enough, in retirement until such time as someone breaks his record

vii   One Edward Hanlan, who was the licensee of the pub at 67 King Street, and was the recipient of letters addressed, mysteriously, to "Champion of the Thames, King Street, Cambridge"

viii   An anagram of "piss artist"

ix   Sic! Though not grammatically perfect, Bunter still insists this was the actual call to arms on the day

x   'Captain's Notes', in *Witless Cricketer's Almanack*, 1st edition, 2001. St Radegund Public House, Cambridge

xi   'Ode to a Night-in-Ale', in *Witless Cricketer's Almanack*, 1st edition, 2001. St Radegund Public House, Cambridge

xii   'Vis – The Business', in *Witless Cricketer's Almanack*, 2nd Edition 2002. St Radegund Public House, Cambridge

2

The Sea

The Sipper had a previous conviction to be taken into consideration, having captained the St Radegund a couple of years previously.

One by one the hopeful travellers approached the desk, handed over their travel documents for inspection and placed their single item of hand luggage onto the scales. The girl in the bright, primary-coloured uniform behind the desk reeled off her list of questions to each of the supplicants in turn with an efficiency dulled into weariness by constant repetition.

"How many bags are you checking in?" she asked.

"One," the traveller replied.

"Did you pack the bag yourself?"

"Yes"

"Could anyone have interfered with your bag?"

"No."

"Has anyone given you anything to carry on board?"

"No."

"Are you carrying any hand luggage on board?"

"Yes."

"Are there any sharp items in your hand luggage?"

"No."

"So, that's gate 39, boarding at 11.30."

Seven out of the eight-strong St Radegund touring party, having been catechised thus and having had bestowed upon them a boarding card, congregated in the main concourse to wait for the last of the group, Beard. After a few minutes it became abundantly clear that he had been found wanting.

"Bugger," Beard said when he rejoined the group. "Five kilos over."

"How much will that set us back?" Highball asked.

"A pony," Beard replied.

"That's a good start," Highball moaned. "Only been on the road an hour and we're already down."

Beard had good reason to be unhappy. Strapped to his back was a 110-litre rucksack jam-packed with cricket equipment. The idea had been to transport as little kit as possible to keep costs down. A single pair of gloves and pads for the wicket-keeper, a couple of pairs of batting gloves and pads, and a few items of gentlemen's protection had been deemed the absolute minimum to be transported, but Highball had failed to factor in cricket bats, examples of which he, Beard and Crabbo Junior had brought along one each. In light of the rather draconian security restrictions on what could be carried as hand luggage (though there was little chance of the bats being used as weapons in the hands of the St Radegund), Beard had generously agreed to further increase his load and allow the other two to unburden themselves, and so they gratefully stuffed their bats into the rucksack on the airport concourse. Unfortunately, this brought the total weight of the rucksack to significantly over the checked baggage allowance, meaning a £25 penalty. With the rucksack on his back, his wild straggles of curly ginger hair and long, bifurcated whiskers whose extremities just sat comfortably atop his barrel chest, it was remarked that Beard looked vaguely reminiscent of the Obelix character from Goscinny and Uderzo's Asterix books. This was enough to momentarily lighten the mood. He unbuckled his rucksack and eased it off his shoulders as Highball handed him some crisp banknotes from the kitty.

"Watch this, will you?" Beard asked, "while I go and pay". And with that he marched over to the main ticketing desk to deal with the surcharge.

Beard was the owner of a local micro-brewery in Cambridge, and so his qualifications for the more sociable aspects of the tour were pre-eminent. He was also the St Radegund tourists' main strike bowler, capable of generating genuinely hostile, out-swinging medium pace from a decent length run-up. A metallurgist by training, he had wandered into the brewing business after an extended jaunt in Afghanistan and northern Pakistan during which time he had chanced his arm at a spot of travel writing. Six months in two of the "driest" countries on earth being shot at by the wily Pathan was enough to confirm anyone's true vocation and he returned to Britain with the idea of going into beer.

It was late September, and strong, bright sunlight shone through the portals of the modern cathedral of Stansted airport. To pass the time while they waited for Beard, the party scanned the newspapers. Out in the wider world, the Hutton inquiry into the Labour government's Iraq dossier was rumbling on. Blair was refusing to rule out a referendum on joining the European single currency. Jeffrey Archer had served two years and two days of a four-year prison sentence for perjury and was now lecturing the Howard League on penal reform. Health officials in Kent were raising concerns about a rise in the number of sexually transmitted diseases owing to the rise in popularity of the social activity known as "dogging". All in all, it didn't seem like a bad time to be getting out of the country for a while, the overriding hope of the St Radegund party being that they weren't leaving behind the glories of an Indian summer for less clement weather ahead. Fortunately, initial forecasts for the Dalmatian coast seemed promising.

Some of the group – Beard, The Yorkshire Sipper, JD's wife Frannie and the team's scorer Jugs – had met in the early morning at the St Radegund before boarding the coach for the airport. At the pub they had been treated to one of Bunter's specialities as a fortifier: instant coffee with rum. It was enough to make one retch. And it did, almost the moment the coach left Drummer Street bus station.

As head of the party, Bunter had allowed his proprietary instincts to surface almost immediately. He had made sure that nothing had been left to chance in getting to the airport in good time, so the group had boarded a nine o'clock coach in order to time their arrival for the precise moment that the check-in desks opened, some two hours before their noon flight. Such efficiency had been expected. The rest of the party, having each travelled in Bunter's company on more than one occasion, had seen him take charge of situations that didn't really need it before. The fact that they were, to a person, independent travellers of no little experience didn't matter to Bunter, and as he issued instructions, over-protective like a scoutmaster with his pack, they bit their lips or buried their heads in a book or looked away.

Their early arrival had given them some time to kill, which they spent watching the great mass of humanity around them as it milled about, craning necks to catch the information on the display screens, sometimes looking lost.

"Look at them," The Sipper said eyeing the party's fellow pilgrims, shaking his head with dismay.

"Dross," Bunter concurred with a hiss. Since the St Radegund party were flying with a budget airline too, they could hardly afford to be picky about the company they kept. Such hubris could only provoke the anger of the gods. Yet they persisted in poking fun at their fellow travellers, and became resigned to the tangible prospect of some as yet anonymous idiot delaying their flight through sheer fuckwittage. How difficult could it be to listen to public announcements, read departure boards, get through security control without trying to carry four items of hand luggage through, arrive at the departure gate at the correct time, follow simple pre-boarding instructions, and retain the boarding card for inspection on the aeroplane? It wasn't, as The Sipper was fond of saying, neurosurgery.

The public address system pealed monotonously, and a robotic voice advised passengers in possession of a boarding card to pass immediately through security control. When Beard returned, Bunter insisted they do just that: get airside as soon as possible and have a coffee and a sit-down. The party negotiated the security checks with no fuss and entered the promised land of tax-free shopping.

▲

Preparations for the trip had begun in earnest only once Bunter had returned from Vis in May. With a green light from the Rokis, he announced that the tour would go ahead after high season was over, more than likely towards the end of September. Further details were scant.

"You'll get an opening dinner, a closing dinner, and a game of cricket," he said conclusively. Other considerations, such as whether the pitch at Plisko Polje would be ready in time, Bunter was neither willing nor able to confirm. Such vagueness was the cue for a jeremiad or two from certain team members warning against travelling such a long way without a strip to play on. Bunter remained convinced that the Rokis would find a way to make it work, by hook or by crook. As feared, a number of mainstays of the St Radegund side had already made up their minds and made alternative holiday plans, or had other commitments that prevented them travelling. Others were simply unable to get the time off work. This included some of the team's better cricket players and some of its more accomplished drinkers. Clearly, getting enough people to form a credible, representative team was going to prove a challenge.

Further incentive – if any were needed – had been provided by the Sunday Telegraph, which had run a piece on the revival of cricket on Vis earlier in the spring. It began thus: "The discovery of a letter from a British naval captain to his mother during the Napoleonic wars has inspired the inhabitants of a remote Adriatic island to take up cricket – despite the fact that the nearest team to play against is 200 miles away."[i] It went on to give a brief account of the history of cricket on the island, mentioned a grant of £7,000 from the European Cricket Council, who had also arranged for a professional coach from England to teach the islanders the rudiments of the game, and Oliver Roki's aim to create "a proper cricket field". There was a quotation attributed to Oliver Roki: "I was inspired by the passion for a sport I had never heard of in connection with our island, and together with other people here we looked into what cricket involved. We'd never played it, but now it is talked about by everyone. The letter struck a chord and it just went from there."

Bunter, reading the article over a cup of coffee prior to the lunchtime shift, was impressed by the progress that had been made by the islanders in such a short space of time. As sundry members of the cricket team duly arrived to claim their first pints of the session, he showed them the newspaper.

"There you go," he said, "If that doesn't convince you, then nothing will." The players who had ventured into the pub that lunchtime made vaguely enthusiastic noises as they read the article with interest. They were quick to point out, though, that the piece on Vis had succeeded in letting the cat out of the bag quite spectacularly: "When the pitch is ready Mr Roki hopes that his club may lure cricket-loving visitors from Britain who want to play in winter."

September was still a long way away, and there was every chance that, with such a high-profile advertisement for cricket on Vis, the St Radegund team would not be the first to play on the island in 200 years, a distinction that was particularly attractive to those who had expressed an interest in going on tour to the Adriatic. This was not something that troubled Bunter unduly: he was more concerned with finding enough players to go on the trip and was determined to get a team out come what may, even if he had to drag in ringers to do it. He had given the Rokis his word, and honour demanded nothing less.

Highball was put in charge of the travel arrangements and general logistics, and during the late spring and early summer he spent many an hour searching for a travel plan that actually worked to the team's advantage. It proved more difficult than he had anticipated. Although Vis is only two and a half hours by ferry from Split, the only airlines with a direct route to Croatia flew out of Heathrow or Gatwick, neither of them the most convenient of airports for Cambridge. Worse, these flights charged full price for a return ticket, so Highball looked for a budget alternative that would lighten the financial burden and encourage more people to go on the trip. Various options were considered and rejected. The quickest route would have been to fly to the Italian Adriatic and take a fast catamaran to Split or, better still, to Vis itself, though this would not be possible out of high season. In the end it was decided that the easiest, though still far from ideal, option would be a midday flight to Pescara, followed by a two-hour train journey up the coast to Ancona to make the ferry, ensuring an outward journey time of well over 24 hours. The return trip a week later would be marginally shorter, if one discounted spending the best part of a day looking round Split, ensuring that the tourists would be back in Cambridge by early evening the following day. As happy as he could be that this was the best of a number of bad options, Highball pinned the details on the pub's notice board and awaited the trickle of responses from interested parties.

The St Radegund's cricket season had started in early June with a six-wicket win over the local Church of England seminary, and ended eight games later in early August with a one-wicket win against a visiting south London pub side Bunter had encountered on a trip to that year's Oval test match. Crabbo Junior had a particularly good season, scoring 30 not out in the third match against another local pub side, and a similar score opening the batting against the Champion of the Thames. This left him at the top of the batting averages, with over 100 runs in six innings at an average of 22.5. Of the other tourists, The Sipper had amassed 93 runs in nine innings, with a top score of 29, to give him an average of 11.62. Beard was averaging slightly lower at 11.16, having played fewer innings, but at least had one score over 30 that accounted for nearly half of his total number of runs. Highball brought up the rear with a fairly unimpressive 14 runs from five innings at an average of a measly 2.80. Simply put, the batting potential was mixed.

Neither did the bowling figures promise much for the St Radegund's first overseas match. Highball and Beard had been the team's workhorses during the season, bowling more than 50 overs between them. Highball's best return in a single match had been two wickets for four runs, but in others he had been his usual wayward self. Over all, he had conceded 146 runs at an economy of 5.62 per over. Beard was no better, and averaged 27.8 with an economy of 5.56 and a strike rate of one wicket every 30 deliveries. Crabbo Junior had had an altogether miserable time. He bowled 20 overs at a cost of 117 runs with not a single wicket as reward.

The team as a whole, though, had enjoyed a marginally successful season prior to leaving for Vis, having won five matches and lost four (including that year's King Street Trophy match). Unfortunately both the current season's captain and the year's best and most economical wicket-taker were among those who would not be able to make the tour. In the skipper's absence, The Yorkshire Sipper was appointed locum captain for the duration of the tour. He had, of course, a previous conviction to be taken into consideration, having captained the St Radegund a couple of years previously and acquitted himself well. His style of captaincy was more Beefy than Brearley: get on with things rather than spend time thinking about them, and he readily admitted that he would be more than happy to delegate the matter of fine-tuning the field placings to whoever could be bothered with it.

The next obstacle was logistical: how much cricket kit to take along and how best to get it there at minimal cost. The team treasurer, drawing on professional expertise, offered to produce a presentation pack to send to around to potential backers in the hope of securing a modest amount of sponsorship to cover such expenses. This was agreed to be a highly useful and generous offer, but was pre-empted – with typical proprietary zeal – by Bunter, who sent a typewritten letter on his favoured beige writing paper to the chief executive officer of the team's chosen airline carrier, asking whether they would be happy to transport, *gratis*, the St Radegund's cricket kit in lieu of sponsorship. The response was predictable, and matched in brevity what Bunter's letter had possessed in chutzpah. It even asserted, to add insult to injury, that a Croatian team could beat a pub team from England. On seeing the letter, the team treasurer, dismayed that Bunter had gone behind his back, promptly refused to offer any further help in trying to win sponsorship.

In the departure lounge at Stansted, over an espresso or two, Crabbo Junior revealed a sartorial statement of dubious tastefulness: a 1970s vintage crushed velvet jacket in black with a Nehru collar. The sight of it was greeted with a mixture of some amusement and not a little covetousness, ditto when he produced a similar garment from his rucksack in a plum colour for The Sipper, who was both surprised and delighted to receive it. Slipping it on over his shirt he gave the assembled tourists what Bruce Forsyth would once have called "a twirl" and struck a pose worthy of Douglas Jardine about to embark the boat for the "bodyline" tour. Sadly, a trawl through the picture archives has yet to turn up a snap of the erstwhile England captain wearing a velvet jacket with sleeves two inches too short for his arms and about to burst out of the buttons like some jazz-age Incredible Hulk.

The Sipper's surprise was genuine. Some days earlier he, Crabbo Junior and Jugs had been passing one of Cambridge's charity shops when The Sipper spied said garment in one of the windows and remarked, in an offhand manner apropos of very little, that he wouldn't mind "one like it". A quick flash of feminine perspicacity on Jugs' part was all that it took, and the offending item was picked up by Crabbo Junior for the princely sum of £4 on the morning of travel before he boarded the train to the airport.

Crabbo Junior had grown up with St Radegund cricket, having played in the very first Rad-Champ match in 1992 when he was thirteen years old, and had turned out for the team regularly throughout his adolescence and early manhood. He even managed to maintain his interest during the distraction of going away to university, missing only one of the annual King Street Trophy fixtures in twelve years. By the time he returned to Cambridge with a first-class degree in sociology, he had blossomed into an accomplished opening batsman of no little elegance, though had yet to settle on a choice of career post-university. Never mind, the loss to the world of work was clearly the St Radegund's gain.

It seemed that Crabbo Junior aimed to cram a lot into the tour's quieter moments. As well as the two jackets, he had packed not only his fishing rod but a number of books, a sketchpad and a set of watercolour paints, all of which he was now struggling to re-pack into his rucksack. Bunter was impressed:

"A Renaissance man. Is there nothing he can't do?" he said, and promptly appointed Crabbo Junior official tour artist.

The Sipper, meanwhile, was asked for his tour aims.

"Well, obviously we want to win," he opined in his broad Yorkshire accent, "but we don't want to rub their noses in it." The sentiment was wholeheartedly endorsed.

In due course it was time to board the plane. When the public address announcer proclaimed the "last and final boarding call" for the flight, eyebrows were raised among the party at this tautology, and they boarded the plane to Pescara with minimum fuss, occupying the starboard aft rows. The flight was busy but not full, and there was plenty of time to board and get comfortable. However, some passengers seemed to interpret the cabin crew's instruction to "pass straight down the cabin aisle taking your seat as quickly as possible" as "stand in the middle of the aisle while attempting to stow more bags in the overhead lockers than you are allowed, so blocking the aisle for all the passengers behind you."

The seats were small and bunched closely together, to Bunter's irritation. Crabbo Junior complained of feeling like "processed cheese: sweaty and vacuum-packed in a controlled and sanitised box with wings", which was a poetic image to play with, if nothing else. The St Radegund party managed to give its complete and very special attention as the cabin crew demonstrated some of the safety features of their Boeing 737-800 series aircraft, the principal object of said demonstration seeming to be to unnerve their passengers:

"Before take-off, your safety is our primary concern…"

"And after take-off…?" asked The Sipper.

"After take-off we'll just keep trying to sell you disgusting food at extortionate prices, and bollocks to safety," finished Beard. This produced a well-earned chuckle and a few knowing smirks from the party. Thankfully, there were no delays to departure and – the safety instructions having been fully digested by the team – the jet was soon airborne.

By way of diversion, Beard had brought with him a global positioning system device. Unfortunately for him, it only worked effectively when pressed up against the cabin window, which meant it was Highball who got to have all the fun charting the plane's route over Germany and the Alps. But why had Beard brought it along? He explained that he hoped to use it to record a confluence of 16° of longitude and 43° latitude near Vis, which he would then photograph from all points of the compass and submit to a specialist website. Sipper buried his head deeper into *The Times* crossword. Highball carried on playing with the GPS device. Bunter needed no toy to tell him where he was, and said as much, before pointing out – accurately as it turned out, as Highball was quick to verify – Lake Como and then Milan below, before the plane banked sharply to broadly follow the course of the Po to the Adriatic.

The mood of the party was upbeat, expectant. Under the patronage and protection of the blessed Radegund (*ora pro nobis*) the two-hour-plus flight passed without notable alarm. The majority of the party eschewed the food, uneatable and over-priced, but did try a cup of tea now and again

– available at a specially discounted price of £1.00 – or simply dozed in the stuffy cabin. If there were any soul-searching to be done, now was the time. When the trip had been mentioned to passing acquaintances, a common response had been that the idea of travelling all the way to a Croatian island to play a game of cricket seemed like an act of folly, a sheer waste of time. Surely you could find something more interesting to do? This is typical of the outsider with little knowledge of or love for the game; for what is cricket if not the most exquisite folly, the most gentlemanly waste of time ever devised? Those in the know, among whose number the St Radegund team counted themselves, were safe in the understanding that for enjoyment, companionship and high jinks there really is no other pastime quite like standing around a large field for an afternoon, attempting to dodge a 5½ ounce projectile, while trying hard to look interested in proceedings.

One could only hope that the players on Vis felt the same way, but it was perhaps a little soon in their development to expect so much. Of them and their ability little was known, save what Bunter had imparted, and he had hardly been forthcoming. The tour demanded a fair amount of trust that Bunter had got it right, if not a downright leap of faith. Aside from The Sipper's specific tour aims, the general hope was to make friends with a good bunch of people who would enjoy the game for what it was and enjoy a beer or two afterwards. The main *craic* – as Bunter would have it – was for the team to play its part in helping to re-establish a sporting link between Britain and Vis that went back nearly 200 years. In that respect, if you really want to be grandiose about it, they were to be cultural ambassadors. But they weren't to be first.

That June, barely three months before the tour, Beard had emailed Highball a link to a story from the European Cricket Council's website, with the comment "That's torn it." That which had been feared following the Sunday Telegraph piece had come to pass. Under the headline "Saumur Strays make dream come true for Croatian Cricketers" [ii] the website described how the Saumur Strays cricket team, "a British team with its roots in France", had made the journey overland to Croatia towards the end of June. Saumur meet "just once a year in unusual or foreign locations not normally associated with cricket". Once their captain had read about the team on Vis, Saumur had "pulled out all the stops to make the game happen".

Having arrived on Vis, they coached the local children at cricket, played and won a match against the islanders, and in doing so became the first visiting cricket team to play on the island since the time of the Napoleonic Wars. Croatian national television cameras were there to record the event, which drew a large and enthusiastic crowd. They then travelled on to Zagreb to play a match against the capital's cricket club, which they again won.

For Highball this was a disappointment. Bunter too felt a sense of grievance at having been gazumped, though he did his best to hide it. The distinction of being the first to play the game on the island since the early 1800s was no longer available. The St Radegund was still struggling to put a team out and Highball had doubts about putting the article on the pub notice board in case it put off the vacillators even further. The matter was discussed at an informal Sunday conclave of the cardinals.

The Sipper, who was serving behind the bar at the time, read the article carefully, as he wiped clean a beer glass. He was diplomatic:

"Well, you can't really blame the Croatians, can you? It probably means nothing to them who their opponents were. If I were playing the first game there in 200 years, then I'd take the first team that came along."

"And they did bring an artificial pitch to play on," Crabbo Junior observed hopefully, "so we should at least be able to get a game if we go out."

Sure enough, some of the club's resident doomsters were now having second thoughts about going, pointing out, by way of illustration, that nobody remembers who the second man on the moon was. The Sipper, always happy to argue the toss, threw in his two penn'orth, and pointed out that *everyone* remembers that Buzz Aldrin followed Neil Armstrong onto the lunar surface in 1969. And, for good measure, he mentioned that Neil Armstrong was now virtually a recluse while Buzz Aldrin enjoyed a profitable living on the after dinner speaker circuit. *Quod erat demonstrandum.*

Highball was reading the article more closely and getting rather het up by it.

"Look at this. It says here that Saumur 'arranged the tour themselves'! Well, who the bloody hell else was going to organise it?" he asked, showing in his irritation his flair for cavilling.

Beard took another look at the piece and questioned the phrase "a British team with their roots in France". With unfailing logic, he suggested that were the St Radegund team populated entirely by Australians they would still be a Cambridge team: *ergo* the Saumur Strays were, in fact, French, and then added – somewhat irrelevantly – that the French are "garlic-smelling, cheese-eating surrender monkeys". The Sipper settled the matter by saying he would be content to go to Vis and lead the first cricket team *from England*.

And what of the Vis team's "dearest wish"? According to the piece in the newspaper, it was the prospect of playing *and beating* a British team that inspired the islanders. Highball was firmly told not to get too hung up on details. Tellingly, though, the article made no mention of Saumur's margin of victory…

▲

The huge glass and steel construction of Pescara railway station, by reputation one of the largest in Europe, was a welcome refuge from the late summer heat of the city. Its marble-floored interior played witness to the tour's first major falling out, between Bunter and Highball's Memsahib.

The Memsahib had first-hand experience of the Italian love of bureaucratic efficiency having, in the course of her research in art history, spent some time in the country. As well as an appreciation for a well-made espresso first thing in the morning, she had developed an instinct for when smoking was and was not acceptable. Memorably she had, whilst researching in the Vatican, taken enormous pleasure in enjoying a sneaky roll-up in the garden courtyard of the library as hundreds of tourists gawped at her from the windows of the Vatican museum on their way to being herded at great speed through the Sistine Chapel. What they must have thought of a single female indulging in such an ungodly pastime in the traditionally male enclave of the Vatican was anybody's guess. The speculation gave her almost as much pleasure as the cigarette.

Bureaucracy, Italian style, worms its way into most walks of life, even the small matter of purchasing railway tickets. The ticketing desk at Pescara sat behind bullet-proof glass. One metre in front of it the floor was marked boldly with a thick yellow line it was forbidden to cross – so the signs helpfully pointed out in Italian – until a cashier was free. Bunter, back on terra firma, had resumed the role of scoutmaster. As the *carabinieri* circled with menace, firearms cocked, he – with scant regard for both the Italian authorities and his own personal safety – crossed the forbidding yellow line to stand at the shoulder of a middle-aged Italian woman who was buying some tickets. Worse, he had lit up a Rothmans in a distinctly non-smoking railway station, a prohibition the *carabinieri* would doubtless be keen to enforce. Highball's Memsahib was familiar with the shoot first, ask questions later proclivities of Italy's law enforcement officers and helpfully, but a little too pointedly, made Bunter aware of the folly of his defiance and the risk at which he was putting himself. Bunter turned spectacularly. His response was of hair-drying intensity: blunt, misogynistic and unparliamentary in the extreme, and forced Highball into the unwanted role of mediator.

Nearly everybody else thought it was a hoot. The Sipper, in particular, came up with an idea for a new money-spinning venture on the spot: a series of travel books authored by Bunter, demonstrating how to be offensive in the major countries of the world, and called "Gruff Guides".

"Yeah, great idea," said a sulking Highball. The Memsahib seethed for an hour or so before deciding that she wasn't going to let the St Radegund's curmudgeon-in-chief spoil what was for her a much-needed holiday. Order was, thankfully, restored in time for the party to make their connection to Ancona and, with tickets purchased and validated, they left Pescara behind; the delights of the Abruzzo region, its wines, medieval castles, fortresses and picturesque hilltop towns never to be sampled, the abiding memory confined to a near ding-dong at the railway station after barely an hour on foreign soil. For the Memsahib, in particular, to miss out on spending time in a part of Italy she barely knew was particularly galling.

The two-hour journey to Ancona took the party along the coast, allowing most their first glimpse of the Adriatic Sea through the dirty windows of the train. It was a ribbon of azure beneath a cloudless sky, the view only occasionally interrupted by an ugly apartment building on the foreshore. Out there, lay their ultimate destination, still the best part of 18 hours away. It was as though they were merely circling Vis without getting any closer. Could they get there without further disharmony?

As some dozed or read a book in the airy carriage, Beard pulled from his rucksack a 1929 edition of *Lyle's Guide to Languages*, a volume no doubt indispensable to the independent traveller of its day, containing as it did some of the most charmingly useless phrases one could ever hope to master, the best of which included such gems as: "Bring me a flask of brandy and some fresh tea. These eggs are bad," "Take these bags to a third class smoker. This way. Enough," and, "Do you speak French and Russian?" "No, but this man speaks Spanish and German." Beard's gleeful rendition of these pearls banished any lingering bad feeling and, committed to memory by all, remained a source of comfort and amusement even on the fourth or fifth hearing.

The Italian rail network being second to none, the party arrived at Ancona in good time. They piled on board a bus that took them northwest towards the port, passed a Roman marble arch at the head of the harbour road and then made a swift descent into the centre of the city. On their left, various merchant ships clustered around the late-18th-century Mole Vanvitelliana, a curious pentagonal building originally designed as a quarantine station. In the main part of town they alighted at the Piazza della Repubblica, which was only a short walk from the ferry terminal. From a vantage point high on a hill at the northern end of the harbour the 12th-century Duomo di San Ciriasco gazed down. In the Middle Ages the city had been an independent republic like Ragusa (now Dubrovnik) with which it often allied, but it had become part of the Papal States in the 16th century, then fallen under French rule in 1797. There was certainly plenty of history to get one's teeth into here but, once again, the St Radegund team would not get much chance to experience it.

Bunter put himself at the head of the queue for ferry tickets. This proved judicious as he managed to bag the last available cabin, an inside double berth. This meant that he and Crabbo Junior, who was second in the queue, would be able to sleep in relative comfort. Crabbo Junior – who had a reputation as something of a ladies' man – was immediately, and predictably, re-nicknamed "Roger the Cabin Boy" for the duration of the voyage, betraying the envy of the others more than anything else. After all it was "Roger" who had a bunk for the night. The rest of the party would have to bed down wherever they could.

There was more bad news on board: the restaurant was full for dinner, a large coach party of German tourists having made a block booking. Bunter began to remonstrate with the maître d', and then, spying a group of Germans close by, began to fulminate at high volume against their country's role in the Second World War. To make matters worse, at his elbow was a Japanese tourist who was making somewhat more polite enquiries about the possibility of obtaining a table. Before you could say "Banzai!" Bunter began to lay into the hapless Asiatic visitor for daring to jump the queue, and for good measure let him know exactly what he thought of the Emperor Hirohito and General Tojo's conduct during the conflict as well. He was mollified only when it was pointed out to him that the Japanese had insisted, politely, that Bunter be seated before him. Further tirades against an Axis plot were spared, though no apology for this outburst was forthcoming.

"Why should I?" he asked rhetorically, "The Japanese government never apologised for any of their actions during the war!"

With no prospect of a sit-down dinner this left only the forward bar which, though spacious with comfortable seats and tables, offered a menu restricted to ham rolls and, for dessert, popcorn. These were, nevertheless, quickly devoured. The party's larger bags were conveniently stowed in Bunter's cabin, allowing everyone the opportunity of a well-earned first drink of the campaign – draught Eurolager. As the only alcoholic drink on offer, it was very welcome and proved to have highly refreshing qualities, particularly when taken repeatedly in large quantities.

Bunter was complaining again, first about people's bags being stowed in his cabin, then about taking the Italian ship with no free cabins, rather than the neighbouring, and no doubt superior, Croatian ship which he was sure was half empty and probably called in at Vis directly en route. For this he blamed Highball for not investigating it further, but Highball explained that the Croatian ferry company had been unable to give an assurance that their direct service to Vis would be operating so late in the season. The neighbouring vessel was more than likely heading for Split as well. Before the discussion could continue, the Japanese from the restaurant came into the forward bar. Bunter broke off long enough to shout "Pearl Harbour!" at the hapless tourist, who promptly turned on his heels and fled the room.

The ferry made its stately way out of Ancona harbour an hour late. As the evening wore on the party was less than delighted to find that the only onboard entertainment consisted of a single CD recording of Dire Straits' *Greatest Hits* that gained nothing in being repeated ad nauseam. In desperation some made their way to the aft duty-free shop to purchase medicinal spirits. For some reason it was only open for one hour, but its prices proved competitive enough and the party eagerly loaded up with booze.

Out on the aft deck as Highball and the Memsahib were taking the evening air their English voices attracted the attention of a young man with rucksack attached.

"You're English?" asked the young man in a strong Australian accent. He was a backpacker on walkabout, making an extended European tour. What, he wondered, were an English couple doing travelling to Croatia? His tone was that of one who had been the first to discover this part of Europe. Highball explained that he was part of a team on its way to Croatia to play cricket against some Croatian islanders. With typical antipodean crowing, the backpacker asserted that the English team would surely lose. This was the cue for a major sense of humour failure on Highball's part. First it was the airline's CEO, now some jumped-up little Aussie backpacker. What was it with these people? Had English cricket's stock really fallen so low? The conversation with the Australian was curtailed abruptly and the Highballs went back inside.

Elsewhere, on the starboard deck, The Sipper and Crabbo Junior, by now well-fuelled on Eurolager, were admiring a full and orange moon, low above the inky expanse of the Adriatic. The tour captain was overcome by the urge to sing, and so the two struggled their way through the first verse of the Navy hymn:

> Eternal father, strong to save,
> Whose arm hath bound the restless wave,
> Blah blah blah blah blah blah blah blah
> Blah blah blah blah blah blah blah blah blah
> Oh, hear us when we cry to Thee,
> For those in peril on the sea!

They followed this with a salute to Selene, the Greek goddess of the moon, in the only appropriate manner. Promptly turning their backs to the celestial orb and loosening their trouser belts…

Those without a cabin who were of a mind to get some sleep made do with the floor of the aft passenger deck. Beard, ever innovative, contrived to wedge his 110-litre rucksack between the jambs of a door so he could rest halfway in and halfway out of the passenger deck, and benefit from what little ventilation there was.

As the soothing strains of Dire Straits' *Sultans of Swing* began to lull the weary party to sleep, Frannie was out on deck taking a last look at the sea before retiring. The low throb of the engines and the churning wake behind the ship were the only intrusions on a scene of absolute calm. Her work regularly took her to Kenya and Uganda where, out on the plains at night, she had known absolute silence and solitude. In spite of the company of her fellow travellers, she was feeling lonely, her thoughts firmly with her husband JD, who had not travelled with the main St Radegund party but was now somewhere at sea on the Mediterranean. He had set out from Menorca a good week earlier with another St Radegund cricketer, El Bow, on board the latter's sailing boat, the plan being that they pilot the boat into the Adriatic to arrive on Vis in time to make the game of cricket on the Sunday. A journey of more than a thousand miles, this meant they would need to sail better than a hundred miles a day. Frances had not heard from JD since he had left the Balearics, and would likely not do so again until he got within range of a mobile phone mast, probably not before he neared the heel of Italy. She thought of the two of them, connected by the same stretch of water, yet apart.

▲

Dawn, its rosy fingers spreading over the mountains of the Dalmatian interior, broke just after half-past six. Most of the party awoke with the light and went onto the aft deck to get their first glimpse of the coast: rocky islands and steep hillsides fretted with sleepy towns unchanged since they were built in the sixteenth century. Such breathtaking vistas at so early an hour were not to everybody's taste: Jugs and a couple of others were instead playing cribbage in the fore bar.

A simple but barely filling breakfast of coffee and a pastry was gladly taken by the starving party, accompanied again by Dire Straits' finest. Highball, irritable at the best of times but at his most irritable first thing in the morning after a bad night's sleep, found the too-cheery-by-half opening refrain of *Walk of Life* too much to handle. He had had enough and began to fantasise long and loudly about the possibility of travelling back in time to break Mark Knopfler's fingers.

Bunter, meanwhile, was having another little difficulty with the locals. He had dressed and left his cabin early to go and breakfast, then decided it would be a good idea to change his remaining euros into Croatian kuna while still on board. He joined an orderly queue at the foreign exchange desk. When his turn arrived, he approached the counter and asked (in

English, of course) if he could change his currency. The helpful cashier was only too willing to oblige and asked for Bunter's passport. This item Bunter steadfastly refused to hand over, and insisted that his possession of a British passport ("Her Britannic Majesty's Secretary of State requests and requires…" etc) should be enough to ensure compliance with his wishes from this minor Italian flunkey. Impasse. Eventually it became clear that if Bunter didn't hand over his document for inspection he would get no money, and so he relented. As Bunter turned from the counter, the vexed cashier made it quite clear what he thought of this disruptive Englishman who was trying to tell him how to do his job: "Signor Mussolini!" he called after him.

Soon enough the ferry had pulled alongside the main dock in Split, and all disembarked hale and hearty, though not without a casualty. As Bunter was making his way from the boat to passport control, he managed to drop a litre bottle of duty-free Export Gordon's Gin onto the dock, where it smashed. After a perfectly observed minute's silence at this unexpected libation to Poseidon, the party carried on, consoling themselves with the thought that Split's municipal cleansing department would be grateful, at least, for the St Radegund's impromptu sterilisation of the harbour side. Then Bunter realised he had left his passport on board the ferry. The rest of the party kindly decided to stick together and wait for their leader while he went back onto the ship to track down the missing document. After a few minutes Bunter re-emerged, passport in hand and, ignoring the rest of the St Radegund party, marched imperiously to the front of the queue for passport control and was already on his second cigarette by the time the rest made it through. With customs formalities overcome, everyone went in search of coffee on Split's bustling, palm-lined *Riva* or waterfront, before boarding the 9.30 ferry to Vis.

The morning was bright and clear, the temperature already in the low sixties. Up on deck people basked in the sunshine, fanned by a gentle westerly breeze. Below, in the main café area, excitement was beginning to build among the group at the thought of their 27-hour journey nearing its end. Beard, who apparently had barely slept, decided to celebrate the team's imminent arrival by making satisfying inroads into a litre bottle of Isle of Jura malt whisky he had bought back at Stansted. The Sipper had been with Beard at World of Whiskies but had declined to buy a bottle himself, even in spite of an attractive thirty per cent reduction on the high-street price. Though no prude, to The Sipper's mind drinking at so young an hour smacked of bad form and he made his disapproval plain with a frown.

"Breakfast of Champions!" enthused Beard, by way of mitigation.

"Breakfast of Tramps, more like," rebuked The Sipper light-heartedly. Just as he was about to issue Beard with a firm, captainly warning along the lines of "everything in moderation, including moderation", Bunter appeared and cheerfully announced the news that Lawrence Dixon had managed to get himself locked in the ferry's lavatory.

NOTES

i   Scepanović, Ivo. *Croatian island re-discovers its history – and takes up cricket*, in the Sunday Telegraph, 23 March 2003

ii   European Cricket Council website (http://www.cricketeurope.net/ECC/index.html), 2003

3

The Three Stooges

Everyone chatted amiably, impressed with the quality and quantity of the food, and the charming setting.

Seated away from the main party on the flight to Pescara were Lawrence, Pete and Mike, all stalwarts of the St Radegund's great cricketing rival, the Champion of the Thames public house, just up the road on King Street. Once it had appeared likely that the St Radegund alone would not have enough players travelling to Vis to make up a full eleven, Bunter had raised the alarm and invited Lawrence Dixon and company to join the party. So it was that they turned up in the departure lounge at Stansted each wearing sunglasses, Bermuda shorts and sandals, their ensembles completed by floral-print Hawaiian shirts in Technicolor of particular violence. As they stood around, uniformed like timeshare reps of the apocalypse, the trio's tonsorial diversity seemed their sole distinguishing feature: Mike had a stubbly beard and closely shaved head, Lawrence slightly thinning sandy-ginger hair, and Pete a thick jet-black mop. Highball immediately spotted a vague resemblance to those nearly forgotten American vaudevillians and slapstick film comedians The Three Stooges, and so were the trio named – Curly for Mike, Larry for Lawrence and Moe for Pete – for the duration of the tour.

At this jibe, Lawrence – Larry – announced with a show of mock petulance that the three of them planned to sit right at the front of the plane to avoid the Radegundians. In fact Larry knew, he admitted, that most airline in-flight trolleys carry no more than three miniature bottles of champagne on short-haul flights, so getting seats as close to the front of the aeroplane as possible would allow them to relieve the cabin crew of said sparkle.

"Good luck, at twenty quid a throw," said a cheapskate from the St Radegund, ever the poor relations whether in cricket or budget air travel. And with that The Three Stooges flounced off to seek out a "stiffener" and stand at the head of the boarding queue. At the nearest bar they ordered three gin and tonics. The requisite number of glasses was produced, iced, sliced and ginned, whereupon the barista announced that the bar was out of tonic. This was not a good start.

Larry's wife had recently taken over as licensee of the Champ and Larry himself worked there as, in his words, "an occasional barman" which translated more accurately to "a most-of-the-bloody-time barman". A bookmaker in a former life he, unsurprisingly, took an interest in most sports and keenly upheld the tradition of the Rad versus Champ game, though he rarely graced the greensward himself. His cricketing ability was, therefore, something of a mystery. Curly and Moe, on the other hand, were more than familiar to the cricketers of the St Radegund.

Moe was well known on the river Cam as an accomplished rowing coach. He had played cricket in the first Rad versus Champ match in 1992, and in nearly every one since. His powerful, clean-hitting batting displays had turned many a match in the Champ's favour and led to him being rightly regarded by the Rad players as their opponents' danger man.

Curly was a more recent addition to the Champ team. A Cambridgeshire-born mathematics graduate, he was once winner of a Brain of Cambridge competition and on another occasion placed third in Mensa's Brain of Britain. His technical proficiency as an opening batsman was only marred by an occasionally ponderous scoring rate. Curly and Moe at least gave the St Radegund tourists the look of something approaching a cricket team. Their other potential contribution to the tour was of a more dubious quality.

Take these regulars of the Champion of the Thames out of Cambridge and transplant them en masse into a foreign country, and disaster pursues them with the relentlessness of the Furies. A number of foreign trips to locations as diverse as Berlin, Cork and Prague (twice!) had produced such a catalogue of missing luggage, lost hotel keys, missed flight connections and general misfortune that the wonder was that they had never been deported or, at the very least, asked to surrender their passports. Their rampages through one European city after another had become the stuff of legend on King Street, not least because of the catalyzing effect that alcohol had played in their misadventures. Make no mistake: their Beer Miles membership had reached platinum status. You name it, they'd been there, done that, and in all probability lost the T-shirt somewhere along the way. And compounding the issue was the fact that, owing to other commitments, the trio's stay on Vis was going to be far shorter than the rest of the other tourists', meaning they aimed to pack as much as possible in to the limited time available. This could only spell trouble.

In the arrivals hall at Abruzzo airport the Stooges were champing at the bit to hail a taxi to decant them at the closest available bar to Pescara's railway station, and were about to disappear and do just that when Bunter tried his scoutmaster routine on them, insisting that everybody stick together and take the next available bus into town. It was his party, his charter. This did not go down well with the more independently minded

Champ boys. As the Stooges aired their differences, one bus was missed, then another. The rest of the travellers could only sit on their luggage outside the airport in the thick afternoon heat and wonder why they weren't going anywhere. As the warring parties retired to their respective corners to fume and sulk and smoke, the Stooges made a point of glancing melodramatically at wristwatches to indicate precious drinking time being lost. When, finally, the party did board the bus to the railway station it inched its way from traffic light to traffic light, making a mockery of the supposed twenty-minute journey time into the centre of Pescara.

It was also at Pescara that the party caught its first glimpse of a phenomenon unique to countries with a high proportion of Roman Catholics, a pair of nuns. As if on cue, Bunter produced one of his famous old chestnuts: "Why do nuns always go around in pairs? So one nun sees the other nun don't get none." The possibility of this being repeated by Bunter at every sighting of Sisters of Christ was too much to bear, but the party managed to put a brave face on it and act as though they were hearing the joke for the first time.

Once at Pescara railway station, and with their tickets bought, the Stooges managed to give Bunter the slip long enough to sink a couple of Nastro Azzuro beers, but joined the rest on the platform for the train to Ancona. Amazingly, given their record, all three had remembered to validate their train tickets. The St Radegund party, in the meantime, had settled for a spot of lunch at a terrace cafe on the town's main drag. Here The Sipper impressed one and all with his command of tourist Italian, as he ordered *un' espresso doppio*, which appeared in due course, thick and dark in its dainty cup and saucer. One slurp of coffee later and its laxative powers took immediate effect. The Sipper rose quickly from the table and moved smartly in the direction of the washrooms. Things were, he said, "heading south".

Aboard the train to Ancona the Stooges were the object of some good-natured ribbing. Larry's hair, once undoubtedly fuller and thicker than it now was (though never a match for Moe's luxuriant thatch) bore the brunt of it. When Highball suggested Larry had been detained at airport security because "his rug contained a metallic weave" Larry shot back a glance that said, quite clearly, "Watch it!" Highball was chastened. Larry was not one to cross.

The train journey was "dry" so Moe, for one, was looking fairly fed up with the whole experience. So bored was he that he couldn't even be bothered to call anybody by their real names, so for convenience's sake addressed everybody as "Dave". The boredom was probably explained by the Rad's unnecessarily circuitous route to their destination. Given that the three of them were going to leave Vis on Monday, their desire to crack on with things was understandable. The Sipper, who had known Larry for a number of years, was entirely sympathetic to their need to pick up the pace and take on fuel at any and every available opportunity.

Things were less cordial between the two as Larry eventually emerged from the locked lavatory on the ferry to Vis. The problem had been a combination of a sliding bolt and mortice lock on the cubicle door, though why on earth you needed a mortice lock on a public lavatory was beyond him. Having shut the door firmly behind him, he had jammed the mortice lock halfway in, and as there was not enough clearance above the top of the cubicle to climb through he spent the next ten minutes hammering on the door like Fred Flintstone, shouting in the hope that somebody who understood English could help him. Then his mobile phone rang. It was his wife, ringing to enquire how he was enjoying his holiday. Larry explained his predicament and added, succinctly, that that particular moment was perhaps not the best time for idle chitchat.

Bunter entered the Gents with the aim of having a shave. As he lathered he heard Larry's voice and asked if he was all right. Larry apprised Bunter of the situation and asked him to find a steward to open the door. Bunter said he would be happy to oblige just as soon as he had finished his ablutions: he was not about to wander the decks of the ship with his chops covered in soapsuds. To Larry this felt like the last straw. Having spent the previous evening trying to sleep under a lifeboat (it seemed, given the Stooges' track record, a reasonable precaution) only to be woken constantly by an ongoing argument between Curly and Beard in the wee small hours, and with a formerly high regard for the works of Mr Mark Knopfler and his cohorts' musical oeuvre having been thoroughly ruined by constant repetition, to be denied his freedom just because Bunter wanted to finish his "dig of the grave" was taking the biscuit. When, thanks to Bunter's brawny intervention, Larry did emerge from his confinement he was, to say the least, not amused. The Sipper was, though, and thinking Larry would appreciate the joke, put a referee's whistle to his lips and produced a yellow card from his top pocket that he proceeded to brandish in the hapless publican's face. Larry turned quicker than you could say "Oh dear, what can the matter be?"

"Which side do you want, port or starboard?" Larry enquired menacingly of The Sipper, who quickly backed down in the face of this offer of assistance in a very premature disembarkation.

Curly, meanwhile, having spent most of the night in conversation with Beard, and partaken in the early-morning cribbage three-hander with Jugs and Larry, was settling in nicely, engaged in merry conversation with the Rad boys. Having seen Beard tackle his bottle of Jura with aplomb, he decided to engage a half-bottle of duty-free Cabernet Sauvignon of vivacious tone and sharp palette. His reading matter on the trip was a book called *The Truth about Wilson*, an anthology reprinting some of the exploits of one William Wilson, a North Country athlete blessed with the secret of long life who managed, in weekly episodes of the *Wizard* comic from the 1940s onwards, an increasingly unlikely array of impossible sporting feats. The St Radegund team were familiar with some of these tales already, having often been treated to a lengthy account of them by Bunter himself. At the end of each story, in which Wilson would set a ludicrously fast world-record time for the 100 metres, or win the Ashes single-handedly. Bunter would laugh heartily at the sheer daftness of it all, "Ho-ho-ho: Wilson!" It was with similar gusto that Curly, pausing only to refer to his vino, dictated from the book to the delight of the gathered throng,

Beard was now generously offering a taste of Jura to the assembled group. As the bottle passed between them, for the most part untried, The Sipper returned and Beard demanded to know, yet again, when he was going to don the helmet. The Sipper, exasperated, maintained that he hadn't forgotten his responsibilities but was merely looking for the most appropriate opportunity to start fining people. With Beard having made many similar requests, this seemed to The Sipper to be as good a time as any to start, if only to keep the peace.

For anyone who has never been on a cricket or rugby tour, a regular element of the social side of things is the imposition of fines for breaches of personal or collective etiquette. The offences come in all shapes and sizes, and cover everything from failing to take a drink quickly enough, or in the prescribed manner (left-handed with the little finger extended is always a good one), to complaining, displays of personal affection, foul-mouthedness, intended or unintended double entendres and the like. According to the St Radegund team's treasurer, the formal rules were codified back in the 1930s and provide for such eventualities as under what circumstances to wear a cravat, the right to appeal a fine and so forth, but the essence of the exercise has been refined by the St Radegund to the following three cardinal rules:

1. Anything and everything will be fined
2. The bank does not give change
3. What goes on tour stays on tour

The bank, in the case of the Rad, was a Cambridge RUFC sock whose powers of elastic deformation had been put to a severe test on the previous year's tour to Gloucestershire. As the fines had accumulated, the sock had become a thing of wonder as, stuffed with a good couple of hundred pounds in small change, it stretched four-and-a-half feet over the treasurer's shoulder, and was memorably described by Bunter as "hanging lower than a Lebanese donkey's dong". Even more amazing was the fact that it had managed to return to its original shape with little or no encouragement once the tour was over and it had given up what remained of its precious treasure.

The Sipper produced from his bag a bright orange, plastic police constable's helmet, the symbol of ultimate authority for the fines master. Back in Cambridge a float of £100, with which to subsidise beer on tour, had been added to the sock, which was now in Highball's care along with a hardcover exercise book in which to record the various infractions. The only instructions issued to the touring party by those left behind in the St Radegund had been to make sure the sock returned to the pub with the same amount as it left with. In other words: what was spent on drink had to be put back into the sock over the course of the tour.

Highball handed The Sipper the fines book, which had been decorated with a pencil and ink image of Vis harbour above the words "St Radegund Pub – Vis, Hrvatska – Fines and Forfeits". On the back was the return address of the St Radegund: "just in case", as Highball put it. While a practical precaution, this nevertheless gave Highball the distinction of being first in the fines book: a penalty of half a euro being awarded for "excessive officiousness". Beard, having repeatedly enquired when the fining was to commence, wasted no time in getting into the book and clocked up several amercements in the first half hour of business for, variously, "arguing with the fines master", "waffle", and, most seriously, "a disgraceful adornment of his King Street Run tie", said item having been tied around his head in the fashion of a bandana. Others soon followed Beard into the book as the process of relieving the party of most of its loose change began in earnest.

The majority of fines early into any tour are usually for such crimes as questioning the fines master and snitching, which can in a lot of cases be put down to a lack of familiarity with the rules. A typical early exchange, then, proceeds in the following manner:

"That's a one euro fine for 'excessive rudeness'."

"But he started it!"

"That'll be a further euro for questioning the fines master, and one euro for snitching. Three euros please."

Snitching, in particular, is regarded as absolutely beyond the pale. The only person allowed to pass on information to the fines master is the official tour sneak, whose identity is traditionally a secret until tour's end. This means the fines master has to be eagle-eyed, alert to everything going on, and on duty 24 hours a day, or at least until such time as he declares the book closed for the day.

Larry was, of course, a prime candidate for fining following his toilet escapade. The book recorded "a shocking sense of humour failure, dissent to the fines master, and refusal to pay. Three euros." Curly was deemed to have infringed for "passing the whisky to the right", an unconscionable lapse of etiquette given that the fines master was at that precise moment sitting directly to his left. So it was that the book started out recording the various penalties with exquisite care and fidelity often in quite florid, descriptive detail. Inevitably, as the day grew long and the drink took hold, this would degenerate into scrawled illegibility and meaningless drivel. As a record of tour activities it was a poor substitute for a well-kept diary, but as an account of the social highpoints of the trip and how easily good intentions are undermined by alcohol, it promised to be an invaluable reference tool and *aide-mémoire*.

A few tables away Bunter was chatting to the newest members of the tour party, Nick King and his father, David. Nick was just about to begin the final year of a philosophy and history degree at Jesus College, around the corner from the St Radegund pub. He was also that year's president of the Rhadegund Society, a college drinking society named in commemoration of the saint. Its motto, "drink to our patron saint in a bumper of wine", was honoured in the observance, and then some. Square-jawed and clean-cut, Nick was a keen cricketer for the College's first XI, where he batted in the middle order with some accomplishment.

Nick's father, in his mid-sixties, hailed from Downham, between Catford and Bromley. After National Service (spent mostly in Hong Kong) in the Royal Artillery, he had taken two firsts in the history Tripos at Magdalene, and was the proud possessor of a King Street Run tie, notable for being "P"-less. From Cambridge he had gone on to a career as a university lecturer, mainly in the north of England, where his main research was on the Visigoths. As he viewed the massed ranks of the St Radegund touring party he could be forgiven for thinking that he was about to spend a week observing the actions of those barbarian hordes' descendants.

The Kings had flown to Trieste from Stansted the day before the rest of the St Radegund party and had managed a good look around the Italian city's squares and cafés, before taking the overnight bus down to Split. This was timetabled to arrive at five in the morning, but actually got into town an hour and a half earlier, bang in the middle of the night. The bus driver woke them loudly, screaming at them "What are you waiting for? We are here! This is your Split!" and deposited them and their bags on the pavement. They had no place to stay and were considering looking for a conveniently placed park bench on which to rough it when they were approached by a man offering a room for the night. They looked at each other, shrugged, and followed him to an apartment where he woke an attractive-looking young girl who showed them to a pleasant enough room.

They woke around eleven to bright Mediterranean light, and were delighted to find their apartment only a stone's throw from Diocletian's Palace and overlooking bustling market stalls. Nick had been to Split a few years previously so considered himself something of an old hand, and was expecting to have to accompany his historian father around numerous cathedrals and palaces while he did his best to act as tour guide. To his great surprise and delight, David's priority was to spend quality time with his son, and so they passed an agreeable day drinking beer and coffee and eyeing up the local talent.

In the evening when they stepped out into the heart of the city to eat, they stumbled upon what seemed to be some sort of political rally that involved dancing and a bloke shouting at people on the *Riva*. Both agreed this was not particularly compelling as an electoral stance, and so they went to dinner. Nick enjoyed a portion of local *čevapčići* or meat rissoles while David, in typical Englishman-abroad-mode, got to grips with an omelette. Unlike most of the St Radegund party on the ferry, the Kings had managed a decent night's sleep, so were fresh and lively. Bunter made introductions.

"A pair of Kings is always worth having in your hand," he quipped, then added to the Rad boys, "better than a bunch of jokers like you lot!"

As a gesture of welcome to the fellow travellers Beard immediately offered the Kings a "morning snifter" of his Jura, which they gratefully accepted. The Memsahib, who had her nose in a guidebook to Croatia, mentioned that *Juraj*, the equivalent in Croatian to George, is the patron saint of Croatia, and then reeled off a number of Mediterranean cities she and Highball had been to that also claim St George as their patron. This information was enough, unsurprisingly, to earn her a one euro fine for swottiness. Having, for the time being at least, completed the pressing business of fining people, The Sipper turned his attention to furnishing the Kings with nicknames for the duration of the tour. He mused aloud in front of David: "King... father... pop king... yes, Elvis..! El-vis! El Vis!" So David became for the remainder of the trip, and Nick, for want of anything better, was christened "Son of El Vis". Genius. The senior of the two Kings felt flattered at such an immediate and unquestioning welcome into the St Radegund's fraternity, and was already enjoying his holiday greatly. He had never been to Croatia before, so when the offer came to join the cricket tour he had jumped at it. Nick was growing up fast and, as a consequence, they were seeing less and less of each other, so an opportunity for father and son to spend more time together was welcome.

Up on deck Jugs, Crabbo Junior and Moe were taking the Adriatic air on a perfect, cloudless day. The temperature was already in the mid-seventies, but a fresh sea breeze brought relief. There was a sudden burst of excitement to port as a small pod of dolphins raced alongside the boat. Soon enough the island of Vis began to dominate the horizon ahead. It seemed bigger than any of the party was expecting and the sight of it quickened the sense of anticipation. As the boat made its way deep into the harbour, it towered gigantically above the tiny houses with their brick-red roof tiles. The ferry rounded a small peninsula and headed for the port, then swung its stern round to come to rest alongside the huge, concrete, and now finally completed, dock whose reconstruction had kept Bunter awake sixteen months before. The stern ramp was lowered, and passengers spilled onto the dock, blinking in the bright sunlight. Their 27-hour odyssey finally at an end, the St Radegund party crossed the narrow harbour road and headed straight for the nearest bar.

Bejbi, or Baby, was almost directly opposite the dock, making it the obvious port of call for the thirsty traveller stepping off the ferry. The interior was decorated in a minimalist fashion with jazzy murals that would perhaps best be described as "cool". A pool table dominated the back room. Signs advertised live music. The number of locals milling around drinking coffee or sipping beer suggested it was a popular meeting-point. To the left of the main bar was an alfresco area, topped with a bamboo and palm frond thatch that provided shade from the ferocious sun. Bicycles were lined up outside, none of them secured with locks, which was a shock to the party coming from Cambridge with its almost daily incidence of bike thefts. At midday on a Friday the bar was bustling.

The tourists eased themselves round a large table in the middle of the alfresco area. Highball stood at the bar and ordered the first round of drinks: thirteen bottles of the nearest thing to a local brew, from Karlovac, south of Zagreb on the mainland. As he opened his wallet on to the bar, much as he would do back in the Rad, he momentarily turned to the party to check his arithmetic. Facing the bar again he was shocked to find his wallet had disappeared. A sickening wave of panic rose in him as he looked around in a desperate search for it. He didn't have far to look for the culprit. Beard had playfully hidden the wallet and was enjoying Highball's discomfort. Highball was not best pleased.

Comfortably ensconced with a Karlovačko each the party, for the most part, spoke their first words of Croatian, a toast. They raised their glasses, and pronounced in unison, though with varying degrees of accuracy, "*Živjeli!*" Light and Pilsnery at 5.4% ABV, the Karlovačko went down very easily indeed, and the happy fact of their arrival with only a few minor mishaps on the way was celebrated. The round of thirteen 50cl bottles was estimated at having cost just over £10. This appeared eminently reasonable, and with initial thirsts slaked it was deemed only right to celebrate again with a further round. It was to be hoped that the bar would not run out.

Beard stepped outside to take a text message from the team's non-travelling captain back in Cambridge. "Any disasters yet?" it asked. Beard fired off a quick reply, mentioning Bunter's dropped bottle of gin but little else. The news came back that those left behind were busy organising an "alternative Vis" party for those who weren't able to go on tour. Beard knew where he'd rather be and reported as much.

Tacked to the wall by the entrance to the bar was an A3-sized poster advertising the forthcoming cricket match between St Radegund Cricket Club, Cambridge, England and Kriket Klub Sir William Hoste of Vis, with a graphic of a batsman defending his wicket.

The Sir William Hoste team's captain, Oliver Roki, and Goran Pečarević from the Villa Kaliopa joined the party for a drink. Over a leisurely beer they divided the travellers into smaller units for the purpose of accommodation. Oliver told the party they would all be billeted in various apartments belonging to team members around town. Apart from Bunter, no member of the party had given any thought to accommodation, so it was a relief to find arrangements well in hand.

In addition to the Croatian for "good health!" another linguistic discovery was made. Bunter had, for the past year and a half, been pronouncing the word "Vis" as if it were that toilet-humorous, Tyneside comic magazine featuring Sid the Sexist, Roger Mellie *et al.* The briefest of chats with Oliver made it plain that the island was in fact pronounced "Veess", with the "v" almost completely swallowed into a "w". This would take some getting used to.

Bunter had promised the tourists an opening meal, which was to be a late lunch at the Pojoda restaurant in the suburb of Kut. The party was given general directions and then Oliver, Goran and Neo Poduje – a waiter at the Pojoda – drove the guests to their respective apartments. The journey proved a hair-raising experience as the cars careered through the narrow lanes at breakneck speed, heading straight for solid stone walls before lurching off at the last moment, left or right as the road dictated. Happily, all arrived safely and found their accommodation to be of a superb standard.

Fate, however, had somehow conspired to split up The Three Stooges. Curly was sharing with the Highballs in Lučica, farthest away from the town in a spacious double apartment that boasted its own basketball hoop in the courtyard outside. Larry and Moe, meanwhile, had a place close by the main square in the centre of Kut. It would have been reasonable to expect some weakening of the powers of the evil eye now that there were only two of them sharing together, but no. No sooner had they dumped their bags and started to freshen up than the toilet seat broke under Moe. Larry went into the bathroom to take a shower and turned on the water only to find that the handle had come away in his hand, leaving a gushing stream of water it was impossible to stop. Larry looked at Moe as they wondered what to do next.

"Let's go and get a drink while we think about it," decided Larry. Tracking down their landlord proved more difficult than they expected, so Larry and Moe were late for the lunch at the Pojoda, the party's first introduction to Dalmatian hospitality.

There they were joined by Rob Dumančić, by profession a freelance journalist and media analyst, who had learned to play cricket out in Australia, and co-founded Zagreb Cricket Club in 1999. Rob mentioned that he had played, only last year, against an MCC touring side. At this Highball's ears pricked up, and Rob was surprised to find out that Highball knew one of his opponents. The world of cricket is a small one.

The previous September Rob had been in Split, having come down from Zagreb where he and his then girlfriend lived and worked, en route to the pretty Dalmatian coastal town of Makarska with an eye to a permanent move there. Having some time to kill he picked up a copy of the August issue of the Croatian language edition of *Playboy*. Skipping through it he found an article extolling the virtues of life on Vis. It also carried a brief mention, in a review of Konoba Roki's, of Oliver's desire to start up a cricket team. Rob took the bait and headed for Vis instead of Makarska. So charmed was he with the island and its inhabitants that he eventually moved there, his (now) wife having found a job teaching religious education at a local school.

Rob clearly enjoyed the opportunity of conversation in English, and in Bejbi had been particularly happy to swap Australian cricketing stories with Crabbo Junior, whose mother was born in Melbourne. When it came time to show the St Radegund tourists to their accommodation he took a lift with the El Vises, Beard and Crabbo Junior in Goran Pečarević's van to their apartment in Kut: not quite as far out as the Highballs and Curly, but still a good fifteen minutes' walk into town. It was an impressive townhouse on three storeys round the corner from the local church. There the tourists were introduced to the owner, a middle-aged man called Tomislav who spoke no English. Rob offered to translate, and so a tortuous, three-way conversation took place. Beard's copy of *Lyle's Guide to Languages* was conspicuously lacking a single phrase that could have helped the situation.

Tomislav, though, had kindly brought his visitors a welcoming gift, a magnum of home-made *travarica*, brandy flavoured with herbs such as lavender and wild fennel that he had picked himself. The huge bottle was suspended between two armatures on a wooden frame, the idea being that tilting the bottle on the frame makes pouring out the spirit much easier. Tomislav demonstrated the operation, filling a number of shot glasses with the cloudy liquid. "*Živjeli!*"

"Sorry, did you say it was called 'Dragon Water'?" asked Son of El Vis, having misheard the spirit's name in Croatian. Knocking back his sample in one, he decided that Dragon Water was about right. The rest made vaguely approbatory noises and paid their compliments to Tomislav, "*Dobra!*"

Glasses were charged a second time. Then Tomislav produced another bottle, pressing it into El Vis' hands (it didn't take much pressing), presumably in view of his seniority in the party. The Visigoth specialist uttered a humble "*Hvala*", or thank you. It was not clear from Tomislav's demeanour whether this bottle was intended for the group or for El Vis alone, but El Vis assumed the latter and decided on the spot to take it home unbroached and at once secured it in his room. This action Beard eyed with suspicion, having surmised that the bottle was meant to be shared. As grateful tenants and honoured guests, it behove them to polish off as much of this free booze as possible before they left, and he communicated as much to Crabbo Junior and Son of El Vis, who nodded conspiratorially.

▲

The Pojoda restaurant proved easy to find. Its owner, Zoran Brajčić, buzzed around a long table under the citrus trees making everyone feel welcome. His waiters, Zoltan and Neo, made sure everybody was comfortable and brought out a round of beers while Zoran cooked lunch. And what a lunch: melt-in-the-mouth tuna risotto with caper sauce, followed by a wholesome, mixed fish soup and helped down with a couple of bottles of Plavac, the local red wine. Everyone chatted amiably, impressed with the quality and quantity of the food, and the charming setting. Then, to everybody's surprise, Zoran produced another course, a huge, whole scorpion fish or škarpina[i] served with the head and accompanied by a substantial pasta and bean salad. The fish was of conversation-stopping ugliness, or maybe it was just that the party had already eaten their fill. Out of politeness to their host, they did the best they could, but it was really quite enough food, and this was only lunch. Bunter grew suspicious.

"Are they trying to nobble us for the game on Sunday?" he asked.

Replete, the St Radegund began to relax and enjoy the tranquil garden setting. There seemed no more civilised way to pass the time than to while away an hour or two under the lemon and mandarin trees. If this was a true reflection of the pace of life on the island, then the party had been, as Crabbo Junior put it, beaten with the lucky stick. All were unstinting in their praise of Bunter for pulling it off and actually getting them there. More wine was ordered, this time a bottle of the white Vugava.

"Is it named after a lady's part?" Crabbo Junior asked insouciantly.

Curly fell asleep at table, which caused some debate. A consensus was reached that, with his shaved head and powerful build, he reminded them of nothing less than a beaten boxer, out on his stool. On cue The Sipper picked up his cloth napkin and started playing cornerman to Curly's prize fighter, wafting the serviette in Curly's face like some latter-day Angelo Dundee. Curly opened his eyes. The Sipper checked them for signs of recognition, then announced to the assembled that Curly was in a fit state to "box on", a performance familiar to the Radegund boys as being one of Bunter's staples for the amusement of the pub's clientele.

Elsewhere, Crabbo Junior and Highball were engaged in a session of competitive mimicry, each trying to outdo the other in vocal impressions of members of the party. There was little to choose between them with Bunter, as both managed to emulate his gruff, North London tones with ease. The Sipper's vocal inflections – all punctured vowels and swallowed consonants – proved easier to take off for the Lancastrian Highball, but Crabbo Junior just edged the plaudits for his take on the absent Eyebrows, capturing the orotund baritone of his tangential digressions ("Ahh, did you hear that programme on Radio Three about Charlie Parker? Turns out he was a Kraut," being a particularly favoured, though fictitious, example) and exaggerated hand gesticulations with stunning accuracy. Beard, who was not a great eater of fish, had been toying with his food and was eager to get in on the act. Unfortunately he was not at his best after a number of pre-, inter- and post-luncheon stimulants. His own version of an Eyebrows impression lacked fluidity. The hand movements were too mechanical, the vocalisations too much like mere throat clearing, and the whole thing curiously redolent of running down clockwork. Beard then topped this by rocking back on his chair and falling off it.

The group left the Pojoda in good spirits. The meal had cost under 2,000 kuna for three courses and wine. It was estimated that this was equivalent to under £200 which, to feed 14 persons well, represented extremely good value. People either dispersed back to their billets or wandered around Kut. Not far from the Pojoda was Vis town's police station, a modern one-storey building in the brutalist style whose outer walls were covered in all manner of helpful community notices, including a poster for Sunday's cricket match.

"I hope they aren't using it as a WANTED poster," The Sipper said. The mere presence of a police station in such a quiet, friendly setting as Vis provoked some questions about the level of policing needed on an island of 4,000 souls. How many policemen did the town possess? What was the ratio of cops to people? What was the most common crime? Jugs speculated it was drunkenness, to judge by the number of foreign-owned yachts in the harbour. Given such a small population, and a more-than likely low crime rate, did the police need to hit crime targets and, if so, what did they do to drum up business?

"Maybe they put a sign on the door saying Open For Crime," the Memsahib suggested drolly. This started Crabbo Junior riffing wildly. He imagined a whole poster campaign devised by the under-employed island bobbies to encourage criminal behaviour. This theme was quickly taken up by others in the party, and produced suggestions along the lines of "Your crime is our business," "Got a job to do? So have we," and "Go ahead, punk, make our day."

Plans had been made for the evening. Bunter suggested meeting at six in Goran's new bar, Lambik, in the main square in Kut for pre-dinner drinks before going on to the Villa Kaliopa. This seemed an ambitious programme so soon after finishing a three-course lunch but most were still following Bunter's suggestions automatically.

It being a Friday night, a meeting of the Vera Lynn Appreciation Society was appropriate, and accordingly the tourists descended upon Lambik at the appointed hour. The society had been founded in the mid-90s in the St Radegund pub by two regulars who liked to unwind at the end of the working week with a gin and tonic or two. Bunter quickly latched onto the idea of serving double measures at a reasonable price for the first two hours of business every Friday evening and, looking for a marketing angle, they came up – between the three of them – with the Vera Lynn Appreciation Society.[ii] Although in truth never much more than an informal aggregation of like-minded aficionados, the society quickly flourished and began to add to its ranks every Friday night, each new member receiving a token of membership in the form of a two pence piece folded into the discarded bottle top of a litre bottle of the spirit.

Vera Lynn herself was soon in on the joke when Bunter wrote to her via the Royal British Legion to request a signed photograph for the pub. He explained his National Service background and the fact that members of his pub had named a society in her honour. To everyone's great surprise Dame Vera responded, showing interest in "your gin drinking club" and enclosed an A4 black and white photograph, signed "To the regulars of the St Radegund pub. All best wishes, Vera Lynn." The photo, once it had been lovingly framed, was hung over the bar of the pub, where it resides to this day as an object of wonderment to regulars and visitors alike. In due course the Vera Lynn Appreciation Society was able to field a team to face the St Radegund in a cricket match. Meant, in theory at least, to be a contest between the pub's gin drinkers and its beer drinkers, in actuality the distinction was somewhat unclear and difficult to enforce, and the match ended up as the St Radegund team playing against second stringers of even more doubtful ability than themselves and, now and again, wives and/or girlfriends. The series, which still survives, has gone heavily in the St Radegund's favour.

Lambik was converted from the colonnaded courtyard of a 16th-century merchant's house. The vaulted interior was decorated with vines and other climbing plants, and lit with turquoise and red lamps. The bar was a frequent haunt of the town's young, and featured local DJs playing music of a kind invariably referred to by Bunter, in a catch-all way, as "Snot and The Four Nosebleeds".

The party settled at a large table inside the door and ordered a round of double gin and tonics. To its delight these duly appeared complete with a slice of lime and individual bottles of Schweppes tonic water, an absolute must in the preparation of the perfect, Vera Lynn-approved, gin and tonic. A slice of lemon or tonic water from the soda gun is unacceptable to the connoisseur. Lime and bottled it has to be. Accept no substitutes.

El Vis and Son of arrived. While the former had caught forty winks since leaving the Pojoda, the latter had managed to get in a swim from outside his apartment up to the north end of the bay and back. Thus he was refreshed and looking smart as paint. He wore around his neck a tie of a distinctive bottle green, purple and silver design, the official tie of the Rhadegund Society. Bunter, as an honorary member himself, insisted on all members of said society wearing their ties in the pub of a Friday night, and often slipped his own tie into his back pocket in case he was challenged. Bunter, Son of El Vis argued, in leaving his own tie at home had fallen foul of his own rule. It was a fair cop, admitted Bunter, and he bought the outgoing president of the Rhadegunds a Vera, which gave Son of El Vis no small degree of satisfaction. With such petty triumphs does one populate a Friday night.

Not far behind Son of El Vis in the sartorial stakes, Highball had, along with the fines sock, seen fit to bring out the Vera Lynn president's cap. It was in all respects like the cap worn by the St Radegund cricket captain except that where the Rad's colours were blood and sand with black trim, the Veras' were lime green and silver, like – if you accepted a double measure of poetic licence – a gin and tonic. What the barman at Lambik made of this paraphernalia was anybody's guess. What he made of thirteen thirsty Brits appearing in his bar and demanding to be drip-fed gin at six on a Friday evening, ditto. The local gin was perfectly drinkable though, perhaps, a little weak. It was to nobody's great surprise then when, after three rounds of thirteen gin and tonics – no, make that twelve gin and tonics: Moe was insistent that there was no way he was drinking gin – Lambik ran out.

No problem, thought Bunter. He was nothing if not resourceful, so promptly dispatched Curly to go and fetch one of the latter's own bottles of duty-free Gordon's Export from the apartment he shared with the Highballs. When Curly returned, Bunter promptly paid him for it and handed the bottle over to the barman, telling him to accept it as a gift, and that he could begin selling it back to the St Radegund over the bar. Larry couldn't believe his ears.

"We give them a litre bottle of gin for them to sell back to us. What's that all about?"

Bunter explained that it was meant as a friendly gesture to people who had been caught unprepared for their arrival. Larry shook his head. Curly, who had decked himself out in a woollen jumper in asymmetrical Christmas colours hand-knitted by his grandmother, looked non-plussed. He had, after all, been the loser in this being now minus one litre of duty-free gin (which not even money could recompense him for), but kept his counsel. The Export Gordon's, as expected, turned out to be significantly stronger than the local spirit, and so double measures of serious strength were doled out. Larry took a sip and grimaced in shock.

"It's like going from unleaded to leaded." he quipped. As the evening wore on and the best part of the donated litre bottle went down, things started to get a little more raucous, edging slowly, ominously, towards being out of control. Son of El Vis accidentally knocked over a couple of drinks. Moe, impressed by Crabbo Junior's silver cigarette case, was examining it closely, turning it over and over in his hands. Then, probing the mysteries of its spring-loaded fastening mechanism, he undid the catch whereupon twenty Lucky Strike shot out over the floor of the bar. By the time the party rolled out of Lambik and went their separate ways – The Sipper, Jugs and Crabbo Junior back into Vis town for more drinks, Bunter and the rest around the corner to dine at the Villa Kaliopa – things were steaming along nicely. The police station, The Sipper noted, was now Closed For Crime, but that didn't stop a whole cadenza of gin-fuelled riffing on the police's poster campaign. The three of them eventually settled down at a pretty vine-covered courtyard wine bar at the head of the harbour road, where they sipped Vugava served by an attractive, dark-haired waitress, for the rest of the evening.

At the Villa Kaliopa, Bunter and company were greeted warmly by Goran who showed the party to a table down in the garden, not far from the exterior wall. This spot was agreed by all to be a little too cosy so they asked to be re-seated higher up the garden at a larger table. Though Goran had been at Bejbi when the party arrived, Bunter formally introduced him to the members of the St Radegund cricket team. At the mention of cricket Goran's eyes lit up, and he suddenly disappeared into the restaurant, returning moments later carrying a cricket bat. He told them, with obvious pride, how he had started to play cricket with the locals this winter, having never seen a game before. Bunter asked if he would be playing on Sunday. Goran shrugged and said that the team would be made up of some of the younger guys on the island, in an "It's a young man's game" sort of way. Bunter commiserated.

Presently Goran went through the menu for the benefit of the visitors, once again, like the first time Bunter had eaten there, from memory. Bunter was recommending the prawns to everybody. Few of the party were ready for another three-course meal, so the ordering was ad hoc with some preferring starter dishes rather than mains. Another enormously ugly fish was shared between some members of the party. Bottles of Vugava were ordered. The food was freshly caught, sensational, delicious. The picturesque garden setting lent a memorable ambience to what was a gastronomic delight. More wine was ordered. Son of El Vis, having seen off a *Dubrovnika* crème caramel which, he swore, was to die for, was idly sculpting the fat candle on the table.

Digestifs were ordered, cigarettes produced. General chatter ensued. Someone asked for a light. Larry picked up the candle. Its sides, remoulded by Son of El Vis, contained a deep reservoir of hot liquid wax. The wax spilled onto Larry's hand causing him to drop the candle on to the tablecloth, which caught fire. Son of El Vis's attempts to put it out with paper napkins only made matters worse. Anxious waiters rushed to extinguish it. Larry blamed Son of El Vis. There were courteous and sincere apologies all round. Bunter, though, was incensed.

A torrent of abuse fell from his lips as he vented his anger on the party. He had brought them all this way to meet his friends, who had had their hospitality thrown back in their faces. Purple with rage, he had half a mind to call a halt to the evening there and then, the stupid arseholes. The tablecloth was ruined, and though Goran had accepted the apologies of the party it still wasn't good enough for Bunter, who stumped off towards the lower part of the gardens.

Though torch-lit, it was still difficult to see. He was blinded by rage and booze, and, missing a step down, he fell heavily on his left arm. Pain shot the length of it. He swore loudly for he knew that he had just broken his elbow. Frannie rushed from the table and a couple of waiters came over to help him up. Bunter cradled his arm, insisting to everyone who asked that he was all right. The arm was already starting to bruise badly. Bunter stubbornly refused to go home but waited until the meal was finished.

Quickly the dinner party broke up. Goran kindly offered to drive Bunter and Frannie, who were sharing the same apartment, back into town. Bunter assumed Goran must know an emergency doctor, but asked no questions. They sped through the narrow streets of Kut, Goran driving with a sense of urgency that made the pain in Bunter's arm feel all the more acute. To the passengers' surprise, Goran dropped them off not at a place offering emergency medical care, or at their apartment, but back at Bejbi. It was better than nothing. Bunter and Frannie knocked back a nightcap before Frannie walked him home and helped him up the stairs to his room where he spent a distinctly uncomfortable night's sleep with a now badly swollen arm.

The Three Stooges, meanwhile, had wandered merrily from the Villa Kaliopa into the warm night air and headed back towards town looking for a last nightcap. Larry was having a little difficulty walking in a straight line. Straying too close to the harbour's edge, he would have fallen in but for the quick reflexes of Curly, who picked him up, threw him over his shoulder and began to carry him back to his digs. As they passed the police station, still Closed For Crime, you could only wonder how long it would be before one of them was banged up. At least it would give the police something to do.

NOTES

i   Like the French *rascasse*, a major ingredient of bouillabaisse
ii The forename of the one-time Forces Sweetheart, now Dame Commander of the British Empire, is rhyming slang for gin. Vera = Vera Lynn = Gin. Obvious, really. But you'd be surprised at how many people still ask.

4

The Waking of the Dead

Farther on through some trees, beyond a small chapel, lay a rectangular walled cemetery.

The members of the St Radegund party crawled sheepishly from their respective pits on a bright Saturday morning, each sporting hangovers of varying intensity and some a not altogether unwarranted sense of guilt. Highball and the Memsahib were first out of the traps, having turned in unpardonably early the night before. They woke equally early, still fuzzy-headed, and decided on a pre-breakfast swim in the waters of the harbour. They walked down the steps from their second-storey apartment in Lučica to greet a sunny and agreeably hot day and, passing their host family's substantial vegetable garden where rocket and tomatoes grew in abundance, crossed the vine-covered terrace down to the narrow road, on the other side of which stood a stone jetty giving immediate access to the pristine harbour waters.

The Memsahib was a strong swimmer and had completed a dozen or so lengths of 25 metres between a buoy and the family's tethered fishing boat before Highball had even managed more than a little uncertain paddling. The water was bracing but not cold. Refreshed and revived, and their hangovers banished, they wrapped their lower torsos in the Balinese batik sarongs (five quid a throw from the St Radegund following one of Bunter's south-east Asian jaunts) they had brought with them in lieu of towels, and wandered in the direction of Kut, allowing the morning sun to dry them as they walked.

A little way up the road, they could see the small bell tower of the church of SS Cyprian and Justine, Kut's parish church. On cue the bell tolled nine, and the pair found the stone steps that led down from the higher road through Kut to the suburb's main square and a small quayside along whose edge were ranged yachts and sailing boats. Seen in daylight and with the benefit of a cold and sober eye, the concentration of restaurants in such a small area was impressive. By one of the walls of the square was set a bench on which sat some older locals. Their conversation became peppered with exclamations and laughter as Highball and the Memsahib passed, and the couple became conscious of their unusual attire. Had these old boys never seen a sarong before?

A quick left turn away from the harbour brought them off the square and out of earshot of the locals, and they soon recognised the small street they had visited the night before when the St Radegund party had met at Lambik. At the end of it was another flight of steps that led up to the main door of St Cyprian's. Next door to Lambik they found a small cafe open, and took a table outside in the sunshine, ordering a *kava espresso* and a *kifla*, a small pastry, each. What the menu lacked in range it made up for in depth, with all manner of coffees and combinations of coffees available, including a *kava bezkafeinski*, which was helpfully, and rather sweetly, translated as "discoffenated coffee". When their order arrived they were delighted to find that their bevarages each had a small piece of rum-flavoured chocolate melting on the top. They were a delicious way to start the day.

They discussed what to do with the morning and agreed that an exploration of Kut and some more swimming was in order. Satisfactorily breakfasted, they walked up the steps to the front of St Cyprian's, which perched above the square. A sign on the door forbade food and drink, cameras, mobile phones and immoderate dress inside the church. Did Balinese batik sarongs count in the last category? The Memsahib, who held a doctorate in art history, was all for going inside, for though the architectural style was baroque it was believed to be built upon the remains of an earlier gothic church. Such questions were academic anyway, as the door was locked.

They went back the way they came, and reached their apartment with its green window-shutters. Curly was descending the steps on his way into Kut for breakfast. The Highballs exchanged pleasantries and asked him if he'd had a good evening.

"Don't ask," was the response.

They walked as far as they could to the end of the road, aiming for the grand-looking three-storey building on the peninsula at the north-eastern extent of the harbour. The building was known locally as the Topić (after the family who built it) or Česka (after the Czechs who later bought it and turned it into a hotel) Villa. The residents of this part of town all seemed to grow their own produce in small terraced gardens set into the hillside. Presently the road became a dirt track. Cicadas chirruped in the trees. They made their way to the sheltered cove in the crook of the peninsula. There stood a single-storey building bordering the water's edge which appeared to be used as a boathouse of some description. A number of sturdy stone walls and jetties met the water and a short walk up the slope brought them up to the Villa. It was deserted. Looking through the broken ground-floor windows they saw graffiti daubed on the walls. It was an eerie place.

Pressing on, they stopped briefly at a small chapel, again closed and named, like the peninsula itself, after St George. They were now sufficiently hot and sweaty for another swim, and walked beyond the chapel to the north shore of the island where the woods gave way suddenly to the shingle beach of Grandovac bay, and there they took a dip to cool off. Once more revived, they made their way back to Lučica, pausing between the bay and the chapel to stop at a garden, enclosed by a six-foot high wall. Daubed on the wall was some graffiti proclaiming *Volimo hrvatska republika*, or "I love the Croatian Republic". They entered the garden via an iron gate that swung open on creaking hinges. A wide path bordered by white-painted stones led to the far wall, broadening out to accommodate a couple of stone tombs and a plinth whose memorial was missing. On the back wall hung a couple of marble plaques, one read:

AFTER MORE THAN ONE HUNDRED YEARS
BRITISH SOLDIERS AND SAILORS
WHO FOUGHT AND DIED FOR THEIR COUNTRY'S
HONOUR
ON THE SEAS AND ISLANDS OF DALMATIA
HAVE AGAIN BEEN LAID TO REST
IN THIS ISLAND CEMETERY
1944

HERE DEAD LIE WE BECAUSE WE DID NOT CHOOSE
TO LIVE AND SHARE THE LAND FROM WHICH WE SPRUNG
LIFE TO BE SURE IS NOTHING MUCH TO LOSE
BUT YOUNG MEN THINK IT IS AND WE WERE YOUNG

THEY SHALL BE MINE SAITH THE LORD OF HOSTS
IN THAT DAY WHEN I MAKE UP MY JEWELS

▲

Sixty years earlier when Brigadier Fitzroy Maclean first arrived on Vis, he came across the cemetery by accident. It was "long since overgrown and fallen into decay", with most of the names on the tombstones "almost obliterated by moss and weather."[i] The earliest memorials dated from the

Napoleonic wars and commemorated British lives lost in a naval battle off the coast of the island in 1811. Set into one of the walls, weathered by time and the elements, a stone plaque indicated the cemetery's original purpose: "HERE LIE INCLOSED THE REMAINS OF BRITISH SEAMEN WHO LOST THEIR LIVES IN DEFENCE OF THEIR KING AND COUNTRY, AD MDCCCXV."

There were others, to those lost in a naval action against the French in 1812 off the coast of Venice, and one commemorating another victory off the coast of Vis, for the Austrian navy over their Italian counterparts in 1866. Those buried within this small plot of land would soon have company, and the cemetery be tended on a more regular basis.

Maclean's early life had followed a well-trodden path of Eton and King's College, Cambridge, followed by the Foreign Office. He saw diplomatic service in the Soviet Union at the height of Stalin's purges but, on the outbreak of the Second World War he decided that he would enlist in the army. This proved more difficult than expected. His superiors balked at the idea of a junior civil servant with only six years' service dropping everything to "go off and play at soldiers",[ii] and his resignation was summarily rejected. Checking the FO's regulations he found a technicality that he could exploit to his advantage, announced to the permanent undersecretary his decision to go into politics – anathema to career civil servants – resigned on the spot and joined the queue to enlist at the nearest recruitment office. He completed his basic training in Inverness as a member of the Cameron Highlanders and made corporal in short order, but to prolong his military service he still had to demonstrate to the Whitehall mandarins' satisfaction that his political ambitions were sincere. In spite of having no experience of the parliamentary or political process he managed, in the best amateur tradition, to get himself elected Conservative Member of Parliament for Lancaster in a by-election in 1941. Before he could take his seat he received orders to report to Cairo where, after a chance meeting with the brother of an old school friend, he ended up in David Stirling's fledgling Special Air Service, serving behind enemy lines in the Western Desert campaign.

A change of location came in September 1943 when he was invited by Prime Minister Winston Churchill to head up the British mission to Tito's *Partizani* in German-occupied Yugoslavia. As Churchill's personal envoy, Maclean had it as his task to make contact with this communist resistance movement in order to assess the "value of the Partisans' contribution to the Allied cause and the best means of helping them increase it".[iii] There were complicating circumstances, however, not the least of which was that the British government was already materially supporting another armed resistance movement in the country.

The Kingdom of Yugoslavia had been invaded by the Axis powers on 6 April 1941, forcing the government of King Peter into exile in London. After two weeks of resistance to the invaders, the regional governors of Yugoslavia signed an armistice. Immediately Germany guaranteed independence for Croatia and set up puppet governments in both Belgrade and Zagreb. The new government of the Nezavisna Država Hrvatska[iv] (NDH) was formed by Ante Pavelić's Ustaše.[v] Originally a radical faction of the Croatian Party of Rights, the Ustaše, like other nationalist parties, had been banned in Yugoslavia since 1929 and subsequently set up military training camps in Italy with the full support of Mussolini's government. That support, though, was driven in part by a desire for greater influence in Dalmatia, which it regarded as historically an Italian possession.

Mussolini invited Pavelić to head the new government of the NDH on terms dictated by the Axis powers, who divided Croatia into specific spheres of influence. Under the Rome Agreement of May 1941, Italy annexed historic Dalmatia between Zadar and Split completely, a move which made Pavelić intensely unpopular.

Armed resistance to the puppet governments in Zagreb and Belgrade gravitated, initially at least, towards Draža Mihajlović's *Četniki*, who were the remnants of the Royal Yugoslav army. Though mainly active in Serbia and Bosnia they occasionally slipped over the border into Italian-controlled Dalmatia where they were able to operate largely undetected. At the request of the exiled King Peter, Churchill's wartime government gave the *Četnik* resistance in Yugoslavia its support (Mihajlović was, after all, defence minister in King Peter's government-in-exile) and was soon supplying it, sporadically in the first instance, with arms.

The German invasion of the Soviet Union in June 1941 also drew the armed resistance of the outlawed Yugoslav Communist Party into the fray. Led since 1937 by a former Croatian locksmith named Josip Broz, but better known as Tito, the *Partižani* movement attracted a broad constituency of Jews, intellectuals and the left. It made an immediate impact against the German occupiers (thanks largely to Tito having made long preparations for resistance), so much so that in those early days of the occupation Tito and Mihajlović even discussed the possibility of a unified command structure. However, the Serbian Rising of the summer of 1941 and its bloody suppression by the occupying Germans led to a tactical divergence between the two resistance movements, and by the end of the year the two were more often than not fighting each other as much as they were the enemy. Worse, by the beginning of 1942, the *Četniki* and Germans had coordinated the expulsion of the communist resistance from Serbia altogether, Mihajlovic's "moderating" policy apparently allowing for collaboration with the occupiers as long as the means justified the ends.

By the time Maclean parachuted into Bosnia and met Tito, the *Partižani* had been fighting a guerrilla war against the German occupation with no outside help for the previous two years, and the British government's support for Mihajlović's resistance movement was already beginning to seem misdirected, though any change in policy was politically sensitive as long as King Peter's government remained in exile in London. As Maclean travelled through the forests and mountain passes of Bosnia with Tito, he witnessed at first hand the communists' campaign against the German occupiers, their living hand-to-mouth with no permanent base, mending and making do in often hostile weather, capturing enemy material as and when they could. He gradually became convinced that their resistance was effective and his reports back to Churchill recommended that the British government throw its full weight behind supporting Tito any way it could.

The capitulation of Italy in September 1943 left a power vacuum in Dalmatia that the *Partižani* gladly filled, and they succeeded in liberating and holding the Dalmatian coast and islands, their material augmented by picking up discarded Italian arms and their ranks even occasionally swelled by deserters. The German command, however, was not prepared to countenance the Dalmatian coastal strip being out of their control for long, and by the autumn an offensive was under way, the aim of which was to retake the coast and ultimately the islands, if need be one at a time.

Maclean's arrival on Vis owed not a little to chance. He was on Hvar and awaiting evacuation by the Royal Navy, but received the message that it was too dangerous for the motor launch to approach the island. He had better go to Vis instead and wait there for passage to Bari. He made the journey at night by fishing boat, arriving in Vis town at daybreak. Having time on his hands before his evacuation gave him the opportunity to look around, and his discovery of the presence on the island of the Royal Navy over a hundred years earlier gave him pause to assess the Vis' strategic potential: "Lying, as it does, within striking distance of the coast and the other islands, yet far enough out to sea to be reasonably easy to hold and, at the same time, easy of access from Italy, it makes an ideal base for anyone wanting a foothold in the eastern Adriatic…"[vi] The harbour, Maclean soon saw, would be a perfect location from which to launch raids on German coastal positions and shipping. If, in addition, an airfield could be constructed on the island it would extend the Royal Air Force's operational range considerably, and allow the Allies to provide Tito with effective air cover. The island had been fortified and held before, he reasoned, so why not again?

▲

The Highballs' sarongs had not gone unnoticed by Curly when they had met briefly that morning, but he had not remarked upon them to their faces: a cup of strong coffee was at the forefront of his mind. He did though, in due course, report the sighting back to The Sipper with glee, telling him that he had seen the pair wearing sarongs *as skirts*, trying to cut a dash like some Dalmatian version of Posh and Becks. The Sipper was greatly amused at this intelligence, and found it sufficient information for both Highball and the Memsahib to incur a fine of ten kuna each in absentia for such effrontery. Curly himself did not escape lightly, and was sanctioned a similar amount for snitching on them.

In the meantime he had much to ponder upon, after an evening in which he had nearly been an accessory to criminal damage at one of Dalmatia's finest restaurants; and after a brief tour of Kut he descended the stone steps from St Cyprian's to the Café Martin, on the Highballs' recommendation. To his surprise, sitting outside the bar was an islander, an older man with a shuffling gait whom Curly had encountered earlier. Each gave the other a nod of recognition, and the islander, who had in front of him a shot glass of cloudy-looking spirits, motioned for Curly to join him. In short order a second glass of spirits appeared, which the islander invited him to partake of. When in Rome, thought Curly. It turned out to be a brandy flavoured with *rogać* or carob, which grew abundantly on the island, even in the lanes and gardens of Kut, where you could pluck the seed pods from the trees by the handful. Flavouring the brandy with carob produced a sensation akin to drinking chocolate-flavoured vodka. Curly smiled his approval and nodded back to the man.

After finishing off his drink, Curly thought it only polite to return the compliment and ordered another glass for his host, and so the two spent an agreeable half an hour smiling and nodding at each other and barely communicating. When the man produced a second glass of the spirits for his guest, Curly started to wonder how he was going to get away. It was, after all, still only ten o'clock in the morning...

The only other notable inhabitant of Kut at such an early hour was a sandy-coated mongrel that wandered the narrow streets sniffing here and there while marking its progress accordingly. Jugs encountered it first in the back lanes of Kut as she began the twenty-minute walk into Vis town, then saw it again as she turned left, away from Kut's only convenience store, close by to the Pojoda. She then passed a small ice-cream parlour and made her way along the main harbour-side road. Over the course of the St Radegund party's stay, the mutt could be seen going happily about its business with a regularity so bordering on dutifulness that it was soon nicknamed the Mayor of Kut by the visitors.

Jugs passed the office of the ministry of sport, in whose window she was pleased to see the poster for the impending cricket match. In all, she lost count of the number of copies of the poster she was to see on her walk into town. With the high stone walls of the Villa Kaliopa and the police station, once again Open For Crime, on her left she carried on past the battery whose cannon were used in anger during the Austrian-Italian naval battle in 1866, to the Church of Our Lady of the Caves, marking the end of Kut and the start of Vis town. From there it was a short walk to the ramp at the head of the harbour road, where a fig tree had spilled its fleshy fruit onto the road.

Here the sleepiness of Kut gave way suddenly to the bustle of the port, whose inhabitants were already busy in preparation for the day's trade. The steps of the Galleria wine bar that Jugs and others had visited the previous evening were being swept, rubbish being taken out. Next door, tables were being set outside a restaurant. Further down, the market traders were setting out their wares: watermelons, aubergines, beef tomatoes, oranges.

All the produce was, presumably, locally grown. The owners of the yachts and sailing boats moored along the *Riva* were busying themselves with small maintenance jobs or jumping ashore to investigate the town.

Jugs found Bunter and Frannie sitting at a table on the terrace outside the Hotel Tamaris drinking coffee, Bunter's being accompanied by the obligatory Rothmans. His arm was noticeably swollen and a particularly fetching shade of puce.

"Good morning, Jugs," he said, cheerfully. She sat down and listened as he recounted how he had fallen on his arm, endured a terrible night's sleep, woken early and had to wait for Frannie to get up to help him down the stairs of his apartment. The night before, Goran Pečarević had given Bunter the name of a local doctor, and as soon as it was a respectable time to do so he had called on the doctor to seek his opinion on the arm. The doctor had concluded that the arm was not broken, just badly bruised. He advised Bunter to take aspirin. Bunter, however, knew full well that the arm was broken, having broken it around the elbow on a previous occasion, and debated with himself whether he shouldn't get a second opinion. The potential risk was that another doctor could recommend evacuation to Split, which would surely mean his missing the cricket match and take a large and inconvenient chunk out of his holiday. He decided it was best to brass it out and ignore the pain, which was considerable.

Bunter had settled upon the terrace of the Tamaris as his favourite place for breakfast, and a good vantage point from which to watch the world go by. All things considered, he was bearing up quite well, and was dressed in holiday mode. This was something of a surprise to Jugs, who was used to seeing him in regulation navy blue St Radegund polo shirt, and grey polyester slacks. Instead, he wore his Panama hat and a short-sleeved cotton shirt. Completing the ensemble was a pair of electric blue shorts that showed off his stocky legs to particularly bad effect. The shorts were a brighter blue than the sea itself, which was quite an achievement.

"And what have you been up to?" Bunter enquired.

Jugs, who had begun to recover some of those aspects of her humanity that had been dissolved in gin and wine the previous evening, told Bunter about the posters advertising the cricket match she had seen on her walk in, mentioning the ministry of sport. Unfortunately, her language-processing skills were still impaired and this came out as "ministry of support".

Jugs tried to talk herself sober, but her words started to take on a bizarre life of their own, battling all attempts to corral them into regular sentences, and sometimes fleeing the scene altogether. She claimed to have seen, on her walk into Vis, "a nun getting into a priest" when what she had in fact seen was a nun getting into a car with a priest. It was going to take some time for Jugs' brain to get into gear and up to speed.

Frannie was suffering in silence. With JD's whereabouts still on her mind, and the extra responsibility of making sure Bunter was okay, she withdrew into herself until such times as the excesses of the previous evening wore off. In time, the three of them made their way along the *Riva*, past the huge, freestanding, 16th-century fortification called the Perasti tower and the small tourist bureau which rented (Jugs here made a mental note to check this out) scooters, bicycles and a gaudily painted vintage Volkswagen Beetle convertible. They then crossed a small park with benches and shaded by huge palms and down past the ferry ticket office to seek respite from the sun at Bejbi.

Bunter was carrying a large, bulky, plastic bag that he was eager to unburden himself of. The bag contained fifteen white polo shirts that he had schlepped all the way from Cambridge. The shirts were of lightweight, aerated polyester cotton, so cool enough for the hot Mediterranean climate. Over the left breast of each was the embroidered upper torso of Captain Sir William Hoste RN, taken from a contemporary portrait in which the subject cradled a naval telescope. On the shirts, this object had been replaced, cheekily, with a facsimile of a 19th-century cricket bat. Around the subject's head was embroidered, in a nimbus, the legend "Sir William Hoste Cricket Club" and, below, "Island of Vis, Croatia". (Oliver had originally wanted "*Captain* William Hoste", but apparently using such a title outside of its military context was forbidden by the mainland authorities, so "Sir" it had to be.) On the back of the shirts were printed the words that Hoste had run up the mast of his ship *Amphion* in naval colours just before engaging the French fleet off the island's north coast on 11 March 1811, "Remember Nelson".

▲

William Hoste, born in Norfolk in 1780, was the third of eight children of the Cambridge-educated Dixon Hoste, rector of the parish of

Tittleshall. The village lies sixteen miles south of Burnham Thorpe, the home town of Lord Nelson, himself also the son of a Cambridge-educated parson. Where parson Nelson was an ascetic scholar, parson Hoste loved to play the part of the country gentleman and enjoyed those sporting pursuits associated with such a station. He rented Godwick Hall from local landowner Thomas Coke, lived a life of some extravagance and was profligate with the money he had.

Through careful use of Coke's local Whig connections, Dixon Hoste was able to secure for his twelve-year-old son William a posting with the young Captain Nelson as captain's servant, with the young naval officer essentially responsible for the education of the boy within the traditions of the Royal Navy, the idea being advancement through the ranks to the ultimate goal of post-captain and the potential riches in prize money that went with it. The young Hoste joined Nelson on HMS *Agamemnon* in April 1793 and accompanied Nelson on many actions in the Mediterranean against the French during the Revolutionary wars, including Toulon, Genoa, Cadiz and Cape St Vincent. Hoste was promoted to midshipman in 1794 and was present at the battle of Santa Cruz at Tenerife in 1797 where enemy fire shattered Nelson's right.

Nelson was responsible for the care of other boys – including his own stepson – of a similar status, but most of them suffered by comparison with the precocious Hoste. Nelson's letters home revealed a clear preference towards William, whom he described in never less than glowing terms. Clearly the most favoured of Nelson's protégés, it was not long before Hoste was soon being groomed as his successor. At the age of sixteen, Hoste won promotion to lieutenant. A year later he was part of Nelson's fleet at a famous victory in the Battle of the Nile, though here under the command of the captain of HMS *Theseus*. By his eighteenth birthday he was acting captain of HMS *Mutine*, and engaging in action against privateers, as well as conducting various diplomatic missions. It was during one of these to the Kingdom of the Two Sicilies in Naples that he met Nelson's future mistress Emma Hamilton, then wife of the British ambassador to Naples. She recorded that the young Hoste would, in the fullness of time, "be a second Nelson. If he is only half a Nelson he will be superior to all others,"[vii] though as she was writing to Nelson himself, it's a moot point who was the intended object of such flattery.

Hoste spent ten years at sea, and did not see his home country at all until after the end of the Revolutionary wars, returning to England in April 1804, by which time he had been post-captain of the *Greyhound* since the previous June.

Britain was soon at war with France again, though this time the France of the Emperor Bonaparte. Hoste was given command of HMS *Amphion*, and was soon involved in the blockade of the French and Spanish at Cadiz. Fate, however, conspired to separate Hoste from Nelson at the latter's final triumph. Nelson himself ordered Hoste on a diplomatic mission from Gibraltar to Algiers in October 1805, and so the protégé missed the decisive Battle of Trafalgar in which Nelson perished heroically. Hoste's grief for his patron and father figure was heartfelt, but disguised with a professional detachment. He wrote to his mother: "I cannot get over the loss of our Commander-in-Chief... Never shall we find his equal and never will the Navy of Great Britain furnish a man of his abilities. I never saw such firmness, such decision, in any man in my life before."[viii]

The defeat of the Russian and Austrian armies at the Battle of Austerlitz in 1805 effectively left Britain and Ireland alone at war with Napoleon. Unable to gain the upper hand over the Royal Navy, Bonaparte decided to wage economic war against Britain, and his introduction of an embargo on trading with Britain under the Continental System led to the Royal Navy taking reciprocal action by blockading Mediterranean ports and seizing merchant vessels.

For Hoste, fighting Napoleon's forces soon became a family affair. In July 1806 the British army defeated the French army at the Battle of Maida in Calabria. Among the British number who fought with distinction was George Hoste, William's younger brother. In support of the action, the *Amphion* blockaded Cotrone and Catanazaro in Calabria, and shortly afterwards William wrote to his father inviting his youngest brother, Edward, to join the *Amphion* as a volunteer or captain's servant, exactly as William had been as a twelve-year-old with Nelson.

With the French holding Venice (and rumoured to be rebuilding its shipyards) and possessing a major naval base at Ancona, Nelson's successor as commander-in-chief, Admiral Collingwood, offered Hoste a command cruising and blockading in the Adriatic, which Collingwood deemed to be of the highest priority. Hoste gratefully accepted, and in 1808 he was soon hard at work plying the seas around the Dalmatian islands, raiding enemy ports and capturing merchant vessels.

With Austria now back in the war against France, the success of Collingwood's Adriatic strategy depended on the Royal Navy being able to hold and maintain a secure naval base in the area. With its sheltered harbours and its outlying position giving easy access to both shores of the Adriatic, Hoste decided to make his base on the remotest of the inhabited islands, Lissa.

▲

The most obvious legacy of nearly 400 years of Venetian rule over Dalmatia was architectural, and during the 16th century the simple stone dwellings of the small settlements of present-day Kut and Luka (the part of town containing the main harbour front) began to be supplemented by grander residences for the Austrian nobility and successful merchants from Hvar. A number of the mansions, from the Topić Villa at the head of the bay down to the end of the Obala Sv Jurja, are still known today by the family names of their wealthy inhabitants, the Jakinova Palača, the Palača Petrinović and, grandest of all, the Palača Gariboldi in whose garden now stands the Villa Kaliopa. Others are still referred to locally by their association with distinguished visitors who used them, such as the poet Petar Hektorović, thus firmly linking them with their Venetian past as much as the baroque balconies and corbels, the terracotta roofs and the weathered family coats of arms carved into the lintels.

It was past such splendours that the members of the St Radegund tour party made their various ways to Bejbi, which, it had been decided, was an agreeable rendezvous and forward command headquarters for the trip. Crabbo Junior had spent the morning sitting in a chair on the balcony of his apartment, making a rough sketch of the bell tower of St Cyprian that he hoped to turn into a finished watercolour before he left the island. Perhaps he should present it to Tomislav, the apartment owner, as a thank you? Later, as Crabbo Junior sauntered down the *Riva*, he caught his first glimpse of the young woman selling Vis tourist T-shirts, and promptly fell head over heels in lust. Fit and tanned, her blonde hair falling onto sturdy shoulders and legs that went all the way up to her hips and back down again, she was a true beauty and a fine specimen. Ding dong, he thought to himself.

When he arrived at Bejbi and caught his first glimpse of Bunter's electric blue shorts, Crabbo Junior was highly amused and decided, in collusion with the newly arrived Highballs, to have some fun at the scoutmaster's expense. They agreed that the shorts were in shocking taste and so, as more of the party began to arrive, they put the word around that Bunter's travelling trousers had become soiled or distressed on the journey. The blue shorts, the Memsahib insisted, were in fact a "courtesy" pair on loan from the Hotel Tamaris. This sounded – coming as it did from the Memsahib – almost plausible, but few rose to the bait.

Another fashion statement was being proclaimed at full volume by Larry and Moe in their Hawaiian shirts. As the talk turned to the events of the previous evening, they retold the story of the near conflagration at the Kaliopa with relish. For those who had not been at the dinner the revelations were jaw-dropping.

Almost everybody had been guilty of overtraining the previous evening. "What's the Croatian for hangover?" Beard enquired when he arrived. It was suggested he look in his own copy of *Lyle's Guide to Languages*, but once again it failed to provide an answer. There then followed a debate as to whether the hangover (either as a concept or materially) exists in Mediterranean cultures, with Beard doing a very thorough job of convincing everyone that it is a phenomenon almost entirely Anglo-Saxon in origin. Very convincing that is, until Toni Luksić – Bejbi's patron – made a brief, halting appearance before withdrawing. Unshaven and hiding behind dark sunglasses, he gave credence to the notion that Friday nights are very much the same for landlords the world over.

Oliver Roki, on the other hand, was looking in good shape. He gratefully took possession of the Sir William Hoste cricket shirts from Bunter, who charged him a nominal 500 kuna for them (though they had cost Bunter much more), and joined the party for a beer. He was looking forward to the afternoon's entertainment, a training session for Kriket Klub Sir William Hoste, just out of town at Samogor, to which the St Radegund team were invited. For the cricket-mad, like Beard, this was an invitation not to be missed.

Rob Dumančić turned up just before midday, and over a Karlovačko he and Oliver filled in some of the blanks about the formation of the Hoste team. When Rob arrived on the island the previous autumn he lost no time in tracking Oliver down. Having established that Oliver's intention to start a cricket club was in earnest, Rob gladly gave him all the information he needed to formally establish it. This included filing certain papers with the town's authorities and with the ministry of sport in Zagreb.

Rob went back to the capital and set wheels in motion. In November Oliver received a phone call. Rob had secured a generous amount of funding from the European Cricket Council's development programme to pay for basic equipment, including an artificial pitch, and the services of a professional coach from Manchester. This was good news except for one small detail. Since Rob had left the island, Oliver had done little to organise the team other than fill in and lodge the necessary forms.

Rob stressed the need to get some sort of a team together in time for the coach's visit, and so Oliver called in favours from pals and local businessmen to avoid embarrassing his friend. So it was that Siniša Vodopija, a geography teacher, Stanko Aleksić, who worked at Konoba Roki's, Toni Luksić from Bejbi, Neo Poduje, Goran Pečarević of the Villa Kaliopa, and a rival wine grower by the name of Antonio Lipanović gathered on the appointed afternoon in the school gymnasium while the coach from Manchester put them through their paces.

Oliver had left Australia when he was four years old, so had no memories of having seen cricket played. The other members of the embryonic team, though curious, were equally ignorant of this bizarre English game. The coach explained with patience the rudiments of the game, and brought some plastic wickets, as well as bats, balls, pads and gloves for them to try out. These the islanders, who could only just tell one end of the bat from another, examined with interest. Gradually, over the course of the coach's stay, Oliver's merry band began to grasp the nuts and bolts of the game, often retiring to the Kaliopa at the end of a session to watch DVDs of real international cricket matches to see how the game worked in practice. The coach, for his part, was put up in a palatial apartment and treated to some splendid hospitality for the three days of his visit, and left confident he had started off the islanders on the right track.

Having brought everyone up to date on the Vis cricket scene, Rob was asked when and why he had come back to Croatia.

"Nineteen ninety-one. I came back to fight for my country." Rob did not elaborate.

"That's a long way to travel to fight a war," said Jugs, aiming to smooth over any moment of awkwardness in the conversation. Rob shrugged. It was an experience unknown to all the St Radegund tourists. The Sipper had former schoolmates in the army, some of whom were now engaged in the business of occupying Iraq, and Beard had experience (not always entirely happy) of dodging the Mujahedin in Afghanistan. Bunter and El Vis, of course, did their National Service in the 1950s. Enlistment in a war of independence, however, was well beyond their ken.

Oliver was only slightly more forthcoming about his military experience, telling how he deserted the Yugoslav army to fight for the independence of Croatia. Oliver and Rob and a few others in the team, now in their thirties, had been of a good fighting age when it all went off in 1991, so it seemed the natural thing to do.

There were interesting political currents to the historical idea of Croatian independence. The original Kingdom of Croatia had existed for less than two hundred years from the 10th to the beginning of the 12th century, since which time it had been a part of successive European empires. By the mid-20th century, under Tito's version of communism, much political capital was made out of the Croat government's collaboration with the Axis powers during the Second World War. Equating an independent Croatian state with fascism became a rhetorical tool for the suppression of long-held nationalist aspirations within post-war Yugoslavia. The canard that "Croatian equals fascist" cast a long shadow, persisting also in Western Europe and resurfacing when the Croatian Republic was declared in 1991. Much was, speciously, made at the time of the revival of the traditional red-and-white chessboard on the Croatian flag, last used during the Second World War, and regarded as the "*Ustaše*" flag. To others in the west it was even more significant that Germany, alone of the European Union's member states, was prepared to grant the new republic immediate recognition. For those of a certain political generation, resentment of those states or populations that collaborated with the Axis powers was, understandably, difficult to shake.

From the vantage point of Bejbi, the St Radegund group could sample the busy comings and goings of the port at close hand. As the party chatted to Oliver and Rob they were joined at the table by a sizeable terrier that wandered in off the street, had a sniff around, and wandered out. All together a feistier canine than The Mayor of Kut, it wandered up and down the *Riva* most of the day, inspecting things of interest. Its doings had an earnest, urgent air about them, and couldn't have made for a better contrast with its counterpart in Kut. For the sake of symmetry, this dog was quickly named The Mayor of Vis.

Out across the bay, the midday ferry from Split slowly appeared from behind the Prirovo peninsula. It looked huge, much bigger than it had seemed when the touring party was on board, and soon dominated the harbour, looking entirely out of proportion with the rest of the setting and reducing the town to a Lilliputian quaintness.

Highball and the Memsahib rose from the table in order to welcome the arrival of the latest Radegundian. They crossed the road from Bejbi, past a line of cars and lorries waiting patiently for passage to Split, and walked up to the dock. As the ferry swung its imposing stern around to berth, the aft observation deck heaved into view. There, dead centre and at the highest vantage point, dressed in sunglasses and a white T-shirt, his rucksack slung over a shoulder, was Eyebrows.

Highball shouted a greeting, and the Memsahib waved to attract his attention. Eyebrows threw a friendly wave back. Then, no doubt realising how magisterial he must have appeared towering some thirty or forty feet above them, he looked around to make sure nobody else on deck was watching and, placing one hand imperiously on the deck rail, with the other he executed a brisk fascist salute.

NOTES

i   Maclean, p 386
ii   ibid. p 183
iii ibid. p 279
iv Independent state of Croatia.
v   From the Croatian verb *ustati*, "to rise"
vi Maclean, p 386
vii Pocock, Tom. *Remember Nelson – The Life of Captain Sir William Hoste*. London, Collins, 1977, p 83. Reprinted in 2005 by Pen & Sword Books Ltd, Barnsley
viii ibid. p 117

5
The Letter

... a small, flat patch of ground ringed by palm trees. It was here that Kriket Klub Sir William Hoste began honing their nascent skills.

At Vis' sports centre, which comprised a number of artificial tennis courts and a football pitch, Larry and Moe – resplendent in their Hawaiian shirts and sunglasses – were watching a junior tennis competition with tremendous interest. As they struggled with prodigious hangovers, they could only admire the skill of the two young Croatian opponents. The technical standard and range of abilities were impressive. Powerful serves were met by equally adept returns, baseline forehands with well-timed volleys as rally followed upon rally.

Larry and Moe assumed that Goran Ivanisović's recent deeds must have proved inspirational to the younger generation of Croatian players. The ones they were watching certainly looked cast from a similar mould, being tall, dark-haired, and powerfully built. Goran's unlikely five-set win over the Australian Pat Rafter in the Wimbledon final of 2001, when he became the first player ever to win the tournament after entering the competition on a wild card, captured the imagination of the British public like few victories in recent memory. Split, Ivanisović's home town, went wild when he won. Nearly 150,000 people thronged the *Riva* to watch his triumphant homecoming. Ships in the port sounded their sirens and church bells rang out as the champion made his way by boat from the airport into the harbour. The party, which had started almost as soon as he won the title the day before, did not stop for days.

Behind the tennis courts and through a rusted iron gate, on a small patch of terraced land known as Martvilo, Vis' ancient past lies starkly, side by side with the present. Here, overgrown with scrub and lavender, are the remains of the ancient necropolis of the original Greek settlement of Issa. Burial tombs in varying states of decay lie around haphazardly, the majority of the site amounting to little more than broken stones and pathways, with anything of greater archaeological value having long since been removed to the town museum.

On from the sports centre the road bends round to the north-east where, opposite the town's only petrol station, stand the remains of Issa's Roman *thermae*. The site had been extensively used and re-used for purposes unconnected with its original function until the 1950s, at which time a more serious attitude to archaeological excavation and conservation began to take hold. In a fine state of preservation, and more easily accessed than the necropolis, the floor mosaics between the baths' forecourt and the main chamber are very well-preserved under the dust, and decorated with the stylised images of playful dolphins in black tiles. Farther along and behind the baths is the hill known as Gradina, the site of the ancient town of Issa.

Although Issa was settled by the ancient Greeks nearly 400 years before the birth of Christ, sculptures dating farther back to the 6th century have also been discovered on the island. Founded by one Dionysius of Syracuse, Issa, and its port, soon became a focus of ancient Greek trade in the Adriatic and thence expansion further into Dalmatia, with Greek Issaeans founding a settlement on the coast at present-day Trogir. The high-water mark of Issa's prominence from the mid-4th century BCE onwards coincided with the rule of Ionios of Issa, who gave his name to the Ionian Sea. Coins of the era bear his image. When Illyrian civilization began to flourish along the Dalmatian coast in the 3rd century, conflict with ancient Issa was inevitable and the island threw in its lot with Rome, playing a significant role in the first and second Illyrian wars. Though Gradina is now officially designated a protected area, many of the stones of the settlement have been removed to be reused for other buildings; and though the historic site is accessible there is, in truth, little to see other than a number of stone walls set into the overgrown hillside.

The foreshore in front of Gradina marks the beginnings of the harbour of ancient Issa. Across the road is a short shingle beach that drops away to deep blue waters that still offer good anchorage. Excavations below the present waterline have produced hundreds of wine jugs, and even the remains of huge pottery vessels that appear to have been used for the storage of non-perishable goods under the surface of the ancient harbour itself.

Beyond the baths the shoreline sweeps round in a 200 degree arc south-east to the peninsula of Prirovo, at whose extreme stands an early 16th-century Franciscan priory and the town cemetery. The outbuildings around the main church describe a gentle semicircular arc marking the outer wall of the 1st-century Roman amphitheatre which, it is estimated, could accommodate nearly 2,000 spectators, and upon whose foundations the priory buildings were built. In the priory's basement there is a relief depicting a *naiad*, traditionally an attendant of the god Dionysus, suggesting that the amphitheatre had been built on an earlier Greek site.

Inland from the priory, where Prirovo joins the harbour road, is a small patch of flat, grassy ground ringed by palm trees. It was here that Oliver Roki and the newly constituted Kriket Klub Sir William Hoste began honing their nascent skills. Once Ivo Scepanović's article had appeared in the *Sunday Telegraph*, it only took a month for Oliver to receive his first letter from another cricket team asking if they might come out and play a match. That letter was from the Saumur Strays.

At Highball's request, Oliver proudly showed off the team's new scorebook, a generous gift from the Strays. Highball was keen to see the details of the club's inaugural fixture against the so-called "British team with its roots in France". It didn't make for edifying reading.

In an innings lasting all of nine overs and one ball, Kriket Klub Sir William Hoste compiled a total of precisely 15 runs for the loss of all of their wickets. In reply, their guests took a shade over six overs to knock off the required runs, winning the first match to be played on the island in nearly 200 years by a crushing nine wickets. A mismatch, for sure.

"And I bet they reversed the batting order as well," offered Crabbo Junior, who was looking in over someone's shoulder.

"Was it really worth them coming all that way just to humiliate you?" Highball asked Oliver rhetorically, indulging in that fine old English art of mixing it.

The Saumur boys, Oliver said with consummate tact, were generous with their time in coaching islanders of all ages, and they did make a gift of the scorebook. The British embassy in Zagreb, Oliver continued, also sent a set of brand-new cricket balls.

"What about the artificial pitch?" Crabbo Junior added.

"It didn't get here in time," Oliver admitted. "I had to go and fetch myself, much later."

In fact the ECC's website article had only ever implied that the match had been played on an artificial pitch. The British embassy in Zagreb had indeed done "everything possible" to get the pitch through customs. But once through, the pitch had stayed in Zagreb waiting for someone to pick it up.

"So where did you play?" asked Crabbo Junior.

"At the sports centre. We set up the wickets on the tennis courts."

Even when Oliver finally managed to bring the pitch over he found himself in competition for the credit. A British ex-pat living on Vis brought some guests of his to watch one of the Hoste team's early practice sessions, and within earshot of Oliver, boasted that *he* had *personally* brought the pitch over.

"Bloody British," Oliver said with a smile. Highball and Crabbo Junior warmed to Oliver immediately.

The finer points of scoring a cricket match, though, seemed of little interest to him. He kept referring to the Saumur game as though "16 to 15" were a close result, as in a game of rugby. Whatever, it was important to the press and to Croatian television, both of which had covered the match. And besides, your average non-cricket playing Croatian was unlikely to know the difference.

"Bloody hell," said The Sipper once he caught sight of the book, "did Saumur actually realise you'd never played the game before?"

Oliver would have nothing said against Kriket Klub Sir William Hoste's first opponents who had, to a man, been thoroughly good people, their only minor eccentricity being to arrive somewhat over-dressed in blazers and ties. In fact, so exacting had been their dress code that when one of their number admitted to having forgotten his blazer, he was ordered to search the boutiques of Split for a replacement. When Oliver admitted to having scored the first duck on the island since the early 19th century, it was with a sense of pride that nobody could find un-endearing.

"Croatian television was there, 200 spectators were there," he said. "Saumur were in their whites, we were playing in jeans and T-shirts. As captain I thought I'd better go out and set an example. This guy runs in and bowls at a hundred kilometres an hour and I look round and the wickets are down."

Here was a kindred spirit. For Oliver the mere revival of the game had been of more importance than the result, so there had been no question of their not accepting the first request for a game that came their way. With Highball's irritation at being the secretary to the Buzz Aldrins of the Croatian cricket scene now partially assuaged, he indicated to The Sipper that it was a good time to put into practice what they had rehearsed. In a matter-of-fact way the St Radegund captain assured Oliver that Kriket Klub Sir William Hoste's second-ever match, to be played the following day, would be a much closer affair, and would give the islanders a chance to show their true potential. Oliver looked happy either way.

As well as the obvious benefits of practising cricket on Prirovo, it being (apart from the sports centre) the only area of flat ground of a suitable size in town, it was appropriate for historical reasons, as the alleged site of the Royal Navy's cricket games nearly 200 years earlier, as was disclosed in one of William Hoste's letters home. That the "cricket letter" came to light at all was down to the perseverance and dedication of Tom Pocock, Hoste's biographer, and not a small piece of good fortune.

Pocock was born in London in 1925, into a solid middle-class family with maritime connections, his father having taught at Dartmouth Naval College. Rather than tread the expected route from Westminster School to Trinity College, Oxford, Pocock enlisted in the Royal Navy at the age of seventeen and saw action during the Second World War on British motor torpedo boats in the English Channel. After his military service was curtailed owing to illness, he strayed into journalism, becoming Fleet Street's youngest war correspondent as a reporter for a sister magazine of *Picture Post.* There followed a distinguished career on a number of London newspapers, including the *Daily Mail*, *The Times* (as its Naval correspondent), the *Daily Express* and later, as travel editor, the *Evening Standard.* In the late 1960s he began to indulge his passion for naval history by producing several books about Britain's role in the Napoleonic wars, including a number of books about Lord Nelson.

It was in the middle of the following decade, as he was researching his book on William Hoste, that he became aware of an auction of Hoste's original letters at Christie's in London. After Hoste's death, a selection of them had been edited and published by Hoste's widow, but the accounts of his life at sea had been somewhat sanitised in the re-telling. The originals, which were brought to light in the attic of a house in Cornwall by a farmer who was, in fact, an ancestor of Hoste, were clearly of great importance. The emergence of such a collection – 2,000 letters spanning Hoste's entire career – was a rare occurrence, to say the least, and the reserve price at auction reflected this: it was out of the reach of Pocock alone. Fortunately the letters' significance was not lost on the National Maritime Museum and, with the help of Pocock's publisher, they agreed to meet half the cost of the bid and allow the biographer a year's exclusive access to them. Unfortunately they had reckoned without the letters attracting a rival bid: "On the day of the sale we were so confident of success that I had made arrangements for the collection of the letters later that day. A distinguished dealer in manuscripts was bidding on our behalf and I went along to watch. As the bidding began the expectant smile was wiped off my face. We were being easily outbid and Captain Hoste's letters were knocked down to an unknown bidder for far more than we had planned to spend."[i]

Bitterly disappointed, Pocock decided he had nothing to lose in approaching the successful bidder, a stamp dealer who was interested in the collection for the value of the letters' individual franks rather than the content of the letters themselves. Pocock feared the collection would be broken up and lost forever to the hands of private collectors. After he had explained his position the buyer happily agreed to give Pocock unrestricted access: "I need not worry, he said. He would not sell one letter until I had studied them all. Moreover he asked me to pick a few of the best letters and he would present them to the National Maritime Museum, also giving them permission to record the whole collection on microfilm."[ii]

As it turned out, the majority of the letters did find their way into the hands of private collectors, but before they did Pocock's study of them gave him both a valuable insight into his subject's character and precious original material for his book. Though he never made a trip to Vis, the island then still being off limits, Pocock managed an imaginative job of picturing it as it must have looked to Hoste in the 19th century. The benefits of the island as a naval base were obvious. The harbour of Vis town, then known in Italian as Porto San Giorgio, was "near-perfect... running from a narrow entrance, able to take the biggest ships, for one and a half miles across a wide sheltered bay to the town of Lissa itself."[iii]

It was from Porto San Giorgio that the *Amphion* mounted raids on merchant shipping and conducted small-scale actions against the French all along the Dalmatian coast, with such success that in the last half of 1809 Hoste had captured or destroyed no fewer than 218 enemy ships. The defeat of the Austrians at Wagram in July had increased the military stakes dramatically, however, and though British reinforcements were sent to the Adriatic the combined forces were unable to stop Rijeka and Trieste being taken by the French. Hoste's letters home that winter are mocking of the enemy and revel in being the underdog: "Can there be any further proof of the pusillanimity of our enemies in this part of the world, than to allow one frigate and one sloop to annoy the trade in the manner we do?"[iv]

There was no question that Royal Navy was outnumbered and outgunned in the Adriatic, but Hoste was supremely confident of his crew's superior skills. The effects of Hoste's attacks on trade in the region were soon felt. Port Saint George, as it was anglicised under the British, thrived as it attracted merchant ships and smugglers, to whom the Royal Navy gave licence to land their goods on the coast of Europe in defiance of Napoleon's blockade. The population of the island rose dramatically, as mariners flocked there for employment. Bonaparte was insistent that British disruption of Adriatic trade must stop, and over the spring and summer of 1810 France deployed more ships to the region in anticipation of the final battle that would rid the Adriatic of his British irritant for good.

A confrontation was imminent, but in the meantime Hoste and his crew were able to pass their idle hours in recreation. In a letter home to his mother in July 1810 he describes how "…we have established a cricket-club at this wretched place and when we do get anchored for a few hours, it passes away an hour very well. Teddy is the head of the party."[v] As this nugatory and rather unflattering description is all that Hoste wrote on the subject, it is unknown whether William played cricket himself. The reference, though, clearly shows the British searching for home comforts in an otherwise hostile environment. In the retelling of the story for the readers of the *Sunday Telegraph*, Hoste's letter gained a little diplomatic gloss in the name of journalistic licence. No mention was made of Hoste's telling description of Vis as "this wretched place," understandable in what was essentially an open invitation to English cricket teams to tour Dalmatia. Elsewhere the story was embellished considerably, as when Hoste was described as having "extolled the island's virtues as a cricketing venue, with year-long sunshine and perfect conditions for the sport".[vi] Nor in Hoste's letter was there any "praise for the islanders who had taken to joining in the sport".[vii]

Pocock has the *Amphion*'s cricket matches taking place on Prirovo: "The promontory, forming one side of a little bay which had already been named English Harbour and on which stood the *campanile* and church of a 16th-century Franciscan monastery, offered enough flat land for a game of cricket."[viii] The presumption – in the absence of documentary evidence – is reasonable enough. The proportions of the land behind the priory did, and continue to, offer enough flat land for a game of cricket, even if the walls and garden of the priory were, and remain, dangerously within the range of a semi-accomplished batsman. The harbour that Pocock names, however, is thought to be a little farther north from Prirovo, at the inlet the islanders now call Stonca, and though few of the members of the Hoste cricket team were aware that it was given the name English Harbour by the

British, it does appear as "Englische Hafen" on an Austrian map of the port from the latter half of the 19th century.

As summer turned to autumn in 1810, a game of cat-and-mouse began between Hoste and the French forces with the English captain trying to tempt the enemy fleet out of Ancona to do battle. On the fifth anniversary of the Battle of Trafalgar, the French fleet, commanded by Bernard Dubourdieu, in many ways as accomplished an officer as Hoste and a worthy adversary, used the opportunity of the British fleet's temporary absence from Lissa to mount a surprise raid on Port Saint George.

On the morning of 22 October, Dubourdieu struck, leading three French ships flying British colours into the harbour mouth. The alarm was raised and many of the villagers and privateers took to the hills around the town, as Dubourdieu disembarked a force of over 700 French troops. The successes that Dubourdieu claimed for his raid – thirty ships taken, double that number burned in the harbour – were at variance with what Hoste himself reported: only three ships burned and three taken. The only thing either side seemed able to agree on was that neither had suffered any casualties. What is certain is that for all Dubourdieu's success, he dared not stay and try to hold the island. Even with superior numbers, he feared the inexperience of the sailors under his command would be his undoing, and when word got back to him late in the afternoon that Hoste was returning to Vis, he had his troops re-embark and his ships leave for Ancona to avoid a confrontation.

For Hoste, however, this was a humiliation and a major setback in an otherwise spotless career. The following day he set sail for Ancona, hoping to tempt Dubourdieu into battle, but the Frenchman refused to play the game. Hoste was replaced as senior officer in the region, and it must have seemed for a time that his chance had gone. Then, once the winter of 1810 had passed, Hoste was surprised to find himself ordered back to Lissa: his experience in the Adriatic clearly counted for something at the Admiralty. By February of 1811 Hoste knew that a final confrontation for mastery of the Adriatic could not be far away.

▲

Eyebrows joined the rest of the tour party for a Karlovačko at Bejbi, whose unhindered view across the bay to Prirovo and the Franciscan priory had many of the party salivating at the prospect of a game of cricket in such picturesque surroundings with such an impressive historical pedigree. That was for tomorrow, though. In the meantime, there were introductions to make and catching up to do.

Eyebrows, like the El Vises, had flown to Trieste, but he had then gone by train to Rijeka on the Istrian coast, and had boarded the overnight boat to Split. No stranger to independent travel in that part of central Europe, he had decided to make the journey apart from the rest of the party. This prompted Highball to try mixing it a little.

Had Eyebrows, he asked, suffered enough of Bunter's moods over the years to know when to avoid travelling with him? Eyebrows gave Highball a withering look, and then smiled. He was not rising to the bait.

"*Au contraire*," he said, his hands gesticulating exaggeratedly, his voice a rich baritone, "I merely wanted to be alone." Crabbo Junior was studying him intently, doubtless for the improvement of his own already excellent Eyebrows impression. The presence on the tour of such a senior St Radegund cricketing worthy as Eyebrows was welcome, particularly as his eminence within the team and generally sound counsel could act as a corrective to any excesses.

He was a few years younger than Bunter, and had grown up in Kingsbury in North London. A strapping six-footer, he had been quite the athlete in his youth though when, in 1992, he had answered Bunter's call to become the St Radegund cricket team's first captain, he was at the end of his playing days. Photographs taken at the inaugural Rad versus Champ fixture showed him with a jet-black moustache and goatee beard combination that bestowed upon him a more than passing resemblance to Frank Zappa. Since then, however, his features had taken a more distinguished turn and as he thinned on top his remaining facial hair began to grow with abandon in all other available locations making his nickname, which had been appropriate enough when it was first bestowed on him back in the 1950s, now even more so.

While he was in Kentucky some time in the late 1970s, he had been introduced to a friend's parents with the words, "This is Eyebrows, but I call him 'Brows' for short." After a couple of days the parents, clearly uncomfortable, asked him if there was a less formal way of addressing him, and asked what the "I" stood for.

"Isaac," Eyebrows replied and so remained – as far as the parents were concerned – Isaac Brows for the duration of the holiday. In the years since, he has rarely corrected anybody under a similar misapprehension and will respond happily to "Brows" or "Eyes" or "Eyebrows" in several Indo-European tongues.

Then there was the small matter of his fascist salute off the back of the ferry. Highball was concerned that Eyebrows would be tactful enough not to offend the natives by repeating the gesture.

"Wouldn't want you to put your foot in, old man," Highball offered in mitigation, worried he might himself have caused Eyebrows offence.

"Duly noted, squire," Eyebrows answered, sounding more like Eyebrows than ever, and let the impertinence pass. He did, though, offer the observation that anybody unfortunate enough to have been evacuated to the dismal town of Preston in Lancashire for the duration of the war, as he himself had been, could not be begrudged a small degree of anti-fascist sentiment. This seemed fair enough. Highball well knew, however, that Eyebrows possessed an encyclopaedic knowledge of all the derogatory names for foreign nationals, and though it was unlikely that Eyebrows would be as gauche as to let slip an offensive name for the Croats, a sub-stantial Karlovačko session was now in progress so any precautions taken against an infelicitous comment were precautions well made.

The feelings of the islanders of Vis on the subject of fascism could not be under-estimated. In the town cemetery on Prirovo stands a substantial monument decked with flowers. It is a simple stone slab incorporating the portraits of ten islanders from Vis town and their names. The monument was erected by the town council of Vis in remembrance of its citizens – de-scribed in the monument's inscription as "victims of the fascist terror" – who had been shot by the Italian occupiers in 1942. The Italians had dis-covered the theft of some arms and, once a deadline for their return had passed, they selected at random ten citizens from Vis and ten from Komiža, lined them up and summarily executed them. This was not to be Vis' last sacrifice during the war. Following Italy's capitulation to the Allies a year later, the island played a major role in the liberation of Yugoslavia.

The decision to give increased Allied support to the *Partižani* was taken at a conference in Cairo attended by Churchill and Roosevelt in late November 1943, and ratified by Britain, the US and the Soviet Union at a meeting of "the big three" in Tehran a few days later. In an attempt to disprove the Royal Yugoslav government's misgivings that the Allies were now backing the wrong side, it was agreed to give Mihajlović's *Četniki* one last chance to prove them worthy of continued material support. They were asked to demonstrate their commitment to the Allied cause by destroying a strategic bridge on the Belgrade to Salonika railway, an act of sabotage that they singularly failed to commit. Allied support went firmly behind the *Partižani*, leaving the king to face the unpalatable situation of having to reach an accommodation with Tito.

On the Dalmatian islands, a number of Communist Party officials had taken matters into their own hands. Vis' population had swelled as the resistance sought to consolidate its presence on the islands in the face of the German offensive, and was short of food. Unable to contact Tito's headquarters for approval, a delegation travelled to Bari without permission to ask for material assistance, food and medical supplies from the Allies, as well as transportation of prisoners of war and wounded off the island. Formal approval for a rear headquarters at Bari for the ongoing resupply of the resistance was given on 20 October, with the first shipments arriving at Komiža a few days later. In due course Fitzroy Maclean pressed on with the idea of fortifying Vis. He arrived after midnight in the middle of December, disembarked his transport in English Harbour and followed the road into town. It being late, he decided to bed down in his sleeping bag at the first convenient location, and turned off the road as soon as he could, went through a gate and settled down for the night. He awoke to find that he had pitched camp in the town cemetery at Prirovo.

With him on this visit was an RAF officer skilled in airfield construction, and together they went off into the hinterland to scout suitable locations. Climbing 500 feet above Vis town they ended up on the road to Komiža and stopped at a farmhouse on the hill above Velo Polje. The house offered them an unhindered view of the island's central plain, and the RAF officer quickly confirmed to Maclean that the spot would make an ideal location for an airfield comprising one main and one auxiliary runway. Maclean now needed to speak to Tito personally about the island, but first had to find a way to make good on an agreement to provide at least one Allied brigade to match the *Partižani* one already stationed on the island.

At a New Year's Eve party in Bari, Maclean met with the commanders of No 2 commando unit. He found them more than happy to commit to operations that involved harassing Dalmatian coastal positions and causing Jerry all sorts of bother. He put the request to his commanding officer in the early days of 1944 only to be told that the whole question of the Mediterranean theatre was to be discussed at a conference in Marrakech, and that no decision could be taken in the short term. It was at this conference that the strategy for the Anzio landings – the massive seaborne invasion of the Italian mainland – was discussed. With huge demands on manpower expected, the best that Maclean could wring from his superiors in the interim was a token detachment from the commando brigade, with the promise of more troops to follow. Accordingly, 150 British troops arrived on Vis in the middle of January. Maclean returned to Yugoslavia carrying a personal letter from Churchill to Tito (and a signed photo of the PM) and instructions to act as personal intermediary between the prime minister and the leader of the communist resistance.

The situation along the Dalmatian coast had not been going well. Korčula, in spite of having a significant *Partizani* force dug in, had fallen to the Germans, and the resistance had withdrawn to Hvar and Vis, where defence of the islands was being organised once again without official approval from Tito's headquarters. Maclean told Tito of the promised increase in materiel as well as further promises of training of air and tank crews, and delivered Churchill's letter, which pleased Tito immensely. With the Germans having gained a foothold among the Dalmatian islands the pair agreed that the fortification of Vis was an urgent priority, and Tito officially declared the island a war-zone garrison at the end of February. This was the cue for the immediate mobilization of every able-bodied male between the ages of fifteen and fifty on the island and the evacuation of the non-combatant population, numbering nearly 4,000, to refugee camps in Italy and Egypt. In addition to field hospitals and maintenance units, defensive trenches were dug, pillboxes built, fields mined, and the coves around the islands barb-wired in case of German landings. The difficulties of maintaining regular communication with the disparate elements of the resistance were weighing heavily on Tito's mind, and he told Maclean he was thinking of moving his headquarters. Indeed, Tito set up his HQ in a cave halfway up a mountain outside the town of Drvar in Bosnia, where it stayed for the first few months of 1944. It was a decision that would prove costly.

▲

Kriket Klub Sir William Hoste's afternoon training session was held up at the helidrome at Samogor, half a mile out of town. It was not a huge distance, so the Rad party decided to walk it. The road took them up a sharp incline, past a purpose-built supermarket – apparently one of the town's few concessions to modern planning – to the junction where the road divided, one branch doubling back around the hills above the town, the other carrying the main bus route straight on across the top of the island to Komiža.

A former parade ground and army barracks stood just off the junction to the right. In essence the site was a rectangular field about 180 by 240 feet fenced off on two sides. Along a third side ran a gentle slope, along which rusting lorry containers sat, up to the old barracks buildings, now overgrown, windows shattered. Bottle crates were stacked haphazardly outside the buildings, whose walls bore elaborate Croatian graffiti tags. In the middle of the field was a square, concrete helipad. With no infirmary on the island, any serious medical case requiring hospital treatment was airlifted from here to Split. Across the diagonal of the helipad the Hoste team had laid their artificial wicket: two pieces of heavy plastic matting each 36 feet in length. A set of plastic wickets matching the bright blue of the artificial strip stood at each end, and the Hoste team were bowling at them enthusiastically.

A tractor was clearing the rest of the field of stubble, and some of the St Radegund boys helped to remove stones and rocks of various sizes. Then the penny dropped. The work that was going on was to prepare the ground for the following day's cricket match which would not, it became clear, be taking place on Prirovo. Several Cambridge jaws hit the ground simultaneously. For the Rad, who had been used to playing on the picturesque, perfectly manicured green sward of Jesus College, this was a culture shock of seismic proportions. There was nothing in the way of facilities. The ramp that passed the side of the field led only to derelict buildings that offered at best only partial shelter from the heat, which was expected to hit the high eighties by midday on Sunday. Also there was no local water source this far out of town. With a sigh the tourists rolled up their sleeves and helped with the effort to clear the ground.

"It's a bloody nightmare," said Son of El Vis. "There are more divots on the outfield than at Cambridge Pitch and Putt." Having The Close, at Jesus College, for his home ground had clearly spoiled him. Reluctantly, he joined in with the clearing up of the outfield. With as much of the field-clearing labour done as possible, Highball, The Sipper and Crabbo Junior stood and watched the Hoste team's practice. There was promise in their bowling, although it seemed like a number of the team could have sent the ball down with a bit more pace than they were managing. Perhaps they were holding something back for tomorrow? Occasionally the ball dropped a little too short, and it popped up off the pitch and was given the treatment by the batsman. Beard offered to send down a few deliveries to the opposition, if only to show them how it was done properly. Here the artificial pitch proved something of a problem: its ends draped over the points of the helipad's diagonal, which were themselves raised a good two inches above the rest of the field. Worse, a half-foot deep depression in the ground just beyond it made attaining a decent length- and rhythmical run up into the bowler's delivery stride very tricky indeed. Beard, though, seemed to cope with it okay.

The home team, too, seemed to overlook the potential dangers of playing the match in this location. The Sipper, though, was thoughtful. Should somebody be injured seriously enough during the following day's game to warrant hospitalization, it would surely be necessary to disrupt the game for a speedy airlift to the mainland. Helicopter stopped play: a cricketing "first" if ever there was one.

Highball, usually happy to throw himself about the field with great abandon and to no great effect, was concerned by the still substantial stubble – was it the remains of sugar beet? – littering the field that looked sharp enough to pierce both clothing and flesh. The Sipper then noticed that the field's boundary on two sides was not just a fence, but a barbed-wire fence.

"Should make for an interesting game," he said with understatement, "All that's missing are the watchtowers and searchlights."

Unworried by such cares, Beard was enjoying his practice session. He had taken to bowling at the opposing team with gusto, and managed to generate enough pace to bend his back on a few deliveries, with the ball shooting through low and hard. Son of El Vis and Crabbo Junior decided to join in as well, and took up the cherry to give their arms a gentle turning over.

Crabbo Junior remained unconvinced by the trueness of the pitch and expressed doubts about the amount of bounce. A protective helmet would seem to be obligatory. Had anyone seen fit to bring one? No. The Hoste team, for its part, continued to be unfazed by the surroundings and was knuckling down to a solid bit of training. The session had attracted more than the customary eleven players, and they took part with more enthusiasm than any of the tourists – Beard excepted – could muster. Their relative unfamiliarity with the game showed in their selection of batting strokes: a lot of stuff played off the legs to the on side, and the occasional square cut behind point, but little in the way of straight or off side drives.

"Anything here to worry us, Skip?" asked Crabbo Junior.

"Not much," confided The Sipper, "but that doesn't matter."

Hands on hips, The Sipper had dressed for exercise and was sporting a black running vest and pair of rugby shorts. He announced he had seen enough, and turned to begin a far-too-athletic-by-half run back towards town. In The Sipper's attire Highball noticed a clear resemblance to a certain larger-than-life sporting character from the pages of Bunter's childhood *Wizard* comic, and as The Sipper commenced a healthily paced run down the hill, Highball called after him, in perfect imitation of Bunter's Rothmans-inflected rasp, "Ho-ho-ho: Wilson!" The Sipper was soon down the hill and out of sight, thanks not to near-superhuman fitness but to a 1:6 gradient.

Presently the session at Samogor wound down and all made their way back to Bejbi for some well-earned beers. Jugs lifted the hem of her shorts to show off a particularly impressive, cricket ball-shaped bruise at the top of her inner thigh, the result of a quick go with the bat. As she was eliciting sympathy for her injury, one of the males in the party offered a particularly hearty observation about lady cricketers and lost balls.

Jugs' was not the only injury that day. During a swim off the beach near English Harbour that afternoon, the Memsahib had put her hand on a submerged rock to steady herself only to emerge with more than a dozen tiny spines from a sea anemone embedded in her hand. Her only recourse was to retreat to the comfort of her apartment with a pair of tweezers and a litre bottle of Chivas Regal, whose anaesthetic and antiseptic properties she was acquainting herself with for the first time. A brief consultation with the Highballs' host family provided an interesting piece of local wisdom: had the waters of Vis harbour not been so clean, then sea anemones would not be found growing there. It was some small consolation.

These mishaps were, of course, minor compared with what Bunter was going through with his broken arm, and he had been keeping a low profile all the Saturday, still harbouring a sense of shame at what had transpired at the Kaliopa. For the rest it was decided that an early dinner at the Buffet-Pizzeria Katarina, next door to Bejbi, would be ideal. Inside, everybody was surprised to see Curly already seated at a table with a half-empty bottle of wine in front of him, and his partly-eaten pizza showing 9.40. He was sitting bolt upright but fast asleep.

This was a puzzle. Was it narcolepsy, inebriation or mere power-napping? A friendly shove and a shout of "Wake up, your pizza's getting cold!" were enough to restore him to consciousness. Curly had at least hit upon an interesting venue: the pizzas at the Katarina turned out to be of decent quality with wafer-thin crusts, a fact probably appreciated by the hundreds of Italian tourists who flocked to the island during the high season.

In short order, Curly's fellow Stooges arrived and gave an account of their day. At lunchtime they had been back to Lambik where they had ordered a couple of glasses of Vugava, only to receive a single one and an apology that the bar was out of wine. A pattern was emerging. More serious than that, Larry was now nursing a grievance against the other St Radegund players: none of the Stooges had known about the training session at Samogor, and Larry, for one, was irritated not to have been invited.

"I thought you knew about the nets? It was an open invitation. All welcome," explained Highball.

"Nobody told us," said Larry and then continued, with fire in his eye: "Ever since we arrived we've been treated like second-class citizens."

"By the Rad?"

"By the Rad." Highball listened in earnest, as Larry reeled off a short list of complaints. Highball, for his part, admitted that the miscommunication over the training was an honest mistake but gave no ground on the second accusation. Larry was not yet appeased, and went off to find a drink. Wearily, Highball sought out The Sipper to report the bones of the conversation and the nature of the complaints back to the captain, who listened with a heavy heart. It was only later that the pair found out that

Larry's entire list of grievances was a cunning device to try to wind people up. As wind-ups went, this one was the mother of them. The Sipper and Highball slowly plotted their revenge.

NOTES

i   Pocock, Tom. "Captain Hoste and his Cricket Club", in *Witless Cricketer's Almanack*, 3rd edition, 2003, Cambridge, St Radegund public house

ii   ibid

iii   Pocock, Tom. *Remember Nelson – The Life of Captain Sir William Hoste*, p 147

iv   ibid. p 151

v   ibid. p 157. Teddy is Hoste's brother, Edward

vi   Scepanovic, Ivo. Op cit

vii   ibid

viii   Pocock, Tom. *Remember Nelson – The Life of Captain Sir William Hoste*, p 157

6
The *Lady Ruth*

They had eleven days in which to travel more than 1,100 nautical miles if they were to make it in time for the game.

It was gone 10 o'clock that night when JD and El Bow rowed across Vis harbour in a dinghy. They had dropped anchor in the small bay between the ferry dock and Prirovo after a gruelling eleven days at sea, and although they had found time to smarten themselves up before coming ashore they were dog-tired. Frannie, ecstatic and relieved to see JD, brought them straight into Bejbi where they wedged themselves behind one of the back tables and, armed with a pizza from the Katarina washed down with a couple of beers, gave an account of their voyage to the others.

They had started out from the Menorcan capital, Mahón, on 9 September on board El Bow's 42-feet Whitby class boat the *Lady Ruth*. Leaving port in the early evening, they set a course due east. Within an hour it was getting dark and they were experiencing high winds and rough seas that would have made for a very unpleasant passage so, with JD and their other crew member lacking experience in handling *Lady Ruth*, they decided to cut their losses and head back to Mahón. They arrived late in the evening, sat down to supper and discussed their plans. Setting off at all had probably been unwise. They had eleven days in which to travel more than 1,100 nautical miles to Vis if they were to make it in time for the game. A hundred miles a day was a tall order but not impossible, and they were determined not to let the team down.

The following day, however, brought no change in the winds and thus no chance of getting under way, so the three of them kicked their heels around town. It was a holiday in Mahón, known locally as the *Festa de Cavalls,* in which horsemen, astride the indigenous Menorcan breed, charge around the city's narrow lanes while the citizens try to get out of their way by ducking into doorways. To the three visitors it looked only marginally less dangerous than the notorious San Fermin bull-running in Pamplona, and they retired to a local hostelry to drink the local *pomeda,* Mahón gin mixed with lemonade or lemon juice according to preference.

By the following day the weather had settled down sufficiently for them to consider making an attempt to get under way. The seas were still giving some cause for concern, but the consensus was that the winds could not possibly stay strong enough to keep them that way and the crew eventually got going at noon. With the wind off the bow they could use little sail so relied on the boat's motor to make progress, splitting their duties into six-hour watches: six hours on, six off, six sleeping. Early in the morning on their second day at sea, El Bow woke to relieve JD at change of watch only to find the boat coping admirably with twenty feet-high waves. JD was coping less admirably. His face had lost its usual colour, and he had not enjoyed the experience of the night watch at all. By noon, though, they had made good progress, having covered nearly 200 miles, and were off the south-east point of Sardinia and the Gulf of Cagliari. Here they had a decision to make. Their original plan had been to go across the northern coast of Sicily to the Aeolian Isles and through the Straits of Messina but northerly winds now threatened to make that difficult, so they opted instead for the southern coast of Sicily which, in the event, allowed them six hours of uninterrupted sailing.

It was to be the only occasion on the entire trip that they were able to shut down the motor for a prolonged period of time. Spirits were up. Free time was spent fishing, and anything reeled in that was edible was slapped on the grill. Most of the fish caught was gurnard: abundant in the Mediterranean in several different versions, so enough – in theory at least – to provide a modicum of variety.

From the evening of the second day they motored along the south coast of Sicily on calm, windless seas. Just before change of watch on the morning of the 13th, the engine started to be uncooperative. The problem was soon identified. There was water in the fuel, and though they managed to solve the problem, a headwind made the going slow. On the third night El Bow was taking watch on calm seas, with the boat making good time under motor, when at three in the morning there was the sound of sudden breaking waves alongside as a pod of about thirty dolphins kept him company for an hour. If nothing else this seemed like a good omen.

By eight o'clock the engine was protesting again, making its complaint with loud, regular splutters. Shortly afterwards it stopped completely. Attempts to revive it met with mixed success. It could be made to start but refused to do anything more strenuous than sit in its "idle" setting. Time, El Bow thought, to put in to port, so they steered for Licata on the Sicilian coast, where they found a berth in a sheltered bay they had all to themselves, and went ashore at midday.

Licata they found to be an unremarkable industrial seaport of some 40,000 souls located roughly midway between the more historically interesting cities of Agrigento and Gela, both of which boast fine ancient

Greek temples. There was little time for sightseeing of any kind though, JD and El Bow's immediate needs being to repair *Lady Ruth*'s engine.

As soon as they got ashore things started to look strange. El Bow's first impression was that, it being a Sunday, the city elders had let the inmates of the local asylum have the day off: a lot of people seemed to spend their time talking to trees and lamp posts. As the afternoon drew into evening, the *passeggiata* began, and the cafes filled with groups of older gentlemen who had probably been having the same conversation for the last forty years. Meanwhile, the young buzzed around on their scooters. El Bow, a keen Italophile, elaborated on the natives' love of speaking with their hands, indicating the four *signori* at a nearby table as an example. As it turned out these gentlemen were, in fact, deaf and merely communicating in sign language. It was all a bit too Fellini-esque.

Thanks to the tourist office (very helpful, though you could not imagine they ever got much business) the crew of the *Lady Ruth* were directed to the Casa Rosa for dinner. The route was complicated. Availing themselves of a few conveniently placed bars en route they proceeded in the general direction of Licata's finest eaterie. It was at this point that the three decided they were being followed. Everywhere they turned they saw the same faces, all trying not to be noticed. At one point they took a wrong turn and were stopped by a local who informed them that their destination was "that way", with the directions given to them at the tourist office repeated almost word for word. Either this was a very small town indeed, or something very strange was going on. At a small intersection there was a man leaning against a wall reading a newspaper just like in almost every spy film the three had ever seen. As they neared they were overtaken by a youth on a scooter who coughed quite audibly and deliberately as he passed the newspaper reader, who returned the cough without looking up from his paper. By the time they reached the restaurant they found a table had been set for three places, in advance.

They exchanged glances, saying nothing, and before long were enjoying a bottle of wine. They discussed, in lowered tones, what had happened. Was the restaurant so well-known that it was obvious where they would be heading, or had word got (quickly!) around that three *Inglese* were in town looking for somewhere to eat? They decided the latter, and although none of them felt particularly threatened, they stayed no longer than they had to.

The following morning the crew was up early, hoping to get to the fuel dock and make up time on the journey, only to find that their boat had been surrounded by fishing nets and was hemmed in. They were going nowhere. At least they now knew why they had managed to get such a good spot at which to tie up the boat the day before: all the local fishing boats had been out at sea and the *Lady Ruth* had taken one of their moorings. If it had all been part of a local plot to keep them there another 24 hours, then they barely let the thought enter their minds. There was, however, nothing they could do until the nets were gone, so they stocked up on provisions and some spare parts and had another session in their favourite local.

On the morning of the 16th the fishing nets had been removed and the boat was free to depart, its crew eager to get under way again. With the motor working as best they could get it to, they now had the better part of 600 miles to go, and five days to get there. No sooner had they got out of the harbour than they were hit by strong head winds and were back under power. They tried ducking in to the coast to get out of the wind but with current and wind against them the best speed they could manage was still no more than two knots. By mid-afternoon they had found anchorage off a sheltered beach near Scoglitti, west of Gela, 30 miles from Licata. The chances of their reaching Vis on time were looking slimmer by the minute. Little prospect, they thought, of any of them opening the batting.

The next day they made a concerted push eastwards, finally rounded Capo Passero, the southernmost tip of Sicily, early in the afternoon and headed east-north-east with the wind coming off the nose of the boat and the *Lady Ruth* making five knots for the first time in days. Thereafter they enjoyed flat seas but no wind almost all the way to Vis, so the engine was back in use. Crossing the Golfo di Squillace off the Calabrian coast at sunset was memorable for a very strange, flat light: lots of colour in the water to the west, but nothing at all to starboard. They rounded Capo Santa Maria di Leuca at five in the morning on the 19th then passed through the Strait of Otranto, before making a brief stop in Brindisi for fuel. The third crew member, who had been travelling with them specifically to come and play cricket on Vis, had by this time decided he'd rather had enough, disembarked and flew back home to Britain. Though they were sad to have lost his company, they had the consolation of having more than broken the back of the journey, and, with over 160 miles to go they cleared Brindisi's harbour at sunset, at about the same time that their friends from the St Radegund were rolling out of Lambik after their Friday night gin session. There was, however, still a lot of work for JD and El Bow to do if they were to make the match. Perhaps if the Rad batted second the two of them could still get a game?

The alternator of the motor, which had driven them heroically for nearly a thousand miles, burned up at about four in the morning on the Saturday and filled the boat with thick smoke. Fortunately the wind was strong enough for them to carry on, and sunset on the Saturday saw them ten miles off Vis, showered and shaved, with the boat fairly tidy and a Vera Lynn each in hand with chances excellent there would be more to follow. All was right with the world. El Bow and JD had averaged better than a hundred miles per day, even with the enforced interruptions and bad weather. It was impressive going, and their audience, huddled around the table in the back of Bcjbi, could only marvel at it all.

"Piece of cake," El Bow said with a broad grin.

▲

Maclean returned to London in the spring of 1944, on a round of meetings whose principal aim was to improve the administrative back-up to his mission. He also found himself inexorably drawn into political discussions about the future of a liberated Yugoslavia. He was summoned for a meeting with King Peter who, among other things, was concerned about his own lack of influence over the destiny of his country from far away in London, and asked Maclean how he could improve his standing with his people. Maclean mentioned a suggestion of Tito's that the king, who was a skilled pilot, enlist in the fledgling Balkan Air Force, then in training in North Africa. The king was enthusiastic, but his aides were less so, and Maclean thought it unlikely Peter would be taking to the skies over his country any time soon. Tito's gesture was, however, matched by one from the king, who publicly distanced the Royal Yugoslav government from Mihajlović and asked the Yugoslav people to support Tito's attempts to liberate the country, much to the anger of some of those within his own government.

The British mission to Mihajlović's Četniki had been formally withdrawn a few weeks earlier, Churchill having confirmed the decision with a speech to the House of Commons on the matter. Immediate supplies of arms to the Partižani in Serbia, the traditional operational area of the Četniki now became a priority, but little was known of the degree of communist strength in this essentially pro-monarchist region of Yugoslavia, or of the degree to which the peasantry would support them. British government support for Mihajlović may have been expedient at the outset but, as Maclean argued succinctly, they had built him up into "something that he never seriously claimed to be. Now we were dropping him because he had failed to fulfil our expectations."i King Peter realised the need for a united front against the German occupation and cleansed his government of the anti-Partižani elements, replacing them with men who would be willing to reach a political settlement with the communists. The former Ban of Croatia, Ivan Šubašić, was chosen to conduct negotiations with Tito. In spite of these promising signs, Maclean did not rate highly the chances of the two sides reaching a mutually satisfactory agreement. The Partižani held all the cards, a fact he impressed upon Šubašić when they met. Šubašić, according to Maclean "a rather flabby-looking man of medium size with his hair en brosse and small uneasy eyes,"ii did not appear to be concerned by this.

Just as Maclean was preparing to head back to Yugoslavia to report, he received some disturbing news: the Germans had attacked *Partižani* positions in Drvar and launched a huge airborne operation against Tito's mountain headquarters, resulting in heavy casualties on the defending side. Members of the British mission and Tito and his staff were believed to be safe though on the run in the woods of Bosnia with German forces closing in on them. By the time Maclean reached Bari he was able to hear a full account of what had happened.

The attack, Operation Rösselsprung, began early in the morning of 25 May when light aircraft began wave after wave of intensive bombing of Drvar and a massive paratroop drop into the town. The *Partižani* stationed in the town managed to beat back the German advance to the surrounding hills. Simultaneously a glider attack on the slopes just below Tito's headquarters allowed the Germans to control the approach to the cave. Tito and his staff escaped by the skin of their teeth through the roof of the cave.

Those *Partižani* defending Drvar had suffered heavy casualties and soon realised that they could not continue to hold the Germans in the face of an overwhelming assault, so withdrew to the hills themselves. The Germans took the town but, having failed either to kill Tito or capture the Allied Missions, they took their frustrations out on the pro-*Partižani* civilians of Drvar, executing the majority of the town's population.

The Germans pursued the guerrillas into the woods, but Tito and his army were forever on the move, always one step ahead of their pursuers. Members of the British Mission were able to establish radio contact with Bari and get much needed air support as well as an emergency supply drop. Even so, a week after the attack on Drvar the situation was no better. In a moment of relative quiet, Tito confided in one of the British officers that he could no longer effectively command all his forces while simultaneously trying to outwit the enemy in the forests. He needed a more secure, permanent base from which to conduct the campaigns. Would he, the British officer, please arrange for the evacuation of Tito and his staff?

By nightfall on the 3 June Tito, six of his staff, his dog Tigger, and members of the British and Soviet Missions waited by an improvised *Partižani* airfield for their plane to land. Eventually it came, a lend lease US Dakota piloted by two Soviets and flown from the British base at Bari. Two hours later they were on Italian soil.

Tito was given quarters in a villa outside the town, and it was here that Maclean visited him to discuss his plans. Tito was all for moving his headquarters to Vis until it was safe to return to the mainland. To Maclean this seemed a sensible idea. Vis had been garrisoned and fortified, had a significant naval force operating out of Komiža and had recently completed construction of an airfield in the central plain. It was as secure a base for his headquarters as Tito could hope for.

Tito sailed for Vis on board HMS *Blackmore*, a Hunt class destroyer. No sooner had he and Tigger embarked than they were taken below to the officers' wardroom, there to be entertained with drinks before dinner. The crew of the *Blackmore* did sterling work in making their guest feel welcome. Not only did they ply him with gin but, when it came time to sit down to dinner, they produced handwritten menus in both English and Serbo-Croatian. Maclean recalled the wine list as "a formidable one: sherry followed the gin, then red wine, then white, then port, then liqueurs."[iii] Tito didn't seem to mind in the slightest and everything that was offered to him, including a glass of champagne he had initially suspected was cherry brandy, was downed with aplomb. When cherry brandy did finally appear on the table, "any distrust which he might have felt for it earlier in the evening had evidently completely vanished"[iv] as Maclean tactfully put it. The biggest surprise – and highlight – of the evening, though, came when Tito showed off a command of English hitherto un-revealed to Maclean, which he demonstrated by rising from the table to recite Lear's *The Owl and the Pussycat*, no doubt inspired by the fine feast that he had just enjoyed.

▲

"Eat, drink and be merry," quoth The Sipper, who was sitting in a com-fortable chair outside Lambik and sipping a margarita. This pronounce-ment was fine eve of battle stuff, but everybody knew full well that eating had a fairly lowly position on the list of the evening's priorities. In defiance of Bunter's great edict "never put your foot in the same puddle twice" (though why anyone should want to put their foot in a puddle a first time he never made clear), the St Radegund's captain had announced a return to the scene of the previous night's crime for the team's traditional bonding session, and the response, from the younger members of the team at least, had been splendid.

The female members of the party had been invited along for drinks, but were given notice that their presence was not required after a certain time. The main entertainment was to take the form of a gentlemen-only exercise, more commonly known as the lads' night out, the principal aim of which was to see what the fleshpots of Kut had to offer, and how long it would take to drink them all dry. For the St Radegund boys this was something of a busman's holiday. The women were canny enough to want no part of it.

Highball pitched up without the fines sock, an oversight for which he was immediately fined one kuna, and sent back to his apartment to fetch it. The Sipper laid his orange policeman's helmet on the table before him, where it rested with ominous intent.

Goran Pečarević passed by the bar on his way to the Kaliopa. He offered a wave and a smile, so it was assumed the tablecloth incident had been forgotten, or at least chalked up to experience, though he politely declined a request to join the party. As the assembled crew waited for Highball to return and sampled Lambik's lengthy cocktail menu in the warm evening air, The Sipper held forth on his options as captain for the forthcoming cricket match. The expected arrival that evening of JD, El Bow and their third crew member – assuming nothing had gone wrong at sea – promised to add a little more robustness to his team. JD had played only four innings for the St Radegund all season, but had a highest score of 38 to his name and was undefeated on two occasions. El Bow had played one game fewer than JD and, though he had contributed only 20 runs to the team's cause, had performed much better with the ball, having taken five wickets in ten overs at an average of 8.88 and a best bowling analysis of two wickets for two runs. Between them, they would add an invaluable degree of experience to the Rad's ranks.

The Sipper himself would keep wicket, as he had done all season, and delegate placing the field to Highball. The bowling, he promised, would be evenly distributed, with everybody who turned up to play getting an over or two, possibly more, depending on the quality of the hosts' batting. Of The Three Stooges, only Moe's bowling was known to him, and even then it was decidedly less memorable than his batting. And what of Curly? Had he ever bowled in a Rad vs. Champ match? No one could remember. Equally mysterious was the nature and quality of Son of El Vis' bowling, but The Sipper was not unduly worried and maintained that there would be enough variety within the ranks to ensure he wouldn't be short of options for a bowling change.

Beard and Highball were, on their day, more than capable of causing batsmen difficulties, particularly if it became necessary to slow the scoring rate. Beard was a genuine medium pacer with a decent out-swinger. Highball was slightly slower but with an occasionally devastating in-swinging arm ball. Crabbo Junior, who was of a similar build to Highball, had been a medium pacer of similar style. Recently, though, he had abandoned this action for the more devilish arts of leg spin, though he had yet to perfect it to the point where he was taking wickets regularly. JD was another leg spinner of reasonable accuracy and occasionally noticeable turn. And in El Bow they had the team's secret weapon.

With the batting, The Sipper was on surer ground, and confidently expected things to take care of themselves in this department. Curly was a steady – at times too steady – opening batsman for the Champ and never allowed himself to be hurried into a shot. Such a patient approach could turn out to be a useful antidote to hot-headedness. Moe, so often the scourge of the St Radegund bowlers, was more than capable of winning the match single-handedly. Crabbo Junior was a fine stroke player, never happier than when working the ball off his legs. JD could be relied upon to score quickly, usually in boundaries. El Bow, Beard and Highball could certainly be expected to chip in with a few runs if needed, and it was to be hoped that Larry would answer the call too, even if his prowess with the willow was merely speculative. That left Son of Elvis, who was reputed to be a fine batsman of sound habits and The Sipper himself, an agricultural specialist of some distinction. On paper, at least, it looked like a reasonable outfit, even by the St Radegund's less than vaunted standards.

Given the condition of the ground they were to play on, fielding on the deck was always likely to be hazardous. At least with anything aerial, he knew there were a few players among the team who could at least hold on to a ball. The key priority, The Sipper decided, was that everybody should get a game and he, as captain, would try to pick the appropriate bowler for the opposing batsman. "Otherwise," he said raising his margarita, "show us your mettle and make yourselves a name in history."

Once Highball returned with the sock, The Sipper turned his attention to the serious matter of revenge upon The Three Stooges for Larry's wind-up of the previous day. In practice this meant fining them at a greater rate than anybody else, the more so since they were due to return home the day after the cricket match. The evening's entertainment began with the usual minor infractions: obscenity (Beard, two kuna), pedantry (Beard again, four kuna), being a jazz bore (Highball and Crabbo Junior were pretty much interchangeable in this regard, four kuna each), and sneaking (the Memsahib, two kuna). The Sipper's fines were not unreasonable in themselves though with the tour's judge, Eyebrows, being somewhere on the other side of town there was no immediate right of appeal. Curly, for once awake, watched with dread as the fines started coming thick and fast, and started to question The Sipper, the object being, he hoped, to slow down the rate of fining by picking holes in the logic of his arguments. He tried every fallacy he could think of, from apriorism to *tu quque* and several points in between. It was a magnificent contest: the two mathematicians were going about it like heavyweights. There could be only one winner though: The Sipper was confident in the ultimate authority of the fines helmet, and it was all the defence he needed as Curly's blows rained down. There was no linguistic subtlety Curly could try that cut any ice with The

Sipper, who merely doubled the fine. Again came Curly, jabbing away, but always well within The Sipper's range.

"You just don't get it, do you?" he asked. Fine doubled again. Further protestations from Curly? Another fine (two kuna). "It's too easy!" The Sipper was gloating, reeling Curly in. Punched out, Curly had exhausted every line of attack to no avail and was getting desperate. Mild vitriol? Another fine (four kuna). Railing against the system? A whopping ten kuna fine, and a further two kuna fine applied retrospectively on Curly's previous fines that evening. The book was a riot of crossed out and recalculated fines. There was no beating the system.

"Are we all fine and dandy now?" asked Highball, incurring upon himself a four kuna fine for very bad punning. Then he dropped the sock, which earned him a further penalty.

Larry and Moe cottoned on to what was happening pretty quickly. Moe realised the easiest way to avoid the findings of this kangaroo court was to take the fifth. Larry, on the other hand, saw little harm in playing along. The Sipper tried to extract more fines for transgressions earlier in the tour, and warned Larry that the toilet incarceration incident had not been forgotten. Larry's sense of humour failure on being released from the lavatory, and his subsequent display of dissent and refusal to pay (three kuna) was now trebled. Neither did the events of the previous evening go unpunished, Larry earning himself a five kuna fine and the temporary moniker "Firestarter" in recognition of his attempt to burn to the ground one of Croatia's finest restaurants. For the most part though, the fines were taken in good part and once the Stooges were relieved of most of their small change and the party sufficiently lubricated, it was decided that a stroll into Vis town to take the air and check in at headquarters would be a good idea.

Once at Bejbi, Curly promptly disappeared next door to the Katarina for his usual pizza and bottle of red vino, somebody remembering to look in on him after half an hour to see if he was all right. Sure enough there was Curly asleep at the table, his pizza going cold and his wine barely touched.

The Sipper caught up with JD and El Bow, and asked if they wanted to come out with the rest of the boys. They politely declined, saying that they were still struggling to find their land legs after eleven days at sea, so would be happier just to sit in Bejbi with a few beers and then turn in for the night. The Sipper understood perfectly well. He enquired about their missing crew member. Had they thrown him overboard as ballast? When The Sipper learned that he had actually disembarked at Brindisi, his brow furrowed. This left the St Radegund team one player short for the following day's match.

There was a brief discussion about how the evening was expected to unfold. As the general object was for as many of the St Radegund's players as possible to wake up on the day of the match with a mighty hangover, the conclusion was something of a no-brainer: stay at Bejbi drinking until such time as people got bored, and then head out to see what nightlife Vis town could offer. By the time the boys got around to thinking about leaving, they were several rounds of Karlovačko beer to the good. It was gone midnight but still pleasantly warm. Off they went in the general direction of Kut in search of adventure, stopping at various places along the way, most of which proved to be shut.

Presently, not far from the Pojoda on the edge of the main square, they came across a two-storey building with green wooden shutters over its windows. In front of the main entrance was a terrace of huge palms and stone troughs containing decorative foliage, with tables, chairs and umbrellas all tidied away for the night. Inside the lights were still on, visible through muslin curtains in the ground-floor windows, and a low buzz of conversation and recorded music was just audible. Larry was confident:

"This pub's open," he said cheerily, then swung open the door and rolled inside, followed by the rest. Inside the Restaurant Val were a number of islanders sitting around tables, open bottles of wine before them. The conversation stopped at the entrance of the tourists. Had there been a piano-player present, doubtless he too would have stopped playing and eyed the interlopers warily. It was a moment of movie-cliché tension.

"Er guys," asked Crabbo Junior, "are we sure this is actually a pub?"

A bemused silence greeted the gatecrashers. Larry decided to brass it out, and bade everybody a good evening. The greeting was returned, and the boys took a table against the wall. The pianist resumed playing. One of the islanders stood behind a small corner counter. Several bottles of wine stood open behind it. The Sipper approached the counter and asked what was going on. He was told it was a wedding reception.

"How much for a bottle?" asked The Sipper, having ascertained that the team was welcome to stay. The wines turned out to be on the house, and so a bottle of Plavac and several glasses duly appeared on the tourists' table. This seemed splendid hospitality, and besides one could hardly complain at gone one in the morning, so The Sipper, ever the diplomat, asked if he could congratulate the bride in person. He was ushered in the direction of a comely young woman sitting with two men – husband? father? brother? – in one of the seats by the window. The Sipper, bold as brass, went over to her and thanked her for the wine. She seemed to care little, but one of the men with her started casting looks across the room at the table of gatecrashers. Larry was alert to the warning signs: "Fellas, we'd better watch ourselves here."

The music started up again, a lively piece of Croatian Euro-pop. As if on cue, Curly got to his feet, strode over to the main party and asked the bride's mother for a dance. Thankfully Curly's dancing amounted to little more energetic than an orthopaedic shuffle from one foot to the other. He took the mother's hand in his own, placed his other at the small of her back and twirled the matriarch around the room a few revolutions before putting her back down. The son/son-in-law watched intently, looking to see if Curly put a hand out of place. The music stopped. The dance ended. Curly planted a wet kiss on the mother's cheek before retiring to his corner for the next round. The husband/father/brother glared. The sense of foreboding was infectious: Highball's head was in his hands.

"We've had it. It's going to kick off," he said, his appetite for more wine now diminishing rapidly. He feared another evening was about to be ruined.

Crabbo Junior had been put in charge of the fines book, having commandeered it from The Sipper, who was glad of a rest from his duties. Highball, having dropped the sock a number of times on their way into Kut, also happily gave up care of the treasury, and was subsequently fined for declaring that he "wasn't that arsed" about it. This and various other infractions Crabbo Junior was attempting to record faithfully in an increasingly unsteady hand. Curly's "inappropriate snogging", at least, managed to make it into the book legibly.

Happily, the rest of the evening passed with no further incident and petered out into mellow reflection, relations with the locals proceeding on a wary, but mutually respectful basis. Further embarrassments were there none. Larry, though, had made such a grand job of stoking The Sipper's anxieties that the captain was convinced he was about to be beaten up by a huge Croatian bloke for having made a pass at the bride. When the time came to leave, The Sipper did so smartly and made his way home at a giddy clip, not stopping to look behind him.

NOTES

i Maclean, p 438
ii ibid. p 448
iii ibid. p 455
iv ibid

The Ascent of Mount Hum

7

The Match

Curly's proficiency was only marred by an occasionally ponderous scoring rate. JD brought to the game a keen eye, good co-ordination and an unfailing reluctance to take the simplest of runs.

The decisive battle for control of the Adriatic was fought on 13 March 1811. Hoste had been back on Lissa for only four days, and was eager to resume his pursuit of Dubourdieu. Early in the morning his small squadron, consisting of the *Amphion, Active, Cerberus* and *Volage* were about a mile off Lissa holding a north-westerly course. They were not alone. Dubourdieu, under orders from Napoleon to seize and hold Lissa, had decided to take the battle to Hoste and appeared ahead in command of a fleet of eleven ships making straight for the British force.

As well as being outnumbered, the British were outgunned and out-manned. Dubordieu's ships boasted 276 guns to Hoste's 124, and the French had 2,000 men to Hoste's 900. The odds were stacked against the British, just as they had been at Trafalgar. Hoste's main advantage, however, was in the professionalism of his crew, and as the French force bore down on them he recalled the message Nelson had sent to the rest of his fleet at Trafalgar: "England expects that every man will do his duty."

With little time to act before the French were upon them, he had a message run up the mast in naval colours; one he hoped his fleet would find equally inspiring. It consisted of just two words: "Remember Nelson."

The battle commenced around nine o'clock. Dubourdieu's plan of attack was to divide his forces into two lines attacking in parallel, the aim being to come alongside the British line and engage them at close quarters. Hoste's response was to order his ships to form a tight line that would be more difficult for the French to penetrate. Dubourdieu countered by trying to cut across *Amphion*'s stern to separate it from the rest of the squadron, but a series of weighty broadsides against the Frenchman's flag-ship, *La Favorite*, forced the commodore into a hasty reassessment, and he decided to risk all on boarding the English ships and fighting hand-to-hand in the hope that his superior numbers would tell.

The British were holding a course directly parallel to the northern shore of the island. As *La Favorite* bore down on the *Amphion,* its bows teeming with boarders with all arms drawn, Hoste unleashed the payload of the quarterdeck cannon directly at the French ship, destroying the fore-castle and killing a large proportion of the crew and officers, among them Dubourdieu himself. Once again *La Favorite* aimed to cut *Amphion* off across the bows, but Hoste immediately ordered his ships hard about, leaving *La Favorite* to drive itself onto the rocky north coast of Lissa.

The second ship in Dubourdieu's line, the *Flore*, now made for

Amphion's stern and came alongside to starboard while the third ship, *Bellona*, did the same on the port side, a tactic Nelson had used repeatedly at the Battle of the Nile. Hoste's response was to cut across the *Flore*'s bows and fire on her starboard side. The *Bellona* came across *Flore*'s stern in support, but she too came under heavy fire. Both ships lowered their colours, but *Amphion* herself had taken significant damage and Hoste had insufficient boats in good condition to send crews over to the French ships to claim their prizes. The captain of the *Flore* raised his colours and made a run for it.

At the same time, the three other ships in the British line had come under attack by the French's second line, with the smallest, *Volage*, the main target. Yet she held her own and was ably supported by *Active*, the most powerful of the British ships, and together they saw off the attack of the French *Danae* and *Carolina*, both of which followed the *Flore* by running for Lesina.[i] The *Cerberus* had also taken on the *Carolina* as well as the *Corona*, the fourth ship of the French first line, and suffered heavy damage in the process. Again the *Active*, still undamaged by enemy fire, arrived in support and the *Corona* too tried to retire from the battle. The captain of the *Active*, however, was dogged in pursuit and followed the ailing *Corona* half way to Lesina where the two ships spent two hours pummelling each other with broadsides until the *Corona* surrendered.

The battle lasted over five hours. British dead numbered fifty, with over 130 wounded. French casualties were much higher, though as the *Flore*, *Danae* and *Carolina* all managed to escape to Lesina, a final tally of the dead and wounded was unknown.

Hoste enjoyed his moment of glory. In late March, as other British ships arrived to blockade the French ships that had escaped to Lesina, he took the now repaired *Amphion* and the captured prizes to Malta and "a round of congratulatory parties, fêtes and balls".[ii] Praise for his victory at the Battle of Lissa was lavish, and the comparisons with his late mentor many. A rear admiral at Palermo, who passed on the news of the battle to both the Admiralty and Hoste's family in Norfolk, wrote: "Your distinguished bravery will forever immortalise your name and make our country of dumplings and dripping rejoice to think they have… a brilliant spark from the shrine of our immortal countryman, Lord Nelson."[iii]

The hero left Malta for Britain in June, with Lord Byron as a passenger, and arrived back in England a month later. His reception was something of a disappointment. Though Hoste was rightly decorated for his heroism by the Admiralty, further honours were not immediately forthcoming and, worse, when he returned to Norfolk what should have been a joyful homecoming was dampened by the news that his father had wastefully spent all the prize money Hoste had amassed since becoming captain.

▲

The day of the match between Kriket Klub Sir William Hoste and the St Radegund happened to coincide with the autumn equinox, but might as well have been high summer. By noon, as members of the St Radegund team made their way from all parts of Kut to converge on Bejbi, the temperature was into the seventies and climbing. It was going to be a scorcher. As the players, identifiable in their St Radegund polo shirts, threaded their way through the narrow streets of Kut many of them were greeted by townspeople and late-season tourists who wished them well in the coming match.

The polo shirts were of a similar weight to the ones Bunter had brought over for the Hoste team. Over the left breast was an embroidered badge of the pub's coat of arms, above it the words "St Radegund Pub, Cambridge, England" and below "Cricket Tour, Vis, Croatia." On the back was printed Hoste's message to his squadron represented in the colours of the Royal Navy's flag signals, copied from the dust jacket of Tom Pocock's book. The sleeves of the shirts were decorated with the insignia of a Cuban rum brand which had been kind enough to offer sponsorship. At least, The Sipper thought as he arrived at Bejbi in his velvet jacket, they now looked like a team. Even Larry had dispensed with his "spiv on tour" look, as Moe put it.

Pre-match training was a St Radegund tradition, so everyone took on a couple of beers at Bejbi as a libation to Nike in the hope of victory that afternoon. For some it was a case of topping up. At least three of the team had stayed up most of the night before, following their return from the wedding party at the Restaurant Val, to investigate the wonders of their magnum of *travarica*. The majority of the bottle's contents were drunk. Crabbo Junior bailed out at gone four in the morning, his excuse being that he had a cricket match to play the next day, and left Beard and Son of El Vis to their own devices. From the balcony of their apartment the pair watched the sun come up, and then decided on an impromptu swim. They made their way down the nearby jetty, Beard leading, and inched their way into the harbour. Beard stepped into the water and onto a slippery, moss-covered rock before launching himself into the harbour's cooling waters.

"This is a good route down," Beard said cheerily. Son of El Vis followed him, putting his foot on the same moss-coloured rock only to lose his balance completely, and entered the water with an impressive pike and half-turn and a loud splash. Beard nearly drowned laughing. When they entered Bejbi it was noted how well they were looking on so little sleep.

The Highballs arrived, having just been to mass at the Church of Our Lady of the Caves, a surprise to some who had not realised they were a church-going couple.

"We're not," Highball corrected.

"What was it like?" asked Bunter, himself a follower of the Church of Rome, though lapsed.

"*Very* Catholic," answered the Memsahib. "Candles. Incense. The works."

As The Sipper inspected his troops, hands in pockets and wearing his tasselled skipper's cap, he made a surprising admission: he had failed to pack a single item of underwear of robust enough construction to hold a cricket box. All the trolleys he had brought with him were of a flimsy, boxer short design. With admirable resourcefulness, he had borrowed a pair of Jugs' knickers to wear for the duration of the cricket match.

Up at the ground at Samogor, and certain of being able to play in some comfort if not style, The Sipper was able to turn his mind to the problem of having only ten players on his team. Noticing El Vis hanging around by the side of the pitch, The Sipper ventured to ask whether the senior King had any cricketing experience. It turned out that El Vis, though now in his sixties, had played for Magdalene College, opened the batting when he played for the Royal Artillery in Hong Kong and been selected to represent the army's South-East Asian Command team, though the proposed match had never actually been played. The last time he had played had been forty years ago when he had turned out regularly for the Old Dunstonians, but he had given it up when…

The Sipper had heard enough. Assured of El Vis' cricketing pedigree, and with nothing to lose, he asked whether he would like to fill the vacant place in the team? It would really help them out in a spot. El Vis eagerly took his chance, having genuinely not expected to be involved in the cricketing side of the tour at all. The Memsahib immediately offered to give him her St Radegund tour shirt to wear during the match. Beard was wide-eyed in disbelief at The Sipper drafting a sexagenarian into the ranks, but any protests were ignored. The St Radegund team was – at long last – an XI.

Oliver Roki and The Sipper shook hands and the Rad captain took a five kuna coin from his pocket for the toss. Oliver called incorrectly and The Sipper invited Oliver's team to bat. Thirty overs per side. Rob Dumančić and a cousin of Niko Roki's, over for the weekend from Split, strode out to the middle to umpire.

Siniša Vodopija, the geography teacher, opened the batting for Hoste with Lenko Marinković, who worked for a local wine grower. All of the Hoste team had been instructed to wear protective helmets. It was not clear whether this precaution had been deemed necessary because of the variable bounce off the batting strip, or whether they had had advance intelligence about the quality of the St Radegund bowling.

The first over, from the end closer to the adjoining fields, was given to Crabbo Junior. Highball, who was charged with organising the field, had opted for a makeshift setting, neither particularly attacking nor defensive. There was a gully (but no slip fielders), point, extra cover, midwicket, mid-off and mid-on and various fielders in deep-lying positions. At least this way the areas that the opposing players had been seen to favour during the previous day's net session were well-covered.

Having opted to bowl his regular medium-quick stuff rather than his new leg spin bag, Crabbo Junior delivered the ball with decent pace, and did enough to have Siniša playing and missing with regularity. When the batsman finally did make contact he wasn't able to hit the ball off the square, or in this case, given that the artificial pitch was laid across the diagonal of the helipad, the diamond. Crabbo Junior bowled a maiden.

The Sipper then invited his most recent recruit, El Vis, to bowl the second over. El Vis looked pretty sprightly for a man in his mid-sixties. He turned his arm over a couple of times in practice before delivering a looping ball that Lenko drove into the hands of a fielder at mid-on. As the fielding side celebrated, Niko's cousin inexplicably called a no ball. There was not enough pace in El Vis' run up for his leading foot to have strayed over the line. Heads were scratched on the Rad side as they resumed their places in the field. Lenko's response to this reprieve was tentative, and at the end of the over Hoste were still 0 for 0.

Crabbo Junior bowled a second over before being asked to take a rest. After three dot balls the Hoste innings suddenly burst into life. Crabbo Junior's control slipped ever so slightly, and Siniša despatched a pull shot to the square leg boundary for four. His confidence rising, the geography teacher followed that up with a shot behind square, returned from the outfield for two, and a handy-looking drive through mid-on for another boundary. This last shot, driven straight-ish, went through the barbed wire at long on and into the adjacent field. Beard went to see if the ball was retrievable, but Oliver shouted for him not to bother, offering a friendly warning: "It's OK, leave it. There are probably landmines on that side of the wire." Beard was grateful for the advice. He went back to his place in the field which he was marking with cans of Karlovačko, a carry-out he had managed to equip himself with from Bejbi, and which were now warming up nicely in the afternoon heat.

It was clear that, even at this early stage of the game, it didn't pay to underestimate the islanders. Even if they were playing only their second-ever game of cricket, it was obvious they were quite capable of punishing any loose deliveries, and while 10 for 0 off three overs was a little pedestrian, it was still potentially useful. Given the whims of the artificial pitch, a score of anything over 100 from thirty overs could be quite defendable.

El Vis pegged the visitors back further with a second maiden over of solid dependability, all six balls being bowled either on the stumps or outside off and giving Lenko great difficulty in getting a shot away. This brought the fifth over and the first bowling change, Beard coming on at the "field" end. With a fairly even approach to the helipad he was able to bowl off something approaching a full length, and fired the ball down with hairy, ginger menace. His loosener was clipped away by Siniša for a single. Lenko, now on strike, had little answer to a bowler of genuine threat and remained without score by the over's end.

A change of bowler: Highball in place of El Vis, at the end that contained the half-foot deep depression. This Highball struggled to negotiate as he bowled a series of shockingly wayward deliveries that were fortunate not to be called wide, before launching one, with woeful lack of control, over the batsman's head. Again, this brought no penalty from the exceedingly generous umpire, but there were ironic shouts of "Good variation,

Highball!" from the field.

A feature of the St Radegund's play during the season just gone had been to liven up their time in the field by interjecting verbal non sequiturs at random points in the innings. This had started out innocently enough on a cold Sunday afternoon in June at Queens' College's ground in Cambridge, when a member of the team tried to gee everyone up by asking them to indulge in a spot of "pointless clapping". Like all good Rad ideas, this one quickly blossomed into the realms of the absurd. Beard, who had been about to commence his run-up, was asked to "put something big in the larder", another bowler was encouraged "Don't just book it, Thomas Cook it!" While all this meaningless banter kept the St Radegund team amused during a particularly dull passage of play, it had an important side effect: it distracted both umpire and opposition in equal measure. Having discovered by accident something quite the opposite of sledging, but with a similarly devastating effect, the St Radegund employed this tactic in every subsequent game.

On Vis, that first shout of "Good variation, Highball!" was enough to remind the fielding side of this strategem, and surreal shouts of encouragement started to come thick and fast. Typically, it was Beard who led the charge with an enthusiastic "Stand by, number two!" What the Hoste team made of it – if they understood it at all – was anybody's guess. Highball duly completed an over entirely comprised of number twos which, nevertheless, left the Hoste team still struggling to score regularly on 11 for 0. The following over, Beard's second, produced the match's first wicket.

Lenko deserved a great dollop of sympathy for the way he doggedly kept trying to work the ball away into a scoring area to no avail. His 20-ball duck, off the third delivery of Beard's over – a sharp catch bagged by Son of El Vis at gully – drew a warm round of applause from the visitors. The St Radegund had all been there and knew full well the frustration he must have been feeling.

Next in to bat was Stanko from the Rokis' restaurant. He started slowly, taking a single off the second ball he faced to put him on strike for Highball's second over. This was another maiden, full of near wides, borderline no balls and rank long hops that the bowler somehow got away with.

Siniša took a single off the first ball of Moe's first over, which was technically proficient and something of a surprise too, as few on his side could recall having seen him bowl before. Meanwhile Stanko, beginning to build in confidence, cuffed a shot through mid-wicket towards Highball. As he stood ready to field it low near his bootlaces, it unexpectedly caught the edge of the helipad on the bounce and sailed three feet over the fielder's head, eventually being retrieved by Beard in the outfield at a cost of two runs. Two balls later Stanko tried the same again, but this time drove the ball along the ground. Highball tried a sliding block but only got caught among the stubble of the field: one run on the total so Stanko retained strike for the next over.

This happened to be bowled by JD, and was comprised of trademark slow right-arm stuff with a little bit of turn. Stanko certainly looked less comfortable against slower-paced deliveries, and he only managed to get one ball away for a single, with Siniša leaving the remaining two balls. Drinks break.

JD's first over had been the tenth of the innings. This was a notable milestone for a couple of reasons. Firstly, Kriket Klub Sir William Hoste had managed to survive a whole five balls longer than they had done against Saumur in their first game. Secondly, and just as auspiciously, Stanko's single meant they had also beaten their team's previous best score of 15 by two runs, and still had nine wickets in hand. It seemed that the hours Hoste had spent practising under the palm trees were beginning to pay off. If anybody among the St Radegund team had had the presence of mind to recall this at the time, it would have been worth a short round of applause, or at least some acknowledgement from the fielding side. As it was, they were grateful to get off the pitch to re-hydrate on what had become a blazing hot day.

Oliver had, thoughtfully, brought a case of bottled water that had been in the freezer overnight, and was lying in the shade of a large slab of stone at the edge of the outfield. Here Bunter, Eyebrows and the non-combatants gathered, and Jugs perched on the top of it as she kept score. El Vis came to the sidelines carrying a limp. He had been fielding in a shortish extra cover position during the previous over, when a ball was wafted, at a catchable height, in his general direction. As he moved to intercept it, he turned his ankle in a huge rut, just as one of his team mates was inviting him to "Look out!" It had been a mistake to concentrate on the ball in the air rather than conditions underfoot. The Sipper showed concern. Was he all right to continue?

"If you've no one to replace me then I'll have to be," El Vis said.

"That's the spirit," The Sipper said, clapping him on the shoulder, "never say die." The St Radegund's captain did his calculations: twenty overs left, 17 runs on the board. If the current pair of batsmen got a move on, they could easily knock off a ton, which would be just about chaseable in the conditions. He saw no reason to change his tactics at this stage.

Play resumed with Moe's second over, during which the tourists made another breakthrough. Stanko took a quick single off the first ball, leaving Siniša to face. He powered the next ball through Highball at mid-wicket, and thought about doing the same with the following one. The third ball of the over was hit hard and low across the diagonal of the helipad where Highball reached down to take a one-handed catch by the toe of his boot. With a bellow of "How's that?" from Highball, Hoste were reduced to 22 for two.

The fall brought Antonio Lipanović to the wicket. Striding on to the pitch without a protective helmet, all six feet plus of him, he immediately prompted a brief exchange between The Sipper and Highball, both of whom, over six feet tall themselves, were amazed at the sight of somebody taller.

"I don't remember seeing him at nets yesterday," admitted The Sipper.

"You'd have a hard job missing someone that size," said Highball.

"What is he, the village blacksmith?"

Lipanović was indeed a giant. As he tapped down at the crease, the thought dawned on the Rad team that he was Hoste's secret weapon, and had deliberately been kept out of sight. He saw off his first delivery from Moe then prodded the next for a single, so retaining strike for the following over, JD's second.

Overs 12 and 13 were relatively quiet, as Lipanović and Stanko tried to steady the ship after the loss of the useful Siniša. Both batsmen scored singles during the first over, and the second, which was bowled by Son of El Vis, yielded just one run off the final ball, leaving Stanko to face the bowling of El Bow.

Having been coached, in all likelihood, in the virtues of the orthodox bowling technique, it was unlikely that any member of Kriket Klub Sir William Hoste could have been prepared for the sight of El Bow and his round-arm bowling action. The nickname derived, perhaps a little unfairly, from the St Radegund's suspicion that the wiry Irish-American's forearm flexed a little more than the regulation five degrees when releasing the ball. Otherwise his action, though something of a rarity in the 21st (or even the 20th) century, was a perfectly legitimate addition to the St Radegund's bowling arsenal. El Bow approached the bowling crease with a zigzagging run up that betrayed the fact that he had still not quite recovered his land legs. Stanko seemed bemused by it all, and was unable to lay bat on ball. In frustration, his concentration slipped and was out off the final ball of the over, clean bowled for eight. The Rad players, as was their wont, surrounded the bowler and offered their congratulations: taking a wicket with such an unusual bowling action was something of a triumph for the cricketing traditionalists in the ranks. Moreover, El Bow had just bagged a wicket maiden.

Lipanović, for his part, looked on the proceedings with dismay. Only 26 runs were on the board, and it was now the 15th over. Time, thought Lipanović, to do something about that run rate. Unfortunately, Son of El Vis felt the full force of Lipanović's frustration, as the Dalmatian colossus peppered the boundary with a trio of lusty blows, one of which had enough momentum to take it into the adjoining field, where it flushed up a pheasant.

"Where's my Purdey?" quipped Larry.

With another three runs taken from the remaining balls, Lipanović had taken 15 runs off the over and put Hoste's score on to a more respectable 41 for three. He also took strike for the next over from El Bow, which amassed a more typical four runs. Clearly, The Sipper thought, an element of containment was needed if Hoste, and Lipanović in particular, weren't to run away with the scoring, so he brought back Beard for the 17th over. Lipanović worked the first ball away for two. The second he drove with some might past mid-on. Curly, in a vain attempt to cut the ball off before it reached the boundary, threw himself full length into the ball's path. Narrowly missing the projectile, he landed full force on top of an ant hill, at which point he was lost to sight in a cloud of reddish-brown dust. He emerged with ripped trousers, wounded pride and a badly gashed knee that was not to see a surgical dressing until he got back to Britain. Lipanović, though, thought it was intensely funny:

"Ha ha ha," he laughed, with stentorian forcedness, "he is ruined." Curly stiff upper lipped his way through both the injury and this puzzling Croatian judgement.

Beard's bowling was taking a bit of stick, with seven runs coming off the first four balls of his third over to bring up a warmly applauded 50 for the home side. Josko, Lipanović's new batting partner, finished the over off in style by getting off the mark with a well-timed boundary. Fifty-five for three, and so much for containment.

Larry was given the ball for over number 18, and proved that while Lipanović liked to get after the quicker stuff, he soon got bogged down when confronted by a ball given a bit of air and time in flight. Larry gave a creditably tight display, conceding only two runs.

This brought Crabbo Junior back for his third over, and it was by far his best of the day. Josko, try as he might, just couldn't deal with Crabbo Junior's pace. All his deliveries beat the bat entirely and at least two for certain would have clipped the bails, had bails there been. The tension mounted and he eventually produced a final ball that stayed low enough to break the wicket. A maiden for Crabbo Junior, and a first wicket of what had been a very long and frustrating season with the ball, gave him some sense of satisfaction.

Oliver Roki came out to the crease. A call of "captain in!" from Highball, and the arrival of Hoste's skipper was greeted with an especially warm round of applause. Oliver fended off four balls of another well-controlled over from Larry, Lipanović having knocked the second ball away for a single to give his skipper time to play himself in. This was the end of the 20th over. Ten more overs to bowl, and Kriket Klub Sir William Hoste were 58 for four.

Lipanović, now comparatively subdued after his earlier purple patch, ran a single off the first ball of Curly's over, and Oliver again took strike. The next ball he hit for two, and the following one for four, but two balls later he struck one on the up straight to Moe in the covers, to leave Hoste on 65 for five. If it was a brief innings from Oliver, it was at least an improvement on his duck in the first game. Not that Hoste's captain seemed to mind particularly: his broad smile was the same as when he strode out to the wicket.

JD was brought back for a last over against the new batsman, Antonio Nad. Once again, slow bowling seemed to beguile the batsman and JD emerged from the over with a maiden. In over number 23 Lipanović hit another powerful four and then a single off Curly's last ball to take the strike for Highball's third over.

From the trench end, Highball tossed down a long hop that Lipanović struck towards the mid-on boundary where it went straight down Moe's throat for a straightforward catch. Hoste's main batting threat had gone for 35, and a prolonged and respectful round of applause marked the end of his contribution to the innings. In truth, though, the Rad were grateful to see the back of him.

Toni Pralija was next in. Highball bowled something in a similar vein that Toni played in the air to mid-wicket where it was eagerly snaffled by Son of El Vis. Two wickets in two balls for Highball, and Toni departed with a golden duck. Alen Agović was next to the crease. His first ball he played and missed at, the second he cut to Curly at point. Three wickets down in four balls, and Sir William Hoste had slumped to 71 for eight.

The Sipper stood impassively behind the stumps, having just seen the game turn, probably decisively, in his team's favour. Nobody ran over to congratulate Highball. By sheer good fortune he had emerged from his spell with a bowling analysis of three overs, three wickets for no runs.

"Not one of those balls deserved a wicket!" Beard called from beside The Sipper, and he was undoubtedly right.

There were now only six overs to go, with Antonio Nad and young Marko Poduje, still in his mid-teens, at the crease. El Bow bowled a tidy third over, conceding just one run (the over also included a bye, the first extra of the innings) to further restrict the home team. Next, Moe was brought back on to bowl, and it was here that Antonio decided to cut loose, smashing two fours and a single off fairly innocuous bowling. Marko chipped in as well, running two to give Hoste eleven runs off the over, their best since Lipanović in his pomp.

Larry's third over went for nine runs, with Marko hitting a four to move the score on to 93. The following over, the 28th, was bowled by Curly. Its first ball to Antonio was spooned up by the batsman into an area between mid-wicket and mid-on that was unprotected by a fielder. An alert Highball ran in from midwicket to take an easy catch.

Hoste were down to the last pair, Damir Mohanović joining Marko at the wicket. Damir quickly returned strike to Marko who, having waited so long to get a bat and perhaps sensing that the innings was not far from being over, decided to do a bit of showboating. The shot in question's only sporting equivalent is in football. In France it is known as "l'Écharpe", in Argentina as "La Rabona",[iv] but there is no phrase for it in English. Among its more notable exponents is the Brazilian master ball player, Ronaldinho. It involves a right-footed player passing or crossing the ball by bringing his striking leg behind the standing leg to kick the ball. This, in essence, young Marko Poduje tried to replicate with a cricket bat.

Curly bowled a delivery that went down the leg side. Marko took his top hand off the bat and swung it with his bottom hand round the back of his legs to try to hit the ball. He missed. Generous and heartfelt applause went round the fielding side at the audacity of the shot. The following ball Curly put in a similar place. This time Marko tried the same shot again, made contact with the ball, sending it backward of square and ran two. He was immediately mobbed by the St Radegund players, who slapped him on the back, shook his hand, and generally congratulated him on a piece of batsmanship they had been proud to witness. Bunter, who had his notebook open and was collecting ideas for a match report for the forthcoming edition of *Witless*, christened young Marko's effort "The Marko Polo Shot", telling Eyebrows, for effect, that the Venetian had been born on the nearby island of Korčula.

Hoste's innings made it as far as the 29th over, which was bowled by Son of El Vis. Damir gave Marko the strike back on the third ball. Off the fourth, Marko hit a straight drive on the up, right past the bowler. El Bow, standing at mid-off, moved quickly to his right and, with all the nonchalance he could muster, plucked the ball out of the air with one hand. Kriket Klub Sir William Hoste had lost their last wicket, all out for 98. This was how their innings looked:

Siniša Vodopija – caught Highball, bowled Moe – 16
Lenko Marinković – caught Son of El Vis, bowled Beard – 0
Stanko Aleksić – bowled El Bow – 8
Antonio Lipanović – caught Moe, bowled Highball – 35
Josko Radisić – bowled Crabbo Junior – 5
Oliver Roki – caught Moe, bowled Curly – 6
Antonio Nad – caught Highball, bowled Curly – 16
Toni Pralija – caught Son of El Vis, bowled Highball – 0
Alen Agović – caught Curly, bowled Highball – 0
Marko Poduje – caught El Bow, bowled Son of El Vis – 9
Damir Mohanović – not out – 2

Extras 1
Total: 98 all out from 28.4 overs

The St Radegund's bowling analysis was as follows:

Crabbo Junior – 3 overs, 2 maidens, 1 wicket, 10 runs
El Vis – 2 overs, 2 maidens, 0 wickets, 0 runs
Beard – 3 overs, 0 maidens, 1 wicket, 13 runs
Highball – 3 overs, 3 maidens, 3 wickets, 0 runs
Moe – 3 overs, 0 maidens, 1 wicket, 21 runs
JD – 3 overs, 1 maiden, 0 wickets, 3 runs
Son of El Vis – 2.4 overs, 0 maidens, 1 wicket, 17 runs
El Bow – 3 overs, 1 maiden, 1 wicket, 5 runs
Larry – 3 overs, 0 maidens, 0 wickets, 12 runs
Curly – 3 overs, 0 maidens, 2 wickets, 16 runs

The Sipper felt reasonably satisfied at this half-way point of the match. The Hoste team, for their part, had put on a respectable enough score for only their second-ever game of cricket. In spite of enduring a number of overs in which they didn't score, they had, by and large, kept their concentration and pushed the score along where they could. Even losing three wickets in one over could be counted as some kind of aberration, or good fortune for the visitors. It was all, thought the St Radegund's captain, set up quite nicely for the boys to finish the job.

For the tea interval a brace of pizzas magically appeared, courtesy of the Katarina, and the players of both teams lounged in the late afternoon sun eating pizza slices and drinking iced bottled water that was, inevitably, warming up rapidly.

Throughout the Hoste innings, Jugs' ability to concentrate on scoring the match had come under severe strain from the attentions of a particularly cute and friendly tabby that had been wandering the ground. Of greater concern was a young kitten, presumably abandoned by its mother, which was emitting plaintive meows from near one of the abandoned barracks buildings. At the interval, Jugs went to investigate. The kitten was starved of mother's milk, little more than a bag of bones, and clearly unlikely to survive for much longer. Out of compassion Jugs fed it some water to better survive the afternoon heat, but any hopes of restoring it looked forlorn. The wretch's constant mewling attracted the attention and irritation of one of the Hoste players who picked up a stone from the side of the pitch with the intention of launching it in the direction of the sickly moggy.

"Don't you dare!" Jugs admonished. The Hoste boy dropped the stone to his side. Pragmatically, Jugs thought it best to devote her attentions to the cute tabby, to the living rather than the dying. She had done as much as she could.

Given the size of the total the St Radegund were seeking to overhaul, The Sipper decided that his batsmen would retire after scoring 25 runs to give as many of them as possible a chance of a game, and chose JD and Curly to open the innings, with Crabbo Junior to go in at number three. This put Crabbo out somewhat as he had, selfishly, been angling to open the batting. Being the St Radegund's longest-serving player, he felt that on this historic occasion it was only right that... etc. The Sipper was having none of it.

JD faced the first over, which was bowled by Hoste's captain. The first ball of the innings, which drifted down the leg side, JD played with accustomed economy of effort down to the square leg boundary for four. Two balls later a similar delivery was similarly dispatched, and rather than embarrass his hosts JD decided to play and miss at the remaining balls of the over.

Lipanović took the second over, and was useful enough with the ball to make Curly play himself in with a series of defensive strokes that, while technically very correct, did little to set pulses racing.

"Get a move on!" shouted Bunter impatiently from the barely adequate shade of an abandoned barracks building on the ramp, which vantage point he now shared with Eyebrows. Had it been a regular St Radegund player who had blocked out Lipanović's maiden over, the "encouragement" would doubtless have been far more abrasive.

Oliver, as uncertain how long this innings would last as The Sipper had earlier been, began mixing up the bowling attack from the off. Stanko took the third over, which produced a collector's item of a run single from JD, but added nothing else to the score. Four an over was a comfortable scoring rate for the visitors, so JD took a boundary, again down to square leg off Siniša's first over, the fourth of the innings. It was as though he intended to make the retirement target entirely in boundaries, with the single of the previous over merely a necessary evil that would allow him to reach it in the minimum number of shots.

Josko came in to the attack for over number five and his first ball, pitched short, allowed Curly to get off the mark with an masterful drive through the covers for four. With five overs completed, the St Radegund openers had made 17 runs without loss, and had expended very little energy in the sapping heat.

If anything, it was a lack of experience in placing the field that was undermining the home side, as the Rad found the gaps with some degree of ease. Lenko's first over gave JD another brace of fours, both, yet again, either at square leg or just round the corner. Curly, meanwhile, had made a quiet start, even by his standards. By the second ball of Lipanović's second over he had faced 14 balls and scored four runs. On the third ball it was as though he had suddenly awoken from his slumbers over a pizza and bottle of wine in the Katarina. He pulled a shortish ball through midwicket for six then, once again becalmed, was happy to block for the remainder of the over.

Oliver brought himself on for a second over, the second ball of which JD hit – where else? – down to square leg for four. With JD having just made the required retirement target The Sipper called him in, and he left the pitch to a smattering of applause from the Hoste team. His 25 runs had come off just 26 balls.

This brought Crabbo Junior to the wicket, complete with a helmet he had borrowed from the Hoste team. He blocked Oliver for three balls then played a delightfully timed stroke off his pads behind square for a single that left him on strike for the next over, bowled by Stanko. This he decided to block defensively, well aware that the St Radegund were in a strong position – at 36 for one after nine overs – that they were unlikely to surrender easily. Curly further emphasised the visitors' dominance in the next over, when he worked a quick single with his batting partner, who then struck a sweet four off his legs through mid-wicket for four. Forty-one for one, with a third of the overs gone.

The next over saw just one run taken, off Marko Poduje's bowling, with Crabbo Junior and Curly bedding in quite comfortably. The following one, bowled by Lipanović, produced a single to each batsman. With less than half the allotted overs gone, the St Radegund team were well on top of the required run-rate and on course for victory. It was then that things started to go awry.

NOTES

i   The island of Hvar, east of Vis.
ii   Pocock, Tom. *Remember Nelson – The Life of Captain Sir William Hoste*, p 177
iii ibid
iv Respectively, "the scarf" and "the cow's whip".

8

The Blue Cave

... a small entrance just above the surface of the sea that looked barely big enough to swim through, never mind pilot a boat through.

In the game of cricket few tasks demand more concentration than that of keeping an accurate scorebook. This is particularly true at the bottom of the food chain, among the lowly exponents of pub cricket, where a single over can last for ten or more deliveries, runs – when scored – are often run short, and umpires give the signal for a bye when they mean to indicate a no ball, or even fail to signal entirely. In Jugs, the St Radegund possessed a scorer of dogged attention to detail who was able to block out the heckling and oafish shouts of the players and spectators around her and get on with the job in hand. In her delicate copperplate, she elevated the chore of recording the ebb and flow of the game into something resembling an art. Belonging to the school of thought that believes a scorecard should tell everything that anybody could ever want to know about a particular game, Jugs meticulously recorded the number of balls faced, incidents of the batsmen crossing, dropped catches (frequent), the bowler's direction and action (where distinguishable), the playing conditions and state of the pitch, as well as making sure all the columns added up and all the scores tallied. If scoring a cricket match were a university subject, Jugs would have had a starred first and, more than likely, a master's degree with her doctorate well underway to boot. All of which made all the more baffling The Sipper's request, as soon as Crabbo Junior went out to bat, for Jugs to put on a pair of cricket pads and prepare to be the next batsman, or batswoman, in.

Perhaps it was supreme confidence in the inevitability of a St Radegund victory, perhaps nothing simpler than a desire to let every member of the party who wanted it have an involvement in the game? The Sipper did not have to justify his decision: it was his to make as captain. So, with Curly now within sight of a retirement total, Jugs handed the scorebook and pencil to Son of El Vis and Highball and began to pad up. Her elegant calligraphy was soon replaced by untidy smudges and furious crossings out as the pair tried, disastrously, to keep tabs on what was going on.

"Was that a four? Did he signal a four?"

"I don't know. I think so."

"What does that make the score?"

"Seventy-one. No, 72."

"Are you sure?"

"No."

What is known, or at least can be reconstructed, from the mess is that there were a further eight overs left in the match. Crabbo Junior's dashing stroke play was curtailed when he was given out, stumped by Toni Pralija off either Siniša's or Lipanović's bowling only two runs short of a retirement total and a not out score. Curly hit a couple of boundaries to take his personal tally to 27 and was called in by The Sipper, with Moe replacing him as batsman. Jugs scored her first ever run for the St Radegund and, thanks to a benevolent overthrow, recorded five runs off a single ball before she was adjudged out leg before wicket to (again) either Siniša or Lipanović. Then Son of El Vis plundered a few runs before Moe, muttering "Let's finish this off and go for a drink," smote a huge, straight six to end the match with the honours going to the visiting English side. Or so they thought.

Before an inquest could be conducted, though, there was the small matter of the post-match presentation party. Bunter and Eyebrows descended to pitch side from the barracks building in whose welcome shade they had been looking down on proceedings like Napoleonic generals. Hands were shaken, backs patted, words of congratulation and commiseration offered. Among the "well playeds" and "bad lucks" it was noted that Kriket Klub Sir William Hoste had come through its second-ever competitive match with aplomb, and what they lacked in experience and confidence had more than been made up for in enthusiasm. For their part, the St Radegund team had contested the match keenly, perhaps too keenly in a couple of individual cases but, true to the Sipper's word, had not sought to embarrass their hosts. And though the result was never likely to go against the tourists, there had been enough ebb and flow to give the home team hope. It certainly hadn't been a drubbing.

As the teams gathered by the edge of the pitch, Bunter congratulated them both on a well-fought match played, as ever, "in the right spirit". At JD's prompting, with his remaining good arm Bunter presented to The Sipper a trophy: a heavy wooden plinth surmounted with a cricket ball and bails cast in brass. An engraved plaque on its face described it as the Sir William Hoste Trophy. The Sipper was gentlemanly in victory, and requested only that the trophy be kept behind the bar at Bejbi until such time as the St Radegund could return to play for it again. Oliver graciously agreed and accepted it for safe keeping.

More rifling in JD's rucksack produced an engraved tankard for the

Man of the Match. Bunter made a short speech in which he extolled the performance of a number of Hoste players, before singling out Antonio Lipanović as having made the home team's most valuable contribution, and drew a flattering comparison between his batting and that of the late, great Gilbert Jessop, a remark which must have passed straight over the heads of the Vis boys. Crabbo Junior remarked, under his breath, that Antonio's batting style bore more resemblance to that of the equally late Colin Milburn, but Bunter was not likely to be corrected on this point. "Jessop", Antonio was destined to remain.

Frannie presented the tankard to the giant along with a British shilling dating from 1815 that had been drilled and threaded with a red ribbon. This Lipanović, towering a good two feet over the diminutive Frannie, received solemnly as though taking an honour from Her Majesty the Queen. Everyone looked on admiringly as Lipanović raised his substantial arms in a victory salute.

Highball, doubtless overly pleased with his own performance, stood between The Sipper and Crabbo Junior. As they looked around the scene of the St Radegund's first overseas international cricket game, he folded his arms in contentment.

"Well lads," he said, "tonight we shall sleep the sleep of champions."

"You what?" The Sipper asked incredulously. Crabbo Junior sniggered. Highball insisted, in earnest, that he merely wished to convey an appropriate sense of occasion, but struggled for something suitable pithy.

"I won't let you forget those words," The Sipper promised ominously.

Back at Bejbi the Karlovačko flowed freely. In keeping with the traditions of the St Radegund, further awards were made, and celebrated with "down downs". The award for the match's Champagne Moment, styled after the oleaginous manner of the commentators of Test Match Special, was awarded to young Marko Poduje for his "Marko Polo Shot". He was required to down a pint (or the metric equivalent thereof) of beer at the appropriate point during the St Radegund's singing of a Hash drinking song, suitably, if clumsily, adapted for the sport in question:

Oh...
Here's to Marko, he's a blue
He's a cricketer through and through
He's an arsehole, so they say

And he'll never get to heaven in a long, long way.
Drink it down, down, down, down, down, down, down, down...

This Marko did with admirable speed and control for a youngster. In the absence of any more official commemorative gifts, Bunter kindly gave young Marko a spare St Radegund tour shirt as a memento of the team's visit. The young man beamed with pride.

The next award was for the Tesco's Discount Lager Moment. The antithesis of the Champagne Moment, it had been instituted as an official post-match award by the Rad a couple of years previously to commemorate a particularly staggering on-field cock-up and had been awarded regularly ever since, with potential candidates often outnumbering those for the genuine award. Bunter had, on this occasion, no hesitation in naming Curly as the recipient in recognition of his valiant diving lunge into the ant hill that gashed his knee and ruined his cricket whites. Curly was not the only one the worse for wear. Crabbo Junior was suffering the effects of heatstroke, and El Vis was still limping rather badly thanks to his turned ankle. Given the Rad's track record since arriving, it could have been worse.

Jugs, meanwhile, was seated in a corner of the bar attempting to make the scorebook add up. Highball sat beside her, patiently copying from the Hoste team's book to the St Radegund's. Jugs shook her head and made sounds of distress. In the end, she threw up her hands in resignation. The finest cricketing minds of the St Radegund went over the figures time and time again, but could work out neither the precise order of the overs following the 12th one nor the final score and actual margin of victory. The bowling analysis could not be made to match the scores of the individual batsmen, which were out of kilter with the running total of the innings. Try as they might, nothing could be made to tally. Son of El Vis and Highball were summarily warned never to come within a hair's breadth of the St Radegund scorebook for the rest of their playing careers, which was a fitting punishment.

For what it's worth, the scorebook recorded that the visitors had scored 103 runs to the home team's 98. The best that Jugs was able to calculate was that the game had ended prematurely, with the St Radegund still a run short of the Hoste total, but with plenty of wickets in hand. She communicated as much to Oliver Roki, who was magnanimous.

"It doesn't matter, your team clearly won. Let's say you scored 99."

It must have looked like a poor show, having come all the way from England just to be undone by arithmetical ineptitude. Oliver was generous in defeat, or modest in victory, whichever way round you wanted to look at it. Once Beard got wind of this his immediate reaction was to push for a rematch within a day or two. This suggestion was immediately slapped down by the rest of the team, particularly as it would have meant the Vis boys spending even more time away from their harvesting duties. Beard's boisterous good-humour and all round enthusiasm had begun to weary a few of the party but, in the main, the bonhomie and camaraderie that had sustained the St Radegund thus far was holding up pretty well. The "victory" in the cricket had been comfortable, and could by no means be compared with the mauling that Saumur had meted out. If the islanders' faith had wavered during that first game, then it was to be hoped that the visiting English had helped the islanders regain a modicum of pride.

The players of both teams were fast becoming friends. They drank together and swapped stories well into the night. Lipanović made complimentary remarks about JD's imposing frame, impressed by his implacability and unhurried batting. Beard's wild hair and eccentric facial stylings made quite an impression on the opposing team, their experience of things ginger clearly being quite limited. Some of them assumed that he was Scottish, a notion Beard quickly disabused them of. Oliver, for one, was impressed by the pace Beard had managed to generate in his bowling run-up never having seen anything that quick before. Lessons were clearly being learned. El Vis, Son of El Vis and Antonio Nad were among the last to leave Bejbi at gone two in the morning. It had been a memorable day, a great game, and a celebratory evening.

Two days later, the game between Kriket Klub Sir William Hoste and the St Radegund made page 51 of *Slobodna Dalmacija*, the main daily newspaper in this part of Croatia. The team gathered around eagerly at Bejbi listening to Oliver Roki as he gave them a translation.

"The heading says: 'Vis cricketers enchanted English visitors'," he began. "'At the field of the Samogor complex on Vis, in front of about a hundred spectators, the second international cricket match between St Radegund from Cambridge in England and Sir William Hoste club from Vis took place. The English won by a single point, 99 to 98.'"

Again, local scoring conventions were suggesting a result closer than it actually was, though it was much better than reporting that nobody knew precisely how the match had been decided. It was fortunate that Oliver Roki himself had been the one to supply the newspaper with the match details.

"'Antonio Lipanović was declared man of the match,'" Oliver continued, describing how Bunter's enthusiasm for the development of the sport on the island and that "three English players had travelled by boat from Mallorca" [sic] were reported. There were approving nods from the St Radegund players. Then came the *pièce de résistance*. Pride of place was given to Marko's behind-the-legs shot as the match's best moment which, the newspaper reported, had elicited the following reaction from the visitors: "...the English players had never seen a more attractive shot in their professional careers." The trowel-laid flattery of the phrase was greeted with guffaws.

▲

Hard by the roadside on the edge of the field at Samogor lies a twenty-feet-long stone slab quarried from the nearby island of Brač. In latter days it stood near the palm-lined park at the water's edge on the harbour front in Vis town. After Croatian independence the government, in an effort to draw a line under the communist era, ordered the slab, known locally as the *spomenik*, or monument, removed. Enough of Vis' townspeople refused, and by way of compromise it was allowed to stay on the island, though hauled up the hill to the former parade ground, there to lie on its side, neglected in the modest surroundings of Samogor away from the bustle of the town.

Erected in 1964, it commemorates a speech made by Marshal Tito on 12 September 1944 while conducting a review of the First Dalmatian Brigade of the National Liberation Army. A phrase from Tito's speech is still visible, carved – though attempts have been made to obliterate it – into the top of the *spomenik* as it rests on its side: *Tuđe nećemo – svoje ne damo* ("What is ours we keep – what is not, we want not"). On the subject of the return of Italian territorial gains in Croatia that had been ceded by Pavelić's *Ustaše* government under the Treaty of Rapallo in 1941, Tito was adamant. The new government of Yugoslavia would have the stolen lands returned. There would be no further concessions to the fascists. *Tuđe nećemo - svoje ne damo.*

Nobody can decide whether the *spomenik* should be broken up or left where it stands. Like Tito's Cave halfway up Mount Hum, it seems an uncomfortable part of an historical legacy that the *Viški* have yet to fully come to terms with. During the course of the cricket match, it fulfilled the rather ignoble role of acting as the visiting team's changing facility, though to be fair the St Radegund were ignorant at the time of the slab's history or significance. As one of the few objects on the parade ground offering any shade from the blazing sun, it was welcome.

Tito spent only three months headquartered on the island in the summer of 1944, but left a lasting mark. He arrived on Vis on 7 June 1944 and having not lost his penchant for caves, in spite of his close shave at Drvar, immediately set about replicating the style of his Bosnian headquarters halfway up Mount Hum. There were two caves, the higher of which was used as Tito's living quarters, and the other as a dining and meeting space and as accommodation for his dog, Tigger. With the rest of his staff down the mountain in the village of Borovik near the Allied command, he used the caves as his operational base until the end of August when, finally tiring of the guerrilla lifestyle, he moved into the Villa Tramontana above Stonca bay, or English Harbour. Maclean was quartered nearby and the two regularly swam together off the north coast of the island.

No sooner had Tito set up his headquarters on Vis than he entered, at the prompting of the British, into immediate negotiations with Dr Ivan Šubašić, the prime minister of the Royal Yugoslav government. These took place in the Gariboldi palace in Kut and were to determine the degree of future cooperation between the government and the *Partižani* following the eventual defeat of the occupying Germans. The agreement, signed on 16 June, recognised the "national and democratic achievements of the peoples of Yugoslavia won during their three-year struggle which laid the foundations for a democratic federal order," and effectively merged both Tito's and Šubašić's governments until Yugoslavia was liberated and free, democratic elections could be held. In celebration of the agreement, Maclean records, Tito took the entire party "out in a motor boat on a picnic to a local beauty spot"[i] on the island of Biševo. They entered the submarine cave on the island's east coast in a small boat and there spent an agreeable time swimming and larking about. Everyone there was a member of one of the two Yugoslav governments, and "there was much shouting and laughter as one... Excellency cannoned into another, bobbing about in that caerulean twilight."[ii] The passage home was rougher than expected and, Maclean notes, a number of the party were sick.

▲

Part of Bunter's original sales pitch to the members of the team had been the attractions of Blue Cave on Biševo, even though he hadn't himself been able to visit it until his trip in the May before the tour. Long before the St Radegund team ever set foot on Vis it had been decided that if nothing else memorable came of the trip then a visit to *modra špilja* was a must.

On the Sunday night following the cricket match, plans had been made to meet by the Tamaris Hotel at nine o'clock sharp to take the boat trip out to the island. On the morning itself, only Bunter, the Highballs and Crabbo Junior were at the mustering-point at the agreed time. No one else of the St Radegund team was to be seen. Bunter bridled at their absence, but boarded the boat anyway: he could hardly keep its pilot waiting on the off chance that more of the team turned up. The craft was small for a pleasure boat, and Highball wondered if it might have been a fishing boat in a prior existence. Bunter thought this unlikely, even though there were now reckoned to be only nine professional fishermen left in Vis and fewer than fifty in Komiža.

The island's second town was the heart of the island's fishing community, being much closer to the formerly abundant fishing grounds of Palagruža that once brimmed with sardine and lobster, but which had been over-fished thanks to intense competition between the fishermen of Vis and the island of Korčula. To make matters worse, Italian fishing boats had recently been straying into Croatian territorial waters to fish there illegally. Highball and the Memsahib's awareness of the condition of one of Vis' traditional industries had been raised by an article that appeared in *The Guardian* during the summer. Under the headline "Tidal Wave of Tourism Threatens the Island Jewel of the Adriatic"[iii] the report described the diminishing circumstances under which the fishermen of Komiža now operated. What drew the eye was the *Komižani* attitude to tourism: they were against mass tourism in favour of something that was sustainable and, most importantly, which they could control themselves. This spirit of fierce independence manifested itself when a plan to place tuna cages off the harbour to service the Japanese sushi market had been mooted. The townspeople mobilised against it and eventually voted the proposals down. Having tasted the power of participatory democracy on a local level, they were determined to keep unwelcome outside interests from interfering in their affairs. Similar sentiments had been expressed to a number of the St Radegund team during the course of the tour.

The pilot of the charter boat took 100 kuna from everybody, which no one could begrudge him, and the four sat on the aft deck, which had been fitted with comfortable benches and was open to the elements save for a white canvas canopy to shield them from the sun. A couple of British tourists engaging in a spot of island-hopping were the boat's only other passengers.

Soon the boat was under way, making steady but slow progress out of the bay. It passed the Česka Villa and the islet with the small lighthouse at the harbour entrance, then bore to starboard to take a clockwise course around the island. A mile had barely been navigated when a high-powered motorboat began to follow them. As it neared, the keel markings became visible. It was a police launch from Vis town. Crabbo Junior and Highball exchanged glances.

"Stopping crime while on the brine?" Highball suggested. The launch sped off in a wall of spray in search of more worthy marine felons and left the small pleasure boat to putter away on its own course.

The coastline was sheer with rocky cliffs of limestone and dolomite almost as far as Komiža to the south-west. Perched upon them at regular intervals were cottages and farmhouses. Few beaches were visible until the boat passed the island of Ravnik, one of the largest of a small group off the south-east coast. Beyond, the boat made a detour landwards and poked its bows between two cliff faces 60 feet high and ten feet apart that looked as if they were squaring up to fight each other. These sheltered a small, secluded beach, perhaps the object of their quarrel. This was the stunningly beautiful bay of Stiniva. Its image – from the beach out to the sea – was used on many of Vis' tourist brochures. Access from land was via the main road in the central plain then along a footpath and a scramble down the hillside to the small, shingle beach.

The boat reversed out and continued on its way, passing the southernmost tip of the Zaljev Komiža, the natural bay on which stood the island's second town. Though distant, it sat prettily, surrounded by its many wine terraces and overlooked by Mount Hum. The boat steered south-west away from Komiža and crossed the Biševski kanal where it joined a small flotilla of other boats of various sizes, all waiting to visit the Blue Cave.

From the outside there was little inkling of the splendours inside. It was just a rugged cliff face with a small entrance just above the surface of the sea that looked barely big enough to swim through, never mind pilot a boat through. In fact the entrance had been widened in the late 19th century when an Austrian noble by the name of Eugen Rausoonet had been so enchanted by the place that he suggested blasting the rock to make access easier.

The pleasure boat pulled up about forty feet from the cave entrance, where a rowing boat equipped with an outboard motor was to ferry the party through the cave's entrance. It soon became obvious that anybody who turned up on spec in their sailing boat or floating gin palace, rather than as part of an organised tour, had to negotiate passage through the entrance from the man who had the concession. In late middle age, he sat in a rowing boat nearby with his companion, a distinguished-looking collie. He rowed around the entrance collecting money and occasionally issued commands to boats that were getting too close to the cave. Occasionally the collie would bark something to back up his master's instructions. More often than not it just sat there looking rather bored.

Once transferred into one of the smaller boats, the tourists were taken to the mouth of the cave where they jostled with the other boats and dinghies from the yachts to enter. Once precedence was established they passed through an opening that could not have been more than a few feet high, into pitch darkness. There was a short, low-ceilinged passage that led into the central chamber, where they were greeted by a stunning luminescence in the water. The main cave was no more than forty feet across. At its far end was a submerged opening in the rock. When the sun was in a certain position it shone directly on the opening, suffusing the water in the cave with an eerie glow. The water was turned a bright cobalt blue, and the oars and edges of the small rowing boat seemed to shimmer with silver. Trailing a hand over the side, you expected to be able to scoop up handfuls of precious metal from the water, only to find it a trick of the light. The water was so clear that sardine fry were visible teeming on the bottom of the cave.

There were two or three other boats crammed into the cave. Camera flashes popped. The visit lasted only five minutes or so, but burned itself into the memory. It had taken over two hours for the boat to make its journey from Vis harbour. The optical effect of the sun was only at its best for a few hours while the sun was in the east and south-east, and by one in the afternoon it had begun to diminish, so the timing of trips to the Blue Cave was crucial.

With the passengers back in the pleasure boat, it set off around the north coast of Biševo, to the west and a little settlement called Porat. Here a long cove led up to a beach of white sand around which little tin-roofed shacks gathered, housing cafés and bar restaurants. It being out of season, only one of them was open. The boat moored up and the pilot announced that he would be leaving for the return trip in an hour and a half's time.

The day was stiflingly hot, so the Highballs and Crabbo Junior decided to go for a dip in the crystal clear waters of the cove before joining Bunter for lunch at the restaurant. The Memsahib was first in, followed by Crabbo Junior. Highball tiptoed in nervously, claiming not to like the cold water. Crabbo Junior remonstrated that it wasn't cold at all, and started flicking water at Highball, who eventually took the plunge after much dithering and splashing about. By the time he was comfortably immersed, the Memsahib had almost finished her swim.

The restaurant was a rickety-looking beach house on wooden stilts, and offered an excellent view of the cove. It was small, though, with room for only three or four tables. The swimmers joined Bunter in a beer or two, before tucking into a lunch of calamari, scampi and mixed salad.

Behind the restaurant were some small hills on which the Mediterranean scrub was reduced to blackened stumps. There had obviously been a serious fire on the island quite recently. Crabbo Junior piped up: "Lipanović told me about this. Apparently he's a volunteer fireman in his spare time."

"He's got the right build for it," said the Memsahib.

"Thing is," continued Crabbo Junior, "there's no natural water source on these islands. It all has to be shipped in and stored, so he came over by boat and just sat there watching the fire burn itself out."

"What would he have done if the fire had got out of control?" asked Highball. Crabbo Junior shrugged, but before he could add anything

Bunter chipped in, helpfully:

"Probably filled up on beer and pissed the fire out."

The return journey took them past Komiža, round the headland and on to the north coast of the island. The landscape of rugged limestone cliffs dropping precipitously down to the sea was by now an over-familiar sight so the party dozed in the afternoon sun. In time the boat passed the site, off the north coast close to the harbour mouth, of Hoste's battle with the French. Bunter pointed it out.

"Are there any wrecks below the surface?" asked Highball.

"I don't know the answer to that," replied Bunter. Perhaps the – still as yet unvisited – museum in Vis town had the answers?

The boat chugged into the harbour, coming to rest outside the Hotel Tamaris in the late afternoon. The plan was to meet at Bejbi at six in the evening and then row across to the *Lady Ruth* for Veras with El Bow and JD. The discomfort Bunter was suffering with his arm had made him tired, so he took his leave and said he would meet the rest of the party later. The cricket match having been done and dusted and, more importantly, played in an honourable fashion, he had finally shed the last of his protectiveness towards his travelling companions. The rest took this as a good sign that he had fully relaxed into the pace of life. Either that or he had given up on the rest of his charges. Or perhaps his arm was more painful than he was letting on? As the Highballs and Crabbo walked back to their apartments they convinced themselves that Bunter would not be making an appearance that evening. Looking across the bay they noted that *Lady Ruth* was not at her anchorage.

When the Highballs arrived at Bejbi two hours later, the bar was busy but lacking a single other member of the St Radegund party. *Lady Ruth*, however, was now at anchor in the harbour. A Karlovačko or two seemed in order while the Highballs awaited further instructions. Eventually JD turned up. He had moored a dinghy to the jetty outside Bejbi, and invited the Highballs back to the boat.

The missing members of the team were all on board and the drinks were in full flow. A litre or two of Gordon's Export gin was produced and served with fresh limes and a little ice. For the Memsahib this was an ambition fulfilled, being the first occasion she had ever drunk a gin and tonic on a floating gin palace. The comparison was slightly unfair on El Bow, who prided himself on running an efficient sailing boat, rather than one of the sea-going refrigerators beloved of Europe's well-heeled layabout class.

The Sipper, for one, was impressed enough with the *Lady Ruth* to offer his services as crew. El Bow said he was thinking of sailing to the West Indies in a year or two's time, and would The Sipper want to crew it? The Sipper admitted to being sorely tempted by the offer.

As the sun set spectacularly behind Gradina and darkness covered the land, it was discussed whether a party should put out to shore and go in search of Bunter. A none too kind soul suggested that were he to come aboard there would be the usual moaning about something, whether the temperature of the ice, the wrong type of limes, or whatever. El Bow emerged from the galley with a tray of canapés that were gratefully scoffed, and tales of the day's activities were swapped.

Son of El Vis had met Beard on the way down to the main square in Kut with every intention of meeting the charter boat outside the Tamaris in time for the nine o'clock departure. Stopping for a quick breakfast coffee was a mistake, and they arrived at the hotel in time to see the boat making its way towards the harbour mouth. They had missed it by a matter of minutes. This was better than The Sipper, Eyebrows and Jugs had managed, however, classic St Radegund miscommunication having left them waiting at the appointed hour outside Bejbi rather than the hotel. As Beard and Son of El Vis hung around and wondered what to do next, JD, Frannie and El Bow turned up and kindly offered to take them to the Blue Cave and so, with everybody on board, *Lady Ruth* eventually got under way at around ten o'clock.

El Vis had not joined them, though now he was happily knocking back gin and tonic. He had had every intention of joining the Bunter-organised tour – and had even remembered the correct rendezvous point – but decided to favour his twisted ankle, which was still giving him some pain. Instead he limped around town, had a few drinks, read and watched a bit of the junior tennis competition, which was still going on.

Beard was proud of the fact that, at his request, *Lady Ruth* had sailed north of Biševo to coordinates of 43° North and 16° East, where the crew spent twenty or thirty minutes faffing around as Beard tried to get El Bow to pilot the boat exactly on the required line of longitude. Though a chore, it was a technical challenge El Bow relished. After several attempts, during which time the rest took a light lunch of cheese and *pršut*, the boat settled on 42 degrees, 59 minutes and 99 seconds, which was as near as damn it.

Besides, JD pointed out, there was likely to be lag on the information from the GPS, meaning that hitting the precise set of coordinates was highly unlikely. Satisfied that this was as close as he was going to get, Beard promptly took photographs of the views north, south, east and west, and another of his GPS device displaying the information as proof of his visit. He had got his promised confluence and was as happy as a sand-boy.

The rest of the day had been spent idly pottering about the Biševski kanal, the passengers occasionally taking the wheel, being shown some rudiments of seamanship, knots and the like before finally arriving back in Vis harbour late in the afternoon, with most having thoroughly enjoyed their day out at sea.

Their trip to Biševo, however, had been of mixed success. The engine of the *Lady Ruth* was still playing up, and as they sailed, Beard kindly offered to give El Bow a hand in the engine room. They worked over the motor for an hour, Beard getting a beard full of diesel for his pains. It was getting difficult to breathe so he went back on deck. Sitting at the bows, he rinsed his facial hair with *travarica* he had brought from the apartment to try to take the smell away. It was overpowering.

They arrived at the entrance to the Blue Cave just in time to see the old man with the concession rowing his boat away from the cave. A couple of other boats were around. The *Lady Ruth* dropped anchor close to the entrance and the passengers descended the starboard ladder to board the dinghy to travel the short distance to the cave. At this, the old man with the concession turned his boat around and started abusing them in a stream of Croatian invective accompanied by barks from his dog. If they wanted to enter the cave they would have to pay him. Attempts at apologising were made and the excuse of ignorance offered but nobody had any cash on them, so Son of El Vis – as the most accomplished swimmer of the party – went over the side and back to the boat to collect the requisite kuna. By the time he had swum back to the boat he was exhausted.

Jugs handed the old man a fistful of soggy currency with which to gain entrance to the cave, and JD and El Bow were free to guide the dinghy towards the narrow opening. Unfortunately, their timing was a little off: the light that so magically illuminated the cave for the earlier visitors was nowhere near as good as expected.

Beard had been looking decidedly green since he came topside after working in the engine room but, his fellow mariners reasoned, when you factored in the team's hectic schedule, Beard's irregular, non-fish diet since he had arrived on the island, and the motion of the *Lady Ruth,* a reaction of some sorts was long overdue. A wave of nausea passed suddenly over him and he was spectacularly ill over the side of the dinghy. It had not been quite the memorable excursion to the cave the party was expecting.

NOTES

i   Maclean, p 469
ii ibid
iii Traynor, Ian. 'Tidal Wave of Tourism Threatens the Island Jewel of the Adriatic'.
    The Guardian, 21 July 2003

9

The Fort

The keystone at the top of the arch had been cut in such a way as to provide a relief of the Union Jack. Above it was a slab with a carved inscription, partly obliterated where the stone had been weathered away.

On the Tuesday, Son of El Vis had the idea of taking his father on a tour around the island by moped. It would be a convenient way of getting around, they agreed, without putting any further strain on El Vis' ankle. By the time they reached the tourist bureau, however, its small fleet of mopeds had already been booked for the day. All that was left were bicycles, and these would be no good for El Vis. A fallback plan was required. After a coffee or two and an assessment of their situation – it was their last day on the island and they felt obliged to do something more constructive than sit around and drink beer – they decided to explore closer to base, and make their way to the west side of the harbour up to Fort St George. Son of was worried his father was not up to the hike, but El Vis was adamant he could do it.

It took longer than expected to reach the fort. Though it only looked a short distance away, the natural parabola of the harbour made it a good hour's walk. Father and son stocked up on water at the small supermarket by the park and set out, passing Bejbi, the tennis courts and the necropolis of Issa, and round the bay beyond Gradina hill and the promontory of Prirovo. The road rose up to the Hotel Issa then fell as they walked past English Harbour, steepening once more round a sharp bend where it dissolved into a stony track that made the going difficult underfoot. They stopped and took a drink at a wall by a charming villa some hundred feet up with a fine view of the Luka. A couple of sharp turns later and the road became nothing more than a dirt track disappearing into thick scrub and Mediterranean pines. The way was still steep but made easier by a carpet of needles underfoot. The canopy provided by the trees lining the road offered them welcome protection from the sun. According to their map, there were three ruined forts on the north-west edge of the harbour: forts Bentinck and Robertson were smaller satellite forts, St George the principal defence. Robertson appeared to be somewhere off to their right, but the track was overgrown and the way unclear. They pressed on to the headland at the mouth of the harbour.

Suddenly they were upon it. From sturdy foundations among the scrub, thick walls of Dalmatian stone sloped solidly up to battlements over fifteen feet high. There was a single entrance on the eastern side overlooking the harbour mouth adjacent to the road they had taken up there. The keystone at the top of the arch had been cut in such a way as to provide a relief of the Union Jack. Above it was a slab with a carved inscription, partly obliterated where the stone had been weathered away.

Filling in the missing information was no trouble for the father and son historians: George the Third – By the Grace of God King of Great Britain and Ireland. The fort, the largest on the island, had at the time of its completion in 1813 been dedicated to the reigning monarch and not to the patron saint of both England and the island of Vis itself, as seemed the locally accepted custom. For the father and son this raised an interesting question. The harbour had been known in Venetian times as Porto St Giorgio, under British rule as Port St George; the little promontory on its eastern side on which stood the Česka Villa still went by the name of Sv Jurja. At what point had the fort's original dedication been, as it were, sanctified? And why? This was worth asking about, if only they had the time.

▲

Hoste returned to Lissa in the late summer of 1812, and found that, during his absence, the small island guarding the entrance to the harbour of Port St George had been named in his honour.[i] It was now fortified and manned with a small barracks, recognition by the Admiralty of the island's strategic importance. Hoste's other recommendations on the fortification of Port St George were also being acted upon. A yard for the repair of ships was being built in English Harbour. Construction of the largest of the new fortresses on the island, commanding the harbour on a hill north of Prirovo, was already under way by Italian and local workers, as was work on three smaller forts in the style of Martello towers, on hills around the harbour mouth. The British had also granted Lissa a governor and a constitution based on a mixture of local and British laws, and one of the towers on the western side of the harbour mouth was named for the first governor, Lieutenant-Colonel George Duncan Robertson. The other fort on that side of the island's harbour was named after Lieutenant-General Lord William Bentinck, the commander-in-chief of the British Navy in the Mediterranean. The single fort on the eastern side, sitting atop a hill 580 feet high, was named after the Duke of Wellington.

Under the British, the island enjoyed a period of economic prosperity it had rarely seen under Venetian rule. The population swelled to 12,000 in three years, the majority of whom were foreign merchants.

Literacy, in decline under French rule, also improved under the British. The waterfront boasted six taverns. Goods from the British colonies and pirate contraband flooded into the port: "Vis offered three brands of bottled beer, the best champagne and Chinese brandy; the finest Turkish tobacco and Cuban cigars were also available, and the pharmacy offered all kinds of drugs, without any prescription, from opium to mescaline… there was plenty of work for tailors, shoemakers, caulkers, carpenters, blacksmiths, goldsmiths… confectioners from Italy, Austria and Germany offered their wares on the island."[ii]

But the signs were that the Admiralty did not consider the long-term occupation of the island a strategic priority in the way that they viewed Gibraltar or Malta, and they blocked further development of the shipyard in English Harbour, viewing as sufficient for their needs the relative proximity of the facilities in Malta. Britain's rule on Lissa lasted until 1815, when the island was returned to Austria following Napoleon's defeat at Waterloo.

That was, however, not the last of the island's involvement in the naval history of the Adriatic. In July of 1866, again off Lissa's north coast, a battle took place in the Wars of Italian Independence between the Austrian and Italian navies, the main Italian objective being to wrest Venice from Austrian control. Like the first Battle of Lissa fifty years earlier, this engagement saw a superior attacking naval force defeated by a smaller fleet defending the island.

The Italian fleet boasted 29 ships to the Austrians' 18. Though defending the harbour with an inferior force, the Austrians decided to take the fight to the Italian fleet, which was unprepared for a surprise engagement, being busy preparing for an armed landing on the island. The speed of the Austrian attack, the first in naval history to feature ironclads prominently in naval combat, made up for their comparative lack of firepower. The battle was also notable as one of the last to feature ramming as a military tactic. An elaborate and substantial memorial to the dead of the second Battle of Lissa stands in the town cemetery, with inscriptions in both German and Croatian below an impressive carved lion couchant, the symbol of St Mark and Venice.

In the larger context of the wars, the battle was overshadowed by a devastating defeat of the Austrian army by Prussia that led to the Italians realising their immediate objective of regaining Venice, after Napoleon III had brought his influence to bear on the defeated Austrians. Nevertheless the battle played an important part in keeping Italian territorial ambitions in check, at least until after the First World War.

▲

The El Vises inspected the crumbling ruins of Fort George. In its day it must have been impressive. They followed the eastern edge of the fortification as far as they could. It was about 200 feet long and surrounded, at least partially, by a shallow moat. They retraced their steps and went in through the archway. Immediately to their right was a small single-storey guardroom with a couple of small windows. All around them, covering the entire site, broken stones were overgrown with scrub, and weeds grew in cracks in the masonry. The place was clearly not well looked after.

The stone steps leading up to the battlements where infantry would defend the entrance in an attack were still in a good state of repair. Son of El Vis hopped up for a quick look, and jumped back down again. Opposite the main entrance was another, larger, building which divided into a couple of rooms on two floors. These were, presumably, either barrack rooms or stores. Farther on, down a couple of steps, was the main building. Again built on two storeys, it contained a number of large rooms in a decrepit state. In one an old sofa rotted away in a corner.

The original wooden beams that supported the floor of the upper storey were exposed and, largely, still intact, but the boards that had covered them were almost all gone. To the right was a flight of stone steps. They climbed up to the first floor but did not venture further than the first room. A second staircase went even higher up. They followed it and found themselves on top of the fort, a flat sixty-foot-square platform of solid stone, presumably where cannon had been mounted. The walls were well preserved and the battlements offered spectacular views. To the north, down below them at the entrance to the harbour, Host Island looked small and insignificant. Beyond, the dark outline of the islands and the mainland beyond were visible. To the west were the north coast of the island and, further round, the ruin of Fort Bentinck with half its cylindrical mass gone. The hill on which the fort stood must have been over three hundred feet above sea level. As a lookout post for enemy ships it could not be bettered.

They descended to ground level. Through the back of the main building was a large open area shaded by pines. Going down half a dozen small steps they found themselves in a large rectangular pit lined with stone. It looked like a large swimming pool, drained. There was a trough at either end of the pit, suggesting that horses or donkeys had been stabled here. After a brief wander round they decided to head back down. It had been fascinating to see the fort, but they came away disappointed to find it in such a poor state of repair.

▲

Jugs had been meaning to hire a moped to explore the island, and that morning presented as good an opportunity as any. There were no group excursions planned, no plenary activities until later in the afternoon. Everyone was free to do their own thing, and that suited her just fine. After breakfast, she presented her driver's licence at the travel agency was given the keys to a small scooter of Italian make and told to replace any petrol she used. The hire rate was reasonable and, armed with a map of the island, she sped off out of town along the new road to Komiža, passing labourers at work in the fields. They were clearing vine husks from the vineyards and depositing them in clumps by the roadside.

Presently, she came to a point overlooking Komiža, and the road began a series of dizzying switchback turns down to the town. She stopped the scooter. From this vantage point Komiža appeared little more than a tiny hamlet hugging the shoreline of a still, blue harbour around which tiny white fishing boats were dotted like flecks of surf. Riding carefully around the hairpin bends, she descended into the town for a look around.

There was some activity on the main harbour-side. Traders came and went, fishermen pottered about their boats, preparing to take them out into the Biševski kanal. Otherwise, it seemed tourist-brochure sleepy, and after a coffee and pastry at a local cafe she was ready to resume her tour.

According to the map, there was a coastal road that went south out of town, more or less straight save for a couple of sharp turns around the hills, and which climbed gradually up to the villages of the island's interior. She followed it and after a journey of about fifteen minutes around cliff tops with sheer drops down to the sea she rounded Mount Hum and dropped into the high central plain and a long, straight road lined with vineyards. A significant dog-leg right took her through Plisko Polje, and past the Rokis' farmhouse and restaurant. A little farther on she came to a crossroads. Rather than head back towards Vis town she took a right turn and after a mile or so began a slow descent to the settlements of the south coast, Podstraže and Rukavac.

The road into Rukavac descended gradually towards a pretty bay with a couple of restaurants. The houses along the route were as modern as anything she had seen on the island: two- and three-storey townhouses outside which were parked cars with a variety of number plates, few of them Croatian. Holiday homes, no doubt, and with good reason. They offered fine views of the bay of Rukavac and the island of Ravnik beyond, which apparently boasted a green cave, or *zelena šplija*, almost the equal of Biševo's blue one. A small regatta of racing boats, their spinnakers flashed with primary colours, was making its way around the island.

The road back into Vis rose gradually, then took a sharp left and followed round until it climbed to a point high above the town. Here, at the side of the road, was a tall stone cross set upon a mound of earth. Not far away was a squat, stone plinth. On one face was a painted inscription in English: IN PROUD MEMORY OF THE MEN OF THE ROYAL AIR FORCE WHO LOST THEIR LIVES WHILST OPERATING OVER CROATIA 1944–5. On the other side was the same message in Croatian. Looking more carefully she saw that the word Croatia looked freshly painted compared to the rest of the inscription. The surface of the stone around it was also seriously weathered. She quickly realised why: the original lettering had said Yugoslavia, and had been quite thoroughly scratched out and repainted. This was a curiosity. The British who had come here during the Second World War had, surely, fought for the liberation of the whole of Yugoslavia, not just the Croatian part of it and, doubtless, not just confined their bombing raids to the Dalmatian coast and Slavonia. She could understand public buildings being renamed after Croatian independence, but a memorial? It struck an odd chord.

Looking back from the cross back down into the valley, she grasped the significance of her location. For two or three miles back along the road she had just driven along were rows and rows of vineyards. From the stone cross she could see them laid out on huge long swathes of flat land. One vineyard in particular was set at a slightly odd angle to the road back near the village of Plisko Polje. It must clearly be the site of one of the Second World War airfields.

She looked at her map. There was nothing marked on it to indicate the vineyards' wartime function. She got back onto the scooter. The road took her along a narrow road hugging the cliff face. She was high above Vis town and tried hard to concentrate on the road rather than become dangerously distracted by the stunning vista before her. As the road dropped, it became a series of hairpin bends. At another junction, she stopped and checked her map again. One way led back along the edge of the hills around the town to the junction near Samogor, the other directly down the hillside, appearing to end up in Kut. This route seemed the more fun and she freewheeled down the incline, slowed as she approached the back streets of Kut, and came out on the main harbour road into town where she just managed to avoid running Beard down.

▲

The Vis that Fitzroy Maclean returned to in the middle of 1944 had undergone huge changes. The "peaceful little Dalmatian island, with nothing more warlike to show than the crumbling battlements of Fort St George"[iii] had been transformed into a fully operational military facility. The central plain, containing the village of Plisko Polje, felt the impact of these changes more than anywhere else on the island: "In the central valley the olive trees had disappeared and the red earth had been flattened out to form a full-sized landing strip, from which fighters and fighter-bombers were constantly taking off on their way to attack shipping up and down the coast or objectives inland."[iv]

The main runway at Velo Polje was nearly 3,300 feet long and over 300 feet wide, with a further, auxiliary landing strip built at Plisko Polje. Support facilities were located farther down the road to Komiža at Dračevo Polje, not far from the command headquarters at Borovik. The first planes landed at the beginning of May 1944: Flying Fortresses, Liberators, British Halifax bombers, and, over the course of three months, more than 200 emergency landings were made by Allied aircraft operating in Yugoslavia. The most notable action of those early months of fortification was the evacuation of nearly a thousand wounded *Partižani* from Montenegro to Vis in a single day in thirty separate sorties. Elsewhere on the island, the

Royal Navy, operating out of Komiža, were likewise busy, and sank 84 enemy vessels during the course of 1944. The commando brigade under Tom Churchill waged a successful series of harassing raids against shipping in the Dalmatian islands, though at the cost of more than sixty dead.

By June there were over 13,000 *Partizani* and 2,000 Allied troops stationed on Vis. In addition to Allied training of *Partizani* in the operation of pack artillery, the two commands coordinated social and sporting activities among the Yugoslav and British troops including diving, water polo, rowing, and swimming competitions (in full battledress!).[v] The famous football team of Hajduk Split even found time to visit the island, where they played and beat a team from the Queen's Regiment by seven goals to one. The one recreation that didn't make it onto the list was cricket, but, with so much else going on, the absence from the programme of such a quintessentially languid game is hardly surprising.

Apart from the women and children who had been evacuated to Italy and Egypt, those who felt the effects of militarisation most keenly were the villagers of the central plain. In all some 75 acres of prime vineyards and olive groves were cleared and flattened to make way for the airfields. After the war ended it was a number of years before the soil was used again for viniculture. Yet the island of Vis played a major part in the liberation of Yugoslavia, not least when Allied aircraft bombed the mainland in support of *Partizani* actions against the retreating German occupiers in September 1944. The attack, which Maclean and Tito planned on Vis, proved successful in cutting and disrupting German lines. With the enemy in flight from Yugoslavia, Tito left Vis suddenly in the middle of September.

▲

Oliver was late. It was gone eight o'clock when he pulled up outside Bejbi with the minibus, and darkness had already settled on the evening. Bunter told everyone to finish off their beer, and soon the party was sardined into Oliver's transport, and heading out of town up the hill to the helipad at Samogor. Here, Oliver hung a left and soon the bus was a hundred feet up, on the gradually rising road that hugged the hills around the town. Directly below, the streetlights of Kut and, behind, Vis town described a parabola familiar from the brochures Bunter had brought back from his visit the year before. Now, in the dark of a warm Dalmatian evening, the majority of the tour party was seeing this vista for the first time, only a handful of them having made the effort to climb the surrounding hills.

Presently the minibus approached the switchback above Kut, and Oliver found another gear to better tackle the gradient. The party tried to spot landmarks in the darkness. The Franciscan priory on Prirovo was floodlit, making for an easy point of reference. The Tamaris was just about distinguishable by its size, and the Church of Our Lady of the Cave was fleetingly glimpsed as the minibus made a number of dizzying turns on the hairpin bends. Somewhere beyond, in the black stillness of the harbour, the *Lady Ruth* lay at anchor. Those who had witnessed Oliver's driving while being transported to their apartments on the first afternoon on the island could be assured their experience had been no fluke. Oliver did drive like an utter maniac, speeding along the narrow hillside road. The darkness only served to make the journey appear even more dangerous.

Eventually the minibus dropped into the central plain, and five minutes later arrived at Konoba Roki's for what Bunter had promised would be the tour's "closing dinner". Oliver eased the minibus down the steep concrete ramp and into the small field that served as the restaurant car park. Everybody piled out, thankful to have made the journey in one piece.

Oliver showed the party past the outdoor ovens and up some stone steps into the farmhouse courtyard. Stanko, wearing a friendly smile, was there to greet the party and showed them through into the house where a room near the kitchen had been set aside as a reception area. A large table had been set aside, on which were displayed a number of different wine bottles and a number of glasses, all decoratively laid out on a red chequered tablecloth. The Sipper, resplendent in his velvet jacket, noticed the resemblance to the flag of Croatia.

"Is that tablecloth gingham or just Croatian colours?" he asked Crabbo Junior rhetorically. Crabbo thought for a moment.

"How do you know the Croats didn't invent gingham?" he said.

Stanko and Oliver invited their guests to sample some of the Roki produce, and poured a glass for everyone. It was a full, rich red wine called Matadur. At 15.5% ABV and 215 kuna per bottle, this was clearly the top of the range. It was certainly strong and powerful for a young wine. Bunter could not resist a pun: "High octane Roki fuel," he quipped. There was approval from the party, whose appreciation of fine wines was mixed, to say the least. The majority bluffed their way through the tasting with a rousing chorus of "*Živjeli!*" while some were making a mental note to call in at the Rokis' shop a few doors down from Bejbi for some souvenirs before the end of the trip.

In time everyone sat at a long table out in the courtyard, where they were joined by other members of the Hoste team. More wine was served, this time the white Volijok at 14%, and a selection of hors d'oeuvres including local olives, cheese (which local custom dictated was always served *before* a meal rather than after it) and wafer-thin strips of *pršut* which melted on the tongue. As people settled down to what promised to be a long evening's feasting, El Bow stood and tapped his glass with a spoon to gain everyone's attention, then cleared his throat.

"I'd like to suggest a format for toasts this evening. Somebody stands up and specifies a toast and who ever stands up must finish off whatever's in their glass." There was a bemused silence as the assembled tried to take in what had just been said. El Bow hadn't finished.

"To give you an example," he continued, "stand up and join me in a toast, anybody who has *caught something* on tour." Glances were exchanged around the table as the company pondered the multiplicity of meanings of El Bow's words then, slowly, JD, Crabbo Junior, Highball and Son of El Vis stood, raised their glasses and drained them in the twinkling of an eye.

"What did *you* catch?" the Memsahib asked Highball, suspiciously.

"A cricket ball, twice," came the reply. This feat was also true of Son of Elvis. El Bow himself remained standing, having taken the last catch of the Hoste innings. JD and Crabbo Junior had, at various times, caught fish. No one else stood.

El Bow's toasting format was deemed to be an agreeable enough diversion. Its principal reason for being was to pick up the pace of the drinking once things started to flag. This appeared lost on Beard, however. No sooner had El Bow and the rest of the toast makers sat down again than Beard shot straight to his feet and embraced the toast-making whole-heartedly.

"Stand up anybody who's dropped..." he began. Before he could continue, he was shouted down by the rest of the table. Beard sat down, suitably admonished. He had been too eager: the toasts had been intended to add occasional spice over the duration of the meal, not over-season the first course. After a decent interval had passed, Beard was allowed to stand up and make his toast to anybody who had dropped something on tour, and others followed in good time: to anybody who sustained an injury on tour, broke something on tour, and so forth. People were up and down like yo-yos for large parts of the evening.

Stanko brought out an intermediate course of octopus risotto. The octopus was lightly cooked, had a smoky taste, and was gladly wolfed down by the ravenous party. This dish, like the main course, was cooked in the *peka* style, the traditional method of the island's villages. Some were intrigued to see how this all worked, and followed Stanko to the outdoor kitchen. It was essentially a work surface holding several raised metal pots with lids. The courses were placed inside the pots in their serving dishes, and then baked from below and above by the burning hot embers of the discarded wine husks from the vineyard. Nothing here seemed to go to waste.

The main course arrived. It was a whole monkfish, even bigger and uglier than the *škarpina* eaten at the first day's lunch at the Pojoda. The Sipper took one look at its sour, upturned mouth and spiny gills. "His mother loved him," he observed.

It was a huge meal, more than adequately filling the hungry mouths. More wine was produced, followed by various desserts for those who still had room. A bottle of home-made brandy flavoured with carob and known as *rogačica* was produced, and a number of more conventional toasts were drunk: to the Rokis, to Kriket Klub Sir William Hoste. The evening was entirely convivial, if beginning to blur round the edges.

Oliver's mother, Valerie, joined the party at the far end of the table opposite her son. Over a glass of wine she began to talk about William Hoste. Few of those at that far end of the table knew much of the history behind the revival of cricket on Vis, though some had a cursory familiarity with the battle thanks to the brief sketch Bunter had outlined in the previous year's edition of *Witless*. Valerie was remarkably well informed and told her guests how the letter that Hoste wrote back to his mother in 1810 was the only reference made to the introduction of the game on the island. She was clearly very interested in the subject and had, she said, begun to assemble a small archive of things relating to Vis and cricket. She was more than happy to talk, and enjoyed filling in the gaps in her guests' knowledge.

Hoste's career after the Battle of Vis saw notable siege actions against the French at Dubrovnik and Kotor (now in Montenegro), which survive in fictionalised accounts in Patrick O'Brian's books about the naval career of Jack Aubrey. Hoste was awarded a baronetcy in 1814 and knighted the year after. At war's end he settled in an England he had barely known from the age of twelve, and married the daughter of the second Earl of Orford, with whom he raised four children.

Captain Sir William Hoste, first Baronet KCB RN, died in 1828 at the age of 48. His body was buried in the churchyard of the chapel on the corner of St John's Wood Road and St John's Wood High Street, a stone's throw from Thomas Lord's Cricket Ground, home of the Marylebone Cricket Club since 1814. Sadly, the exact location of his grave has been lost and there is no longer a stone to mark it, but a statue of Hoste stands in St Paul's Cathedral as part of his mentor Lord Nelson's memorial.

As things began to wind down Oliver and Stanko appeared with two cases of Roki wine and presented a bottle to each member of the touring party. This was generous. Bunter, perhaps wary of the evening going on too long, asked The Sipper whether he judged it time to call the evening to a close.

"You're the skipper. What do *you* think?" he asked.

"Two more bottles," The Sipper winked. This disappointed Bunter, who had been looking for The Sipper to agree to draw a veil over proceedings.

"You don't see the big picture," he chided, "just your own personal point of view," then reminded his captain that the Rokis were working people for whom this was the busiest time of the year. The two extra bottles went un-ordered.

Oliver drove the party back to Vis town in the minibus. This proved even more alarming than the outward journey, with Oliver driving far too quickly for most people's comfort. The Sipper decided to quieten the party's growing anxiety by performing his party piece, a rendition of *Don't Fence Me In*, Cole Porter's hokey paean to a life unfettered by the cares of the world. No sooner had he begun singing in a rich baritone, complete with Bing Crosby ba-bumm stylings, than everybody began to join in. If the St Radegund team were to go out in a fireball of twisted metal and charred flesh at the bottom of some ravine, then at least they would do so with a song on their lips.

NOTES:

i   It appears on local maps as "Host island", having lost the final "e" at some point.

ii Paravić, Janko (trans), 'The Golden "British Years"' in *The Island of Vis*, Zagreb, Fabra 2004, p.32

iii Maclean, p 457

iv ibid

v   Paravić, p 66

10
The Blacksmith

Antonio hoped his son Petar would take up the game in time.

The St Radegund's number was dwindling. The Stooges had already left Vis the day after the cricket match, taking the midday boat to Split in good time to make their overnight ferry back to Italy. El Vis and Son of left the day after the meal at Konoba Roki's, though slightly later than they had anticipated. Even the crew of the *Lady Ruth* was planning to weigh anchor and sail round some of the islands as El Bow looked to find a port where the boat could winter at a reasonable rate. Waking up late on the Wednesday morning, after that memorable evening of lavish and generous hospitality at Konoba Roki's, brought home to the St Radegund the all-too sobering realisation that the tour was nearly at an end.

There was the consolation of its being the Memsahib's birthday, and the distaff members of the party made sure they marked it. Frannie presented her with a card she had bought locally and which, she hoped, actually said "Happy birthday" rather than "With deepest sympathy" or "Get well soon" or some similar greeting in Croatian. Jugs gave a souvenir of the island: three small ceramic plaques joined together by twine and depicting a seashell, a sailing boat and an anchor, with the single word Vis inscribed into the middle lozenge. The Memsahib was touched by the thoughtfulness, which was in marked contrast to that demonstrated by the male members of the party who offered no more than a perfunctory congratulations and the offer of a drink. It was better than nothing.

The Memsahib thought sharing lunch at the Kaliopa, whose delights on the first night of the tour she and Highball had missed, a fitting way to celebrate the passing of another year. Unfortunately, it was only once the couple had arrived outside the garden gates that they realised the Kaliopa does not open for lunch. Leaving a hastily scribbled note for the others wedged into the brickwork by the entrance to the garden, the Highballs headed back to their apartment with a sense of an opportunity gone begging.

For the rest of the party, each did his or her own thing, trying in their own way to find one last unseen part of the island to cherish. Crabbo Junior, not for the first time, decided to – as his Australian mother would say – "go bush". He had already, the day before, acquired a fishing licence from the main information bureau and had had some success with rod and line. Following the road beyond Bejbi round to the north-west side of the harbour to fish off the rocks by the Hotel Issa he was pleasantly surprised to be rewarded with a catch of two fish that looked like perch, and one, long and silver in colour with a pointed nose, unidentifiable to him.

Now he decided to spend his last morning on the island in equally reflective pursuit. Armed with his watercolours and brushes, he started from where he left off the day before and climbed the steep and winding roads beyond English Harbour up to Fort George. There he made a sketch of the town, with Prirovo in the middle distance and the *Riva* and Tamaris behind, and also managed a watercolour of the fort in a style he later described as "abstract and expressionistic, rather than abstract expressionist". Satisfied with his work, he clambered down in the sticky heat of the midday in search of refreshment, preferably non-alcoholic: it had been, all told, a pretty big week, and he was in need of some serious detoxification.

The previous day, their last on the island, as they walked back down from Fort George, Son of El Vis had mentioned to his father that he, Beard and Crabbo Junior were wondering whether the bottle of *travarica* Tomislav had presented to El Vis on the day they arrived hadn't been intended for all of them, and not just for his exclusive enjoyment. El Vis realised that he might well have misunderstood Tomislav's intentions and admitted as much: but why hadn't anyone said anything? Perhaps, Son of offered, the others didn't think they knew you well enough to insist. El Vis determined there and then that the bottle should be opened for general consumption on their last night and so, following the dinner at Konoba Roki's, once Oliver had decanted his passengers in the middle of Kut and sped off into the night, there was a general invitation to tackle this monster bottle of Dragon Water that a number of people gladly took up. It turned into another in a series of very late nights.

By early afternoon Beard too was treading the now well-worn path up to Fort George. As he climbed the slopes of the headland he saw, to his right, various yachts, fishing smacks and sail boats coming and going in and out of the wide expanse of the harbour. One boat made its way slowly out of port from the little bay on the far side of Prirovo in front of Gradina hill. He recognised it as the *Lady Ruth*. JD and El Bow were leaving Vis to tour some of the neighbouring islands. Beard pulled out his camera to get a shot of it as it left port.

▲

Tito's departure from Vis was unexpected and unexplained. He left on 19 September 1944`without informing the British command either that he was leaving or where he was going. Maclean's first thought was that the marshal had flown to the mainland to take personal charge of the effort to liberate Belgrade. In fact, he had left in a Russian transport aircraft, his destination Moscow and a meeting with Stalin, the purpose of which was to secure the assistance of the Red Army in the final push towards liberation. Maclean's reaction, like Churchill's, was one of anger and disappointment. They had, they reasoned, carefully built Tito up into a major military and political force in his country, and now he was throwing this back in their faces by going behind their backs. Worse, co-operation between the Allies and *Partižani* on Vis had deteriorated suddenly, and this too was being blamed on Tito's flight. When Maclean and Tito next met, in newly liberated Belgrade, they had a frank exchange of views about the manner of Tito's departure. Maclean began: "'....you don't seem to understand that what did the most harm was the way in which you yourself slid away without letting us know where you were going.' But Tito could not or would not see this. 'Only recently,' he replied innocently, 'Mr Churchill went to Quebec to see President Roosevelt, and I only heard of this visit after he had returned. And I was not angry.'"[i]

Tito, easily making the transition from guerrilla leader to statesman, was no fool. His negotiations with Ivan Šubašić on the form of a united government had concluded with Tito accepting the compromise of Yugoslavia remaining a monarchy in name until elections could be held, although the king himself would remain in London, represented at home by three regents. This was all political expediency. Tito merely wanted recognition of the new government by the Allies, which came in due course at the Yalta Conference.

Zagreb was liberated in May 1945, the *Partižani* – their numbers swelled by *Četnik* deserters under an amnesty of 1943 – harrying the Croat army all the way to the Austrian border. At Bleiburg the remnants of the *Ustaše* army tried to cross the frontier to escape the vengeance of their pursuers. Their way was barred by a small force of British troops, to whom the 50,000 strong *Ustaše* surrendered to prevent themselves falling into *Partižani* hands. Their respite was short-lived: the British loaded the fleeing soldiers onto trains and delivered them back over the border to the waiting liberators and annihilation.

The consolidation of Tito's political power occurred in November 1945 with long-promised elections. By this time the monarchist elements of the government had been eased out – King Petar's three regents having been ignored from the start – and anti-communist opposition intimidated. A rigged election produced an overwhelming result in favour of the left, the Tito-Subašić agreement was put out of its misery, and Yugoslavia was proclaimed a Federal Democratic Republic. Mihajlović was eventually tracked down to a village in Bosnia, put on trial and executed in June 1946. Pavelić escaped, only to die in exile. Collaborators, or suspected ones, even within higher echelons of the Catholic Church, were dealt with ruthlessly.

Tito broke spectacularly with Stalin in 1948, having decided that Yugoslavia should follow its own path, not one dictated by Moscow, and so Tito's Yugoslavia became a member of neither the Warsaw Pact nor Comecon. Yugoslavia, unlike the Soviet Union, also recognised the existence of the state of Israel. Three years later, with relations between the United States and the Soviet Union now icy, he took a typically independent course and became one of the founders of the non-aligned movement with India and China.

Vis, briefly his wartime headquarters, was not to get back onto a civilian footing but remained in a state of militarisation. The pillboxes and gun emplacements that had sprung up during the war merely increased in number. The island became wrapped in miles and miles of barbed wire fences. The airfields in the central plain that had served the island were decommissioned and gradually returned to their original use as vineyards. The problem was that there were fewer and fewer people willing to work them, as a wave of emigration took hold.

Before the last major period of emigration in the 1920s, the population of the island was over 11,000 inhabitants; by 1947 it had dropped to just over 8,000. At the start of the 1960s, when the controls on emigration were relaxed, the population stood at 7,000 and, twenty years later, at just over 4,000. The villages of the central plain suffered most during this most recent period, with Podšpilje and environs dropping from 1,500 inhabitants to under 200 today.[ii]

Prior to 1961, illegal emigration was a risky business. Inhabitants of Komiža often tried to escape to the Italian mainland, some in craft no bigger than rowing boats. The lucky ones made it to places as far flung as Canada, the United States and Australia, where there were plenty of jobs.

Anybody caught trying to flee by the Yugoslav navy faced lengthy imprisonment for treason.

As the rules on emigration were relaxed in the 1960s, Dalmatia began to enjoy some of the benefits of foreign tourism when the Yugoslav government opened up the coast. While Hvar and Korčula thrived as holiday destinations in this more open climate, Vis, still denied foreign visitors in spite of a brief opening up of the island in 1972, fell behind. The hotels of the Dalmatian coast were able to generate large amounts of foreign exchange in the process, although the majority of it ended up in the hands of the government in Belgrade. This example of the central government's apparent exploitation of Croatia directly fed the aspirations of the reform movement of the Croatian Communist Party, whose platform of Croatian autonomy, combined with the *Masovni pokret*, the mass movement of the "Croatian Spring" at the beginning of the 1970s, laid the foundations for Croatian independence.

Life on Vis, however, remained frozen in time. While there were occasional improvements in the quality of living, such as the water and power supply systems that were introduced in the 1960s, they were often for the principal benefit of the military personnel. It was only in 1988 that foreign tourists were permitted to visit the island, after pressure was brought to bear by local dignitaries. Even after Croatian independence in 1991, the Yugoslav army tried to retain control of the island, finally leaving only at the end of May 1992. The barbed wire, which had been newly erected to keep tourists off sensitive military sites, is still there. A number of minefields remain on the island but they are, thankfully, well-marked.

▲

In the late afternoon, the remaining members of the St Radegund party made a rendezvous at Bejbi. They had, Bunter told them, all been invited by Antonio Lipanović – the Jessop of the Hoste team, as Bunter insisted on calling him – to visit his "wine caves". This seemed a splendid idea. The team had been exposed to a number of the varieties of wine the island had to offer, but had still only scratched the surface. All of them were rich and strong, the Vugava being, in addition, naturally sweet. One of the few happy consequences of forty years of isolation was that all the viniculture on the island was still organic.

The islanders of Vis made no secret of the fact that wine has been in continual production on the island since about 400 BCE. It was something of which they were understandably proud, as almost every locally produced piece of tourist literature informed its readers. Also frequently reproduced was a 2,400-year-old public relations puff from one Agatharchides of Cnidos: "…and at Issa, which is an island in the Adriatic, Agatharchides says that wine is made which is superior to every other wine whatever." ＼

The goblet training of the vines – a technique which had served generation upon generation of wine growers since the time of the Greeks – had only recently given way to more modern methods, including a degree of mechanisation. Wine-growers' co-operatives, which were established in the 1920s and later incorporated into Tito's collectivisation programme, continue to operate today, but in many other respects, the basic wine-growing techniques remain largely unchanged. This has, inevitably, given rise to a debate between traditionalists and modernisers, particularly on the question of the varieties of grape grown. Among the former, there is a desire to preserve and cultivate as many of the island's indigenous grapes as possible; the latter favour alien varieties with higher fruit yields, and so the two compete for space among the vineyards. Nowadays, a dozen major producers cultivate less than 370 acres of land for wine growing, compared with 7,500 acres at the island's peak of production in the late 19th century.

Once The Sipper and Crabbo Junior had arrived back from a long walk towards Komiža, the party started on its way to Lipanović's. The road taken ran parallel to the familiar approach to the helidrome at Samogor, separated from it by a narrow valley of vineyards and the occasional 1960s concrete structure of monolithic architectural brutality. At the road's end was a villa whose gates were adorned with a small shrine to the Virgin Mary. Thereafter it became a rubble-strewn ramp which rose twenty feet to reveal, overlooking the helidrome, a large opening gouged from the hillside and guarded by huge metal gates. To one side stood an old, wooden wine-press. A barrel was perched above the entrance. No other sign indicated ownership even if the nature of the business was obvious.

To call what lay within caves was somewhat wide of the mark. In fact they were a series of man-made chambers cut deep into the hillside, each about twenty feet high and fifteen wide. The first chamber, about a hundred feet long, led directly to a long corridor, separated from the second by heavy metal doors. Off the corridor were a number of smaller chambers. After the Second World War the complex had served as a military bunker.

Antonio was waiting inside, inspecting a number of huge stainless steel vats in which he was preparing this year's vintage. He seemed, improbably, dwarfed by the huge caverns in which he worked. At Beard's request he opened one up and showed off the blood-red broth within, which seethed as it fermented. As Beard and Antonio swapped oenological titbits and broadly compared brewing and wine-making techniques, Bunter sat down on a nearby stool, hoping that the conversation would move on. Antonio conducted the party on a brief, informal tour of the premises, and showed one of his more experimental efforts. He explained that for four and a half years he had been trying to produce a sparkling wine to sell alongside the usual whites and reds. It was still not quite finished, and he had his reservations about his chances of success given the high sugar content of the local grapes, but still hoped to start producing it properly within a couple of years.

Antonio was using one of the small chambers as a reception and tasting area. Soon the party was seated around a large table on which had been laid some wine glasses. On a nearby sideboard Antonio proudly displayed his tankard and medallion from the cricket game a few days earlier. Next to it stood the Sir William Hoste Trophy, behind photographs of family and framed awards for his wine growing. Antonio uncorked a bottle of Vugava at 13.5% ABV and his Sv Juraj red at 14%, and poured several glasses out.

The party's first impression of Antonio had been formed at the cricket game when The Sipper had cast him in the role of the village blacksmith. This had been a kind of compliment as the St Radegund captain often found himself fulfilling a similar role. In person, Antonio defied such simplistic attempts to characterise him. He was particularly vocal about politics and the history of the island. His father had been among those islanders evacuated to Egypt during the war. After their return, his family left the island and moved to Split. As a child, Antonio had once declared himself to be so hungry that he could eat a *Četnik*, and from the size of him you wouldn't doubt that he would be able to do so. The resulting nickname of "Četo" had stuck to him even after he returned to the island, though no one among the St Radegund party felt sufficiently familiar with him to address him so. Besides, to Bunter at least he was still, and would always be, Jessop. As the remaining tourists sniffed and sipped politely at Antonio's wine, Jugs asked him how long he had been in the bunker.

"Since the end of the war," he replied.

"You fought in the war?" asked the Memsahib. "What was that like?"

"I lost a few friends," he said. The helmet he had worn in battle rested on the sideboard next to his cricket memorabilia. The conversation moved on.

"When I opened for business in 1993, an old widow came to see me and offered me six five-litre jugs of dessert wine her husband had made back in the sixties."

They followed Antonio into a small store room beyond the one they sat in, cut even deeper into the hillside. Inside were wine racks ranged from floor to ceiling. He pointed out the wine donated by the widow. It lay stacked in dozens of slender bottles, gathering dust.

"She said she was so pleased that someone was taking up wine growing again she thought she'd offer them to me as a gift."

"Was it any good?" asked Crabbo Junior. Antonio smiled.

"I thought it would have turned to vinegar in all those years, but it was actually very good. I decided to bottle it all. Not for sale, you understand." And then, almost as an afterthought, "Want to try some?"

Everybody shrugged as if to say "Well, as long as you're offering." Antonio pulled one of the slim bottles from the rack and picked up a couple of spare glasses. The wine poured slowly into the glasses showing a good degree of viscosity, and settled into the bowls with a golden, amber glow.

"I have 120 bottles left. After that it's gone."

Everybody sipped at the forty-year-old wine. The taste was syrupy, honeysweet and fruity, like nectar.

"It's like a bloody good Sauternes," opined The Sipper, who liked to think he knew a little about wine. It was, truth be told, the rarity of what was being drunk as much as the quality that impressed, and there followed an inexpert attempt at putting a value on an individual bottle. £300? £400? It was difficult to say. Whatever, all agreed the circumstances under which the wine was being drunk made the experience beyond price. It was humbling, and Antonio was told what a privilege it felt to have been allowed to try it.

"Finish it off," he said hospitably.

They did so, and Antonio presented Bunter with another bottle to take back to Cambridge. Eyebrows complained that the appreciation of wine of such quality would be beyond most of the regulars of the St Radegund.

"Caviar to the general," he muttered, though it was equally true that once transported to England it would lose a great deal in being drunk so completely out of context.

Unfamiliar voices speaking in English were heard coming from the main chamber of the bunker.

"Who's that?" someone asked.

"Visitors from England," Antonio replied. "Customers, actually."

The Memsahib spoke up: "It's very kind of you to offer us all this wine to taste, but we wouldn't mind at all paying for a bottle or two to take back."

Antonio smiled. "Sorry, it's gone."

"What do you mean?" Highball asked.

"There's nothing left. I've sold all of it. Last year's vintage and this year's too."

This was met with disbelief, but Antonio explained he had indeed pre-sold all the coming year's wine stock before it had even been bottled.

"How much do you export?" Beard asked. Virtually nothing, was the reply. Without preservatives a good number of his wines would not travel well.

"Can you produce any more?" asked Beard. Antonio sighed.

"It's tough. I'm almost at capacity now. Twenty-five thousand bottles a year. I could possibly squeeze another 5,000 out but not much more." He opened another bottle, this time one of his reds, then excused himself while he went to attend to his visitors, who had come to the island specifically to buy up his stocks for their daughter's wedding. In his absence, the party sniffed, sipped and swilled.

"Are there many British living on the island?" Jugs asked when Antonio returned. There were a few, mainly moneyed types who had bought apartments as holiday homes, but the cost of living here was so negligible to them that Antonio was sceptical they contributed anything at all. Worse they made little effort to integrate. Vis was very much still a working island. If it weren't, it was doubtful it could survive.

"It's fine here in the summer," he said. "When the Italians and Germans are here in July and August and when the yachtsmen come here and we make our money. But out of season there's nothing."

There were already disturbing signs, he continued, that the way of life that people like him and Oliver and others of his generation had fought for and come back to Vis to preserve and protect was under threat. Some islanders had already been selling property to German and British visitors seeking holiday homes, and in the process were setting themselves up for life and enabling themselves to retire to Split.

"It's difficult. It brings more money to the island, but if it goes too far it could upset everything: people who have lived here for years selling up because they can make a fortune out of their homes, and only foreign tourists living here."

This unwelcome dilution of the island's traditional character was resented by a great number of islanders, though seen as inevitable. The paradox was abundantly clear: Vis needs tourist income to tide the islanders over the winter but increased exposure of their island to foreign visitors will only fuel the property boom and encourage more incomers.

The Memsahib was sympathetic, drawing a parallel with English country villages like the one she grew up in, where incoming Londoners with little appreciation of rural life were driving up property prices and pricing out young people whose families had lived there for generations. The two were in agreement: lose the traditional working life of a community and you lose its heart, its soul.

Antonio was concerned that the full effects would not, ultimately, be felt by his generation but by the succeeding one, that the youngsters of his son's age would in time be unable to buy their own homes on the island.

There was another complicating factor, and that was Europe. Croatia was a poor country and desperately needed to be a member of the European Union to move forward. At the moment the country's fairly stringent residency laws were holding large-scale immigration in check. Join the European Union and the conditions become a lot easier. Antonio scratched his chin.

"So," Highball said reflectively, "where does the cricket fit in?"

Antonio and the others in the Hoste team saw the commercial exploitation of Vis' links with the British and cricket as an opportunity they could control. Here again they could, in the long run, only be making matters worse. Highball spoke up:

"So are we – the St Radegund – part of the problem, then?"

"No, definitely not." Another bottle was uncorked and poured, glasses charged.

"Whatever comes along we will be ready to face it, and fight it. As long as we do what's right for ourselves". And with that Antonio struck a note of defiance and pride that had been heard in many a conversation since the tour began. It was not a million miles from the phrase carved into the top of the huge stone slab at Samogor: *Tude nećemo - svoje ne damo.*

Antonio started talking about how much he enjoyed playing cricket, and then how he hoped his son Petar would take up the game in time. He started asking Beard for advice on his bowling. By the time the remnants of the St Radegund team left Lipanović's, several bottles to the good, Beard had been showing the wine grower how to bowl outswingers in the longest corridor of the installation.

Later in the evening, as the rest prepared their bags for the following day's departure, Crabbo Junior, Jugs and The Sipper met with Rob and Oliver at Bejbi. As they sat around drinking Karlovačko, Oliver asked the visitors what they had seen of the town. Crabbo Junior mentioned his painting expedition up to Fort George. Neither The Sipper nor Jugs had managed to visit the ruined fort. Would they like to go up there that evening, Oliver asked? A quick exchange of glances between the three of them seemed to say "Why not?" and soon enough Oliver was driving them in the darkness of the warm night up the road past English Harbour to the fort. They unloaded a supply of beers and a couple of pizzas bought from the Katarina, and approached the structure, silent and ominous in the moonlight.

For the benefit of The Sipper and Jugs, Crabbo Junior tried to illuminate the carved Union Jack-decorated keystone above the entrance with his cigarette lighter. In the gloom they could just about make it out. They went carefully into the first courtyard and then, following Oliver's lead, mounted the stone stairs up to the battlements.

The moon was bright, and they could just make out the dark form of Host Island to the north. The lights of Kut and Vis town twinkled in the darkness. All was peaceful and still. They sat down on the battlements and broke bread together, washed down with bottles of beer. The Sipper reflected on their surroundings, effectively one of the few remaining reminders of the British legacy on the island. Oliver was quick to remind him of the others: the English cemetery near Grandovac, and the various Second World War memorials dotted around the island, but, yes, along with the other ruined forts, George was certainly the oldest, and largest, British-built structure. Then Oliver smiled.

"Of course, there's one thing you're forgetting," he said. "In the future there will always be something British on the island, as long as we continue to play the game." Glasses were raised. A final toast was made to the Kriket Klub Sir William Hoste and best wishes expressed for cricket's continued revival on the island.

"I don't doubt you'll make a good fist of things," The Sipper said, clinking his bottle against Oliver's, one captain to another.

▲

It seemed that no sooner had the St Radegund team arrived on Vis, relaxed into the pace of life, explored the island, dined and drunk well and found new friends than, inevitably, it was time to leave. They gathered at Bejbi at six in the morning on the Thursday after the cricket match for a last espresso and a cigarette before boarding the fast catamaran to Split. Oliver Roki and Rob Dumančić came along to say goodbye. One by one the team processed up the gangway and lugged their bags on to the catamaran. There was a slight commotion behind as Stanko, Hoste's genial number three batsman, jogged breathlessly up the ferry dock where he made straight for Eyebrows and informed him that he needed to pay for his room. This was news to Eyebrows.

"Nobody mentioned anything about money," he said with the requisite flourish of his hands. When the idea had entered his head that accommodation on the island would be free was anybody's guess. Stanko, though, was still smiling, and the matter was settled almost immediately. Goodbyes were said, hands shaken firmly, promises to keep in touch made. Oliver, Rob and Stanko waved as the catamaran pulled slowly away from the dock. The engines kicked in, churning the water into a froth behind the boat as it began piloting its way out of the harbour and into the Viški kanal where it picked up to its cruising speed.

The crossing was choppier than expected but not unpleasant, and soon enough the party was strolling down the gangplank directly onto the quayside in Split. Immediately opposite was a well-proportioned café-bar. Some of the party stopped here for breakfast, while others pressed on farther round the harbour to the small left-luggage office by the railway tracks, there to dump their bags for the day: the car ferry back to Ancona did not sail until later that night.

The café-bar was huge; so huge, in fact, that the menu told you it was huge. "Welcome to F-Café. Megacafé. Biggest café in Split," it began, "located on the beautiful place where the sea and Diocletian's palace are touching each other." The unintended eroticism of that descriptive detail produced sniggers aplenty at such an early hour of the day. Several *espressi* were ordered, and some even attempted a couple of the local breakfast pastries before moving on to explore the city.

Behind the F-café, as one moved away from the beautiful place, was Split's main drag, the *Obala hrvatskog narodnog preporoda* or, familiarly and doubtless for the convenience of the natives, *Riva*: a spacious, palm-tree-lined avenue with benches looking out onto the sparkling waters of the harbour and a broad, gently sloping pavement terrace of cafés set into thick limestone and marble walls. The palace had once been the home of the emperor Diocletian, who had renounced his position as head of the Roman Empire to retire here, some four miles from the Roman city of Salona, and grow cabbages. While the original walls and vaulted substructure remain, a lot of the interior stones were cannibalised and reused as the medieval city of Split slowly took shape within and, ultimately, without the palace. The site of Diocletian's mausoleum, within the central courtyard, was now overbuilt by the octagonal cathedral of St Domnius, and its bell tower dominated the skyline of the old city, whose walls now enclosed restaurants, hotels and shops.

The party entered a huge portal in the outer walls of the palace. Descending centuries-old steps through a dark vaulted underpass containing a number of fancy goods stalls, they emerged on the other side into the peristyle of the palace itself. By mid-morning the bell tower of St Domnius had begun to attract a queue, and visitors were allowed to ascend it in groups of four or five. Jugs and Crabbo Junior decided to try it. The entrance was narrow, the stone steps somewhat worn by use, but numerous tight anti-clockwise turns later the stone gave way to metal steps. It was a disorienting, vertiginous ascent. At the top, though, the views of the harbour and the islands beyond were stunning, Crabbo Junior began to feel dizzy, then queasy and he decided to go back down as quickly as possible. Once back at sea level he was glad to gather his wits and pull himself together. His reaction puzzled him. Perhaps it had just been the claustrophobic tightness of the ascent, or maybe was he just run down after a week of over-indulgence? Why, only the day before he had made a climb much higher than a mere 200 feet and everything had been as right as rain. Except for one small detail.

NOTES:

i   Maclean, p 519
ii Paravić, p 229
iii Athenaeus of Naucratis, *The Deipnosophists*, Book I

The Ascent of Mount Hum

11

The Ascent of Mount Hum

Komiža sat in an impressive natural harbour bound by two horns of headland.

I t had all started out innocently enough. On the Wednesday, just before lunchtime, Crabbo Junior had been sharing a beer with Highball, The Sipper and JD outside the Tamaris Hotel, when he mentioned in an off-the-cuff sort of way that he wouldn't mind having a go at climbing Mount Hum. He thought a bracing walk across the top of the island and a hardy climb up its highest peak might be just the thing. Highball too showed interest and mentioned in a casual way that he had read in a guidebook that from the summit of Hum one could see as far as Italy. JD was sceptical, and asked how high the mountain was.

"Five hundred feet?" Highball said uncertainly, having plucked the figure from the dusty corners of his memory. JD maintained that at that height the mountain wouldn't have sufficient elevation to be able to offer a view of the Italian coast, which was well over eighty miles away and went on to explain how, at ground level, the farthest you could see in any direction under optimal conditions was under three miles, owing to the curvature of the earth. Highball had to take all this in good faith, being in no position to argue the toss and having no head for trigonometry. It was more likely that he had confused metric and imperial measurements. No matter, The Sipper and Crabbo decided there and then to make an assault on the peak to settle the issue.

So it was that in the mid-afternoon of their last day on Vis, the pair made their way to the tourist office on the *Riva*. They took a look at a map of the island and conned the mountain's location. "M. Hum," the map told them, was two-thirds of the way along the road to Komiža, and turn right. Emboldened by what looked like a straightforward route, they headed out of town on foot.

They soon passed the helidrome at Samogor and began the long walk over the top of the island. Though to the eye it appeared quite a gentle 1:8 incline, it was deceptively tiring in the heat of the day. By the side of the road, discarded vine husks lay rotting in the sun. The stench (was it cyanide?) was overpowering, making the walk even less pleasant.

They whiled away the time in conversation of a philosophical nature. Crabbo Junior enquired about the subject of The Sipper's PhD, and The Sipper happily gave him a quick primer on fluid mechanics and turbulence. Crabbo Junior nodded politely without understanding much of it. They talked about their great expedition, of the peak they were about to scale, drawing comparisons between themselves and the great mountaineers of old. The name of George Mallory cropped up more than once and The Sipper mentioned "Mallory Syndrome" on the off chance that Crabbo Junior was unfamiliar with it (Q: "Why do you want to climb Mount Everest?" A: "Because it is there!"). Crabbo Junior knew perfectly well.

Not far along the road they came across a small house whose perimeter fence was roughly constructed out of chicken wire. Attached to it at various parts was a collection of mutilated puppets and dolls' body parts, a head here, a torso there. It was an unnerving sight, like something out of a voodoo ritual, and so the pair picked up the pace of the walk.

After about an hour and a half they reached the winding road above Komiža. They consulted the map again, realising they had missed the route up the mountain. They retraced their steps and found the off-road track they wanted. Numerous broken stones lined the route as they began their slow climb up a manageable gradient. The day had become slightly overcast, so the heat was becoming more bearable. As they climbed they saw an abandoned shopping trolley and some discarded, rusted gun cartridges. After an hour's climb they reached the summit.

Crabbo Junior sat down and sparked up a Lucky Strike, while The Sipper, in his Wilson of the *Wizard* running vest and shorts, admired the view. Crabbo Junior pulled out a hipflask of whisky with which to toast their success, evoking once again the spirits of Mallory and Irvine. To the north and east, the huge islands of Hvar and Korčula were visible, and beyond, the vague outline of the Dinaric Alps of the interior. To the southwest was Komiža and beyond, shrouded somewhere in the sea haze, Italy.

"Hang on a minute", said The Sipper. "That mountain over yonder, doesn't it look higher than this one?"

"A good hundred feet higher, maybe more." said Crabbo Junior.

The two of them exchanged glances, then laughed. They had climbed the wrong mountain. They found out later that the "M. Hum" they had seen on the tourist office's map was in fact not Hum but *Mali Hum*, meaning Little Hum.

"Shall we go over and climb the right one?"

"Nah, sod it. Let's go back to town."

Taking solace in the thought that their descent would at least be quicker than the climb, the intrepid adventurers went down the way they came, down the dirt track, past the shopping trolley and the spent cartridges and back on to the road to Vis.

"What was it Bunter kept saying?" asked Crabbo Junior.

"About what?"

"You know. You have to aim for the moon... "

"...to reach Mount Everest." The Sipper concluded, and the two walked along in silence for a while, contemplating their spectacular failure and the chilling thought that Bunter, for all their ribbing of him, actually did know a thing or two after all.

▲

After his alarming climb up the bell tower of St Domnius in Split, Crabbo Junior decided he had rather had enough. He was tired and wanted to get home and so, after the most cursory of glances around Diocletian's Palace, he and The Sipper decided that their last day in Croatia could be most profitably spent whiling away a good number of hours drinking beer on the *Riva* and watching the women go by.

As the pace of the day picked up and lunchtime approached, the main square of the palace's peristyle became a hive of activity. Guided tours were conducted, backpackers milled around the ruins. Bunter and Jugs stopped to watch a group of buskers decked out in what could only be traditional Croatian national dress playing what they assumed were traditional Croatian folk tunes on traditional Croatian instruments: balalaikas or whatever the Croatian equivalent was. Some of the numbers were quite tuneful, and Bunter handed over a few kuna for the troupe's CD recording.

Beard, meanwhile, was emerging triumphantly from a nearby café a couple of storeys up overlooking the square. In danger of being caught short, he had managed to make it up two flights of stairs, handed over his two kuna to the attendant who kept guard outside with her knitting to find, to his delight, that he had stumbled across some of the most exquisitely appointed toilets it had ever been his pleasure to grace. Having been expecting the traditional Elephant's Footprint he was instead greeted by cool marble floors and walls, and potted fern fronds. Beard was lavish in his praise, and thought them worthy of comparison with any of London's finest. The facilities in Split were right up there, fit for a Roman emperor though obviously not contemporary.

"So we're not talking bog standard, then" quipped Bunter, jadedly. The party was weary and looking forward to getting home, so the rest of the day was spent in leisurely sightseeing – largely of a sedentary type – outside various cafés and restaurants.

The sartorial highlight of all that people-watching was a T-shirt worn by a particularly busty young *Splićana*, on which was embroidered a stylised ass, eyes closed, braying. Above the cartoon animal was written – the letters picked out extravagantly in sequins and glitter – the words "Happy Donkey". True, the beast of burden depicted on the shirt did look happy, but for what reason remained mysterious. Beard and Highball toyed with the idea of trying to find the shop that sold the shirts so that they, too, could sport this magnificent item of stunningly kitsch apparel.

As they killed time, the party had their first sighting of the Dalmatian dog breed – native, as it were. For some reason this was not something anybody had expected, and it prompted a vague discussion about the likelihood of seeing an Aberdeen Terrier in Aberdeen, a Labrador in Labrador, or even a Mexican Hairless in Mexico.

As dusk began to fall, the St Radegund party gathered on the palm-lined *Riva* where The Sipper and Crabbo Junior had ensconced themselves for most of the afternoon and had become quite satisfied, as they said, with the quality of talent on display. The *Riva* was busy. People sat outside cafés eating, drinking and enjoying themselves. Bats began to flit between the trees. It was soon time to go.

For the return ferry journey there were, thankfully, plenty of cabins available. Crabbo Junior drew the short straw of sharing with Bunter and was, once again, Roger the Cabin Boy. Beard and Eyebrows shared a twin berth. No Dire Straits marred the journey back. Everybody got a good night's sleep.

The tourists disembarked at Ancona at seven the next morning and though rested the party was a little slow to get going. They had four hours before their train left to take them back to Pescara so they sat on the terrace of a café on the Piazza della Repubblica to take in caffeine and nicotine. Here Eyebrows bade the rest farewell. He was going to take a train to Trieste whence he would take his flight home. The party wished him "bon voyage et bonjour Trieste." As he boarded the bus to the railway station, he waved goodbye with a theatrical flourish. This Crabbo Junior took as a cue for a last impression, which he managed with some accomplishment, if a little wearily. They could barely wait to get home.

The journey back to Pescara was spent dozing or gazing wistfully out of the windows. At the airport the party were reminded of the small matter of the case of Roki's wine that Oliver had given them to bring back to Britain. Most of the bottles had been stowed in Beard's 110-litre rucksack. This made it even heavier than it had been on the way out when an excess baggage charge of £25 had been incurred. How to get around this one? Beard looked at the luggage conveyor by the desk, then back at his bulging rucksack. It was so full that it looked unlikely to fit on the conveyor. Then he noticed the two side pockets, also full.

"Leave it to me," he said, and with that approached the check-in desk with supreme confidence. Laying the rucksack on the conveyor he managed to position it so that the already full side pockets sat on the raised retaining edges of the conveyor in such a way as to transfer a significant load of the rucksack off the belt. The scales recorded the weight of the rucksack at 18 kilos, but the girl at the check-in desk let it go through without penalty.

The aeroplane departed on time, and soon the St Radegund party was winging homeward over the Italian Alps and heading for Stansted. Once they had passed through the baggage reclaim area, Beard took a moment to weigh the rucksack. It tipped the scales at a whopping 42 kilos. They boarded a pre-booked minibus to take them the 25 miles straight to the front door of the St Radegund pub in King Street.

It was Friday evening. The Vera Lynn Appreciation Society was doing its thing in style. Numerous non-travelling members of the team were waiting to welcome the tanned travellers back. Tales were swapped, ales were sunk. Larry, or more correctly Lawrence Dixon, put in a brief appearance on a quick break from his occasional barman duties at the Champ. Mike – Curly as was – arrived wearing a pair of shorts. The very professional job which had been made of dressing his gashed knee when he returned home meant he could now no longer get a pair of trousers on and so was reduced to walking around in shorts, as he put it, "looking like Lawrence".

Lawrence and Mike talked with Highball about their trip back. Before they left Vis, Larry had sent Curly on a mission of the utmost delicacy. Resentful of having been strong-armed into putting so much of their loose change into the fines sock two evenings before, Larry thought it would be a good wheeze to relieve the St Radegund of their beloved treasury, change the kuna back into euros and spend as much of it as possible on the way back to Blighty. How they would laugh as they raised a glass or two on the boat, in Italy, and on the plane home as they toasted the Rad's mounting panic, then frustration and, finally, despair as they conducted a futile search for the missing funds. Yes, that would keep the three of them smiling throughout the long journey home. They would have the last laugh come what may. It would have been a great idea were it not for the fact that when Curly went through the Highballs' apartment he couldn't find the sock anywhere. Highball, either suspecting some such high jinks or perhaps just being careful, had hidden the sock too well.

▲

Once the dessert plates were cleared away, the out-going captain of the St Radegund cricket team stood up from the table and, tapping a teaspoon against a wine glass, called the party to order. Prior to this the oak-panelled Parker Room in Corpus Christi College had been awash with chatter, as those who had been on the trip to Vis told those who had not all about it at length and with enthusiasm. In fact, this had been pretty much the case throughout the month since the return from Croatia, and those who were unfortunate enough not to have gone had probably heard enough about it already. Now, on the occasion of the St Radegund's first end-of-season cricket dinner, they were going to hear about it again. Too bad.

Under the stern gaze of King Edward IV and other luminaries immortalised in the portraits that hung on the walls around them, the captain gave a brief account of the highs and lows of the season just gone, and made reference to a number of individual and team performances that stuck in the memory, usually for all the wrong reasons. He then handed over to The Yorkshire Sipper, "for a report on the St Radegund's first overseas tour, to Croatia".

The Sipper rose to a smattering of applause and, reading from notes, began an amusing five-minute recap of the events, cricketing and otherwise, that had taken place on that remote island in the Adriatic. There was the ferry from Ancona with the Dire Straits music and Larry's incarceration in the lavatory on the way to Vis, the Veras at Lambik and the debacle that was dinner at the Villa Kaliopa. All those from the trip, apart from El

Bow, El Vis, Larry and Moe, were there, and the Champion of the Thames pub was, at least, represented by Curly. They smiled or nodded in recognition as The Sipper recollected the dinner at Roki's, the trip to the Blue Cave on Biševo, and the abortive attempt to climb Vis' highest peak.

Crabbo Junior's perfected impression of Eyebrows drew particular praise, and The Sipper invited him to repeat it for the assembled diners. Crabbo Junior made a modest apology that he could not possibly attempt to do such a thing in mixed company, all the while precisely in the style of Eyebrows, complete with flailing hand gesticulations, requisite facial tics and vocal inflections, and in the approving presence of the old man himself. The place fell about. Then, just for good measure, The Sipper made reference to Beard's own execrable attempts at Eyebrows mimicry at the Pojoda on the first afternoon. Rather than allow him to share the limelight, The Sipper instead invited Highball to offer his own interpretation of the Beard's lack of skill in the gentle art of impressionism.

Highball rose from the table, cleared his throat and pulled on his shirt cuffs. He produced a sound from his larynx like an old washing machine grinding its bearings to powder, and moved his hands palms up in a circular motion like a window cleaner doing double-duty with a chamois. The place fell about again.

Highball, however, wasn't getting away lightly. The Sipper turned to the subject of the cricket match, and recounted the various exploits of the day. Highball's thoroughly undeserved three wickets for 0 runs was mentioned, in good humour, as having ruined what would have otherwise been a much closer match. Boos and hisses from the diners. Worse, continued The Sipper, Highball had been guilty of overbearing hubris when he declared at the end of the match, that he would "sleep the sleep of a champion". The place laughed and groaned in equal measure at this outrageous claim. Highball vociferously protested The Sipper's version of what happened, but had genuinely forgotten saying the offending phrase. No matter, the damage was done and, as The Sipper is often wont to say with a wink and a smile, why let truth get in the way of a good story?

There was, however, one story missing from The Sipper's account, one final tale of travelling disaster that, had he been able to call upon it, would have made a worthy addition to the litany of cack-handedness. It proved, once and for all, if doubts remained, that the whole expedition was cursed from the outset in some way. This involved David King, El Vis. His son,

Nick, recounted the bare bones of it over a bottle of college port and later, after the Parker Room was vacated, back at the St Radegund, with David himself fleshing it out when he visited the pub in the spring of the following year.

David had come up to see Nick, then approaching the end of his final year at Jesus, for the weekend and decided to drop into the St Radegund for a quick pint at lunchtime. Bunter, reading his newspaper behind the bar, looked up from the sports pages and greeted his erstwhile travelling companion in a friendly manner. The guest book was brought out for David to sign, and they sat at the bar together over a pint and caught up with things. Then David told Bunter about his return trip.

The Kings' departure from Vis had not started well. Nick had failed to set the alarm in time for them to catch the early-morning catamaran to Split, so they had to settle for the car ferry departing just after noon. From Split they took a coach to the capital, Zagreb, 250 miles north, arriving late in the evening, and checked into a hotel before sallying forth for a look around the city. It was near midnight, little was open, and there were few people around.

Out of the corner of their eyes they caught a glimpse of an illuminated sign bearing the silhouette of a familiar figure, none other than Sir Winston Churchill. The establishment styled itself the Churchill cigar coffee club. To David this was a godsend as his main regret while on Vis had been the non-availability of a decent cigar. As they sat in luxurious comfort in deep-sided armchairs drinking excellent coffee and smoking a satisfying cigar each, they thought they had indeed reached a state of bliss. This was about as good as it was going to get for quite a while.

The next morning father and son were to go their separate ways, Nick on via Salzburg to Munich where he was to meet up with The Ferrets, a Cambridge University drinking society, at the Bierfest, and David on to Klagenfurt and the flight home. David made a point of revisiting the Churchill in order to stock up with sustenance for the journey home and beyond. The helpful staff put loose cigars into special Churchill-branded packets produced for the club, which was, apparently, one of a chain of such establishments, though David had never seen them before. From there they went on to Zagreb's Central Station to catch their respective trains. Then, as the moment of parting neared, the nightmare began to unfold.

Nick had been looking after the pair's cash ably enough throughout the trip but all David had with him was a card he had only ever used to withdraw cash in the United Kingdom, and his credit card. He had never used the latter to withdraw cash and so had no idea of the pin number. David's itinerary required an overnight stay in Klagenfurt so he would have to dip into the euros Nick had changed in Trieste on the way out. David had urged his son to dig the money out of his bag back in the hotel, three-quarters of an hour before David's train was due, but Nick insisted – with slight irritation in his voice – that he had the money safe. As they waited on the platform at the station, Nick made another search of his bag for the currency but couldn't find the banknotes anywhere. They both searched and re-searched the bag with increasing desperation but to no avail, so Nick went into the ticket office to pay for David's ticket with kuna. Time was tight. David waited on board his train and was relieved to see Nick running from the ticket office clutching David's ticket, which he thrust into his father's grateful hands through the open window scant seconds before the train pulled out of the station. That, thought David, was too close a call.

As he settled into his seat he considered his predicament, and hoped that the banks would be open at Villach where he had to change trains. In the meantime he was able to enjoy the views of the Croatian countryside from a compartment that boasted separate air-conditioning for each of the eight comfortable seats, as well as ashtrays, unheard of now in Britain. He puffed contentedly on a cigar.

At Ljubljana a group of English football fans boarded the train and began to inflict their boorish behaviour on their fellow passengers. They ran up and down the corridors, shouting obscenities, opened compartment doors loudly, sat down with their cans of beer and put their feet on the seats opposite. David tried to ignore them by looking out of the window or talking in German to the people sharing his compartment, hoping the fans would think he was not English and simultaneously praying they weren't in the mood to take their pent-up aggression out on a German. It all made for a decidedly uneasy journey.

David alighted at Villach to find, predictably enough, that the banks were shut. Settling on board his connecting train he now had to contemplate arriving in Klagenfurt with no cash. His first idea had been to stay in a hostel but he couldn't really imagine that one would be happy to take a credit card, so a hotel it would have to be. Then there was the question of how to get to the airport the morning after. Could he set off early and walk there? Perhaps, but he remembered that it was some way out of town down the autobahn, and he was reluctant to rely on hitch-hiking. As he considered his rather diminished options, salvation appeared. From elsewhere in the carriage he overheard people speaking English. They were a young couple sitting some distance away. There was nothing for it, he thought, but to beg. It was clear from their conversation that the couple were also getting off at Klagenfurt, so David positioned himself behind them as they left the train and opened proceedings with an exceedingly ill-chosen comment:

"Hi, you're English, I think?" They bridled immediately, and the response was stern.

"No, we're Scottish," said the young man with a scowl.

Good start, thought David. Oh well, in for a penny, and he embarked on a rambling explanation of his plight ending with a lame "so if you could just spare me a few euros, just enough to pay for the bus to the airport tomorrow, I'd be exceedingly grateful".

The young man looked at him with the same sort of suspicion on his face that David's would have worn had the situations been reversed. Fortunately his partner was made of softer stuff and started to open her purse, even shushing her companion as he protested. She pressed a single euro coin into David's hand and moved off. One euro? This was not going to get him very far at all, and as the couple walked away, he ventured his thanks and wondered aloud whether the money would – did they think? – be enough for the bus. The young man tried to hurry his partner along, but she'd obviously taken pity on the hapless older gentleman and she led him gently to the bus stop outside the railway station, pointed out the times of the buses, read out the cost of the fare and then gave him another three euros. David expressed to her his sincere gratitude, and they went their separate ways.

He had at least acquired the fare to the airport. The next step was to find somewhere to eat and sleep. It was now about six in the evening but Klagenfurt was bound to be a quiet place in September and he expected no problem finding a room in a small hotel. Two hours later he had visited over a dozen places, and in each the answer was the same: all rooms were taken. Eventually David discovered the reason. Volkswagen were unveiling their newest model and had chosen no less a location than Klagenfurt itself for the launch.

Foot-weary, and with his twisted ankle giving him considerable discomfort, he slogged on with no success. He found a small park with a fountain, which dealt immediately with his thirst, and there was a bench conveniently near which he earmarked for the night should all else fail. By now he seemed to be going round in circles, but then stumbled upon a small place tucked away up a side street that he had yet to try. Once again it was full. As he turned away to leave, the phone rang and the receptionist ran after him into the street.

"There is a room!" she shouted. "Hotel Geyer, but you must hurry!" Hurry he did, albeit with a lumbering, limping trot. It turned out that the Hotel Geyer's owner was a friend of the receptionist and was ringing up to lament the fact that she'd just had a cancellation and that it was now too late to expect the room to be taken. The hotel had no restaurant, but the owner made David a ham sandwich. There was a small bar as well, and, most important, it did take credit cards. He had been spared the bench in the park. God had finally decided to smile upon him.

Bunter listened to David's story with amusement.

"Apart from that, Mrs Lincoln, how did you enjoy the play?" he asked.

Very much. He had wanted to spend to some time with his son, to see a country he had not seen before and have a break after several years without a holiday. To be a part – if only the drinking part – of a cricket outfit again after such a long time was a bonus, but to actually play in the tour match was way beyond his expectations. And more, the company, the hospitality, the drinking, the food, the cricket, the sights, everything had been first class. He thanked Bunter again for the St Radegund tour shirt he'd been presented with and which he said he would treasure.

"That's all right. You played in the match, so you earned it," Bunter said matter-of-factly, stubbing out his Rothmans. Then, looking down at the bar, he fixed his eyes on David's nearly-finished pint.

"Something similar?" he asked. "Come on, brush the flies off it."

Epilogue
The Pitch

Rob, Tom and Oliver – supervised by a junior member of the team – get to work on the new pitch.

Little by little, the dream of a permanent cricket pitch next to the former Second World War airfield, among the vineyards of the Rokis' farmhouse at Plisko Polje, in the high central plain of Vis, became a reality. With the outstanding questions of land ownership settled once and for all, the field of rich, red earth began to be cleared of rocks, old vines and long-established roots. During the winter it was turned, and flattened. A hundred foot-long trench was dug in the centre of the field. It would form the base of the concrete under-structure of the batting wicket. Once it had been filled with rubble, smoothed out to create an even surface and overlain with steel mesh, concrete was mixed and spread on top. As the members of Kriket Klub Sir William Hoste waited for their brand new artificial batting strip to clear customs in Zagreb, they went to work making the area around the pitch as flat as possible before grass seeding it in the late winter, when rainfall – already scarce on the island – was at its highest. In time, with the batting strip in place and the grass around it coming along nicely, they decided they were ready to play.

Contact between the St Radegund and the cricketers on Vis had been sporadic in the intervening time. Memories of the trip lingered long as the tour's misdeeds were reported ad nauseam and grew in stature in the retelling. The whole madcap folly was given one last rousing send-off in the pages of *Witless*, where it was commemorated with ten pages of photos, match coverage and intermittently amusing articles on the tour's shenanigans.

The section, which occupied the centre of the magazine's sixty pages, commenced with a parody of the traditional cover of *Wisden* renamed – what else? – *Visden*. Here Bunter exercised his proprietary right and took responsibility for laying out the whole ten pages. On the first two he wrote a scene-setting article describing the background to the trip in his trademark style: "Who would have thought a read through a travel guide would lead to the St Radegund playing a game of cricket on the Croatian island of Vis two years later? In the chapter of the book about Vis there was a brief and obscure mention of cricket being played there during the Napoleonic Wars and an island wine grower with a dream to revive it."[i]

The rest of his article mentioned the original feature in *Playboy* and the various routes the party had taken to arrive on Vis, and sat above a reproduction of Crabbo Junior's sketch of the town, made when he had climbed up to Fort George. Opposite was a spread of photographs of the group at the Villa Pojoda, The Sipper wearing the fines helmet on the ferry to Vis, the *Lady Ruth* at anchor in the harbour, and various members of the party with Antonio Lipanović in his wine caves.

The next two pages covered the match at Samogor. Lipanović's batting was described as "recalling the heyday of Jessop". There really was no point in trying to correct him now, the name had stuck. Apart from an aside at the expense of people from the Indian sub-continent, and taking El Bow to task for bowling out Stanko ("In some past life did he teach the IRA how to lob hand grenades?"), he gave a fair account of the game, heaping praise on the likes of Marko Poduje and, reporting the St Radegund's efforts with becoming detachment, concluded that "there were no winners or losers in this much enjoyed and unusual game." That really depends on your point of view, the scorebook either endorsing or undermining this sentiment completely. Below his piece were, respectively, a photograph of the game in full flight at Samogor, and a few small advertisements for Lipanović's wine business and the Villa Kaliopa.

The following two pages were the centrefold of the magazine, and were devoted entirely to pictures of the game at Samogor: the trophy presentation, the *spomenik* and the ground, and one taken during the match itself, in the centre of the two pages, in which JD loops a delivery to Lipanović.

The next pages featured Tom Pocock's article, which was a generous gesture on his part and much appreciated. It was accompanied by advertisements for the Pojoda restaurant, and for Konoba Roki's whose picture featured a youthful Oliver next to his mother, Valerie. On the same page was a piece of verse written by Sir William Hoste's father, the Rev Dixon Hoste, and taken from Tom Pocock's book:

Swift glides the vessel o'er the sporting main,
Proud of her freight, exulting in her Fame;
And well she might – for noble Hoste she bore,
Those deeds outrival those in days of yore;
Amphion is her name – From Lissa's strand
She longs to gain once more her native land...[ii]

The final pages of the *Visden* section, above a small advertisement for Bar Bejbi, took the form of Bunter's diary notes, cobbled into an impressionistic story of the social aspects of the tour, most of which need no repeating here.

Bunter had found the whole experience inspirational, and his enjoyment of the trip shone through. He hoped that the Vis section would, in giving the reader (as he put it in his introduction) "a flavour of what others missed", inspire others around Cambridge and beyond to pay a visit to the island's shores. It was a small thank you to the islanders for their hospitality and a modest contribution to helping their cricket team flourish. It was the least he could do.

Bunter dutifully sent a number of copies of *Witless* to Oliver Roki to distribute to members of the club. Unfortunately a printing error caused a number of typographical characters to drop out of the final version of the magazine, including most of the Croatian accents that Highball had painstakingly included. Bunter inked them in on a copy himself before sending it to Oliver. He also wrote to the Royal Navy's cricket team to suggest that they might be interested in going to Vis to play a game of cricket in the next few years, mindful as he was of the (not too far off) bicentenary of Hoste's defeat of the French.

The only other contact Bunter had with the island was when a Croatian journalist rang him in the spring of the following year wanting to ask a few questions for a follow-up article on the Hoste team he was writing for Croatia's *Playboy* magazine. Bunter detected Oliver Roki's hand behind this, and gladly supplied some quotable copy. He was certain, he said, that cricket on Vis would be a success because the Croatian people seemed "natural sportsmen". He was also complimentary about the enthusiasm for the game he had witnessed in the players from Vis. When the magazine finally printed the article – a handsome, full-colour piece featuring high-quality photographs of Stanko and Oliver (not naked, but in their Sir William Hoste polo shirts) – Bunter's contribution, boxed on the third page of three, sat below quite possibly one of the least flattering photographs of him ever seen. It had clearly been taken after a few beers while the party was on Vis. Hair dishevelled, brow beaded with sweat, eyes wide and glassy, Bunter was clearly one or two Karlovačko beers the worse for wear. Next to the other more artfully posed shots that accompanied the piece it looked amateurish.

"I wonder what odds I could have got on Bunter appearing in Playboy," The Sipper commented when he saw it.

Oddly enough, it was Curly from the Champ, whose somatic episodes (now diagnosed as a form of sleep apnoea) on Vis had aroused so much interest, who was the first to go back. The year after the trip he returned to the Adriatic on holiday and called in to Vis to say hello to Oliver and the boys. In the main, though, he was staying at a friend's place on the island of Hvar, and while there he somehow wound up on the judging panel of the Miss Universe beauty contest. This he enjoyed immensely although, he ruefully admitted, he hadn't managed to sleep with any of the finalists.

Of the other St Radegund tourists, El Bow left the *Lady Ruth* to winter in Rogoznica, west of Split, for a year. The following August he sailed south through the Dalmatian islands and down the coast, arriving in Dubrovnik in early September. There he met up with The Sipper, who had caught the sailing bug while on board *Lady Ruth* at Vis, and had agreed to crew the boat back as far as Gibraltar. The original plan had been that The Sipper would work doubly hard to finish his PhD before leaving for Dalmatia, and enjoy a recuperative cruise on the way back with El Bow. The plan worked perfectly apart from the part about the PhD, which remained in Cambridge, still unfinished, its legend by now having grown to near-mythological proportions.

The voyage to Gibraltar took a month, a far more leisurely excursion than JD and El Bow's dash across the Mediterranean to make the game on Vis. *Lady Ruth* called in at Menorca, and it was here, in Mahón, that El Bow and The Sipper met JD and Frannie, who were just about to take their boat, *Carinata*, over to Alghero on Sardinia. The four shared a meal together as El Bow told them of his plans to sail across the Atlantic to the Caribbean the winter of the following year. This he did, with JD and Frannie as crew. The *Lady Ruth* currently resides in Bequia in the Grenadines, where El Bow plays cricket more or less every weekend in a team made up of expats and locals.

The St Radegund team, meanwhile, continued to ply its modest cricketing trade. In time Crabbo Junior served his stint as captain, some thirteen years after he had made his debut in the very first Rad versus Champ match. Under his leadership the St Radegund played ten games, with Crabbo Junior emerging as the victorious skipper on only three occasions, which was about par for the course. His transformation into a leg spinner by now complete, he was even able to hold respectable rankings in the averages for the season in both the bowling and batting tables. Another notable feature of his captaincy was the spawning of an occasional St Radegund Ladies' cricket team made up of various spouses and partners of the men's team, including Frannie, the Memsahib and Jugs, the last of whom also continued to be the St Radegund's official match scorer.

Witless Cricketers' Almanack flourished under the direction of Bunter and Highball and, having had its production values and size upped in the years since it was first published, found its reputation spreading far beyond Cambridge.

During a trip to India with his wife, to watch England's third Test match in Mumbai, Beard fell into conversation with MA Atherton of Cambridge University, Lancashire and England, over expensive gin and tonics in the England team's hotel and promised him a copy of *Witless*. During the following day's play at Wankhede Stadium, Beard presented himself at the press box, and was just wondering how to begin to blag his way in when Atherton himself came down the steps towards him. A copy of the previous year's magazine was handed over, and Beard retired triumphantly to his seat in the stands. Later in the game Beard watched the press box through field glasses and saw none other than DI Gower of Leicestershire and England intently reading his copy, shoulders heaving with laughter. This was quite an endorsement, and there are even rumours that the magazine is read, and tolerated at least, by members of the board of *Wisden* itself.

That same year also saw Beard awarded the captaincy of the St Radegund Cricket Team, and the 15th annual King Street Trophy match. In a thrilling contest which went down to the last ball, the St Radegund contrived to turn a near win into a near defeat only to salvage a tie – the first in history of the contest – from the final ball of the game. The occasion was also the more poignant for assembling some of the original players from the very first match, and so Bunter, Eyebrows, Crabbo Junior and his father Crabbo, Moe and Ted Bates mugged for the camera on the steps of the newly refurbished pavilion at The Close, much as they had done fourteen years earlier.

That September a couple of St Radegund newlyweds, both of whom were occasional players for the cricket team, spent their honeymoon in Dalmatia, taking in Korčula, Brač and, on Bunter's and others' recommendation, Vis. They went armed with contact names and numbers for their trip to Vis and enjoyed themselves so much that they stayed there a whole week. They met Oliver and other members of the team, and brought back the news that Kriket Klub Sir William Hoste were keen for the St Radegund to go back and play them again. This was welcome news to some, though Bunter was, if not sceptical, then cautious. His response was all too predictable:

"Never put your foot in the same puddle twice." The only reason he could see for making a return to the island would be if the Hoste team had a pitch – a proper pitch – to play on. This had been Bunter's hope the first time the team had travelled to Vis but they still went with no finished pitch to play on. The question demanded to be asked: if there was still no pitch to play on, would the Rad go?

To mark the beginning of his 15th year in business at the St Radegund and, coincidentally, his fast-approaching seventieth birthday, Bunter embarked on a two-month trip around the world, travelling first to the United States, then to New Zealand, Australia and Bali where he looked up old friends before heading home. As a farewell tour, it worked disastrously and succeeded in only increasing his wanderlust. So late that same year, Bunter indulged a long-standing interest in visiting Eastern Europe, and made a trip to Poland and, shortly after, the Ukraine. As far as a return to Croatia was concerned, anything now seemed possible. Highball decided to investigate further and rang the President of Kriket Klub Sir William Hoste.

"*Molim?*" answered Oliver over a crackling mobile line. Highball reintroduced himself. Oliver was excited.

"We're coming over."

"The Radegund?"

"No, just the two of us."

"When are you going to bring the Radegund over again?"

"We can talk about that when we get there," Highball said. Oliver told him that a mere fifteen days before their conversation, a cricket team representing the Royal Navy had arrived on Vis, and Hoste had beaten them! Highball congratulated Oliver on Hoste's first win against foreign opposition, and arranged to call him when he arrived on the island.

On Midsummer's Day, the Highballs arrived on Vis to find temperatures in the nineties. The couple had left Cambridge to some of the heaviest rainfall in years, and a host of washed-out cricket fixtures, in the hope of good weather in the Adriatic, but the temperature on Vis was still a shock. In the evening at Plisko Polje they sat down at a table with Oliver by the family farmhouse and caught up with things over a bottle of Volijok.

Since that first trip to Vis, Kriket Klub Sir William Hoste had gone through inevitable growing pains. While the core of the team – Stanko, Antonio Nad, Antonio Lipanović, Siniša, Lenko and the others – were still playing, some of the others had moved on, including young Marko Poduje of the audacious Marko Polo Shot fame. In spite of a good deal of publicity for the team, including a spot on BBC Radio 4, the anticipated flood of teams from England had not yet materialised. A team from HMS *Montrose*, whom Oliver had mentioned over the phone, had become only the third foreign team to play cricket on the island since the game was revived, and although Hoste scored a rare win against the tars, the lack of visiting teams was something of a concern for Oliver and the rest of the boys, and keeping the interest up was proving to be a struggle. The bread and butter of their cricket had been the Croatian League, of which Rob Dumančić had been the prime instigator. As well as Vis, the league now boasted teams from Zagreb, Split and, more recently, Ivanić Grad, a town east of the capital. There was even a nascent side in Komiža on the other side of the island.

Within the time that it takes to drink one bottle of Roki's Volijok, Highball had been co-opted into travelling with the Hoste team to a cricket tournament in Zagreb at the weekend, leaving the Memsahib to a weekend of cricket widowhood, swimming and sketching. So it was that at 5.30 in the morning on the Saturday, Highball sat at a table in Bejbi with Rob Dumančić as they shared the traditional cricketer's breakfast of a cough, a coffee and a cigarette. As the other members of the team turned up at the ferry dock to board the catamaran to Split, Rob made introductions and re-introductions. From the original Hoste team, there was Oliver and Siniša, Antonio Nad, Lenko Marinković and the unmistakable figure of Antonio Lipanović. Among the new faces was an Englishman or, rather, a Yorkshireman. This was Tom Howard, who had recently moved to the island from Liverpool after hearing a broadcast of the Radio 4 programme *From Our Own Correspondent*, specifically a segment narrated by BBC News correspondent Alex Kirby.

"You might not suppose," it began, "a small island in the central Adriatic would have had much to do with Britain. I didn't, and I kept finding out how wrong I was."[iii] Kirby went on to describe the topography of the island and its historical British connections, before turning to Kriket Klub Sir William Hoste's revival of cricket on the island: "The club's rebirth is the work of a Croat, Oliver Roki: he learnt to love the game from his father, who lived in Australia. It has been going two years, and has 20 adults and 50 younger members."

The broadcast went on to describe Oliver's pride in having scored "the first duck on Vis in 200 years". "But there have been visits," it continued, "by teams from France and a pub in Cambridge." In time the islanders, Kirby continued, were hoping for a game "with their Ionian neighbours on Corfu, where cricket is a much older tradition". In conclusion he talked about the potential influx of incomers to the island, and mentioned a British couple who had recently bought a house there, "unfazed that the sale was taking place late at night and they had yet to see the property in daylight".

Acting on a hunch, Tom arrived on the island, fell in love with it instantly and bought an apartment. He had been there more than two years and was quickly learning the Croatian language, a gesture appreciated by his new neighbours. Tom was now Hoste's first-choice wicket-keeper.

After a very quick and comfortable passage to Split, the Hoste team was soon on board an air-conditioned van heading out of Split and on the motorway to Zagreb. The tournament Hoste were to play in, the Hrvatski Kriket Kup, happened to take place on a holiday weekend. The Friday had been National Anti-Fascist Resistance Day and the coming Monday was Statehood Day. The volume of traffic was heavy and cars from as far afield as the Czech Republic and Slovakia, Germany, Austria and the Netherlands all jostled for position in the lanes. At several points along the route, the road cut through the imposing hillsides, and here the lanes narrowed from three to one, and the traffic began to queue to enter the tunnels. The tailbacks were immense and the van started to get seriously behind time, considering the team had a match to play against Zagreb at three o'clock in the afternoon.

To pass the time, Highball asked Rob about the Croatian cricket setup. In the August following the St Radegund's visit, Croatia's national cricket team took part in the European Cricket Council's representative tournament in Ljubljana. Five games in five days, against teams from Bulgaria, Finland, Luxembourg, Slovenia, Switzerland, seemed a gruelling prospect but the reward for success was significant: promotion to the

European championship division three and a chance to take part in the
ECC Trophy competition the following year. Croatia won all five of their
matches, and Siniša and Antonio Lipanović, who were both called up to
the national team, took their first international wickets along the way.
Amazing, for players who had barely played the game twelve months
before.

The following year saw the inaugural season of the Croatian Cricket
League. One of the qualifications for continued funding from the
European Cricket Council was the instigation of a national development
programme whose aim, Rob said, was to set up various clubs across the
country and train indigenous players. A significant part of the programme
was to concentrate resources among the existing four teams in Zagreb, Vis,
Split and Ivanić Grad, with each club expected to construct a permanent
ground and develop its own youth team. It all sounded very impressive
and very structured.

What about the Hoste team? How had things been coming along
there? Rob handed Hoste's scorebook to Highball. The fixture against the
St Radegund had been Hoste's last of its debut season. The following year
they had played two fixtures, five weeks apart, both against Zagreb, and
both lost. The year after, they had managed another match against the
capital side, and three (all of which Hoste won) against their neighbours
and local rivals in Split. Then, disaster. No games at all the following year.
This was when a few people found an excuse to leave the club. With no
matches, those remaining concentrated their energies on coaching the
youngsters of the island to fulfil their part of the development plan.
Happily, things had picked up for Hoste in the current year. Their first
match had been the win against HMS *Montrose* in April, and between
then and June they had managed two matches against Split and one against
Zagreb.

Eventually the van arrived in Zagreb or, rather, at a sports facility on
the outskirts of the modern part of town. The journey had taken close to
six hours, so as soon as the van parked up, it was a question of getting out
and getting on with the game. Not exactly the best possible preparation.

There was another new face at the ground. This was Ben Heywood, a
Brit in his early thirties who, with his wife, had recently purchased a three-
storey apartment behind the Hotel Tamaris in Vis town. Ben was in Zagreb
to write a piece on the Hrvatski Kriket Kup for *Spin*, a recently-founded

glossy cricketing magazine. Ben had also been responsible for an email to *The Guardian* website during that April's Cricket World Cup match between Ireland and Australia. It had asked, simply enough: "Would any of your multitude of readers be interested in bringing their pub or village team over to a Croatian island in the middle of the Adriatic for a game of cricket? The William Hoste Cricket Club on Vis is looking for sides of sufficiently amateur ability to give them a game this summer. So far VCC [Vis Cricket Club] has been spanked by a Royal Navy Representative XI, a pub from Cambridge and a band of travelling Aussies who bowled them out for 15 [Saumur Strays?]. They're desperate to have a game against – ahem – more modest opposition and thus record a rare win. Does anyone think their outfit could fit this generous bill? Vis is a gorgeous place for some cricket with a holiday squeezed in…"

The email produced more than twenty offers from English cricket teams to come and tour Vis. Ben had also been working on a website for the Hoste team, one feature of which was information for prospective touring teams. Rob's ultimate idea, Ben said, was to offer a number of fixed itineraries to fit the needs of visiting teams, whether they were coming for just the weekend or staying for the full week. As well as a game of cricket, these would include wine tasting, trips to the Blue Cave and local beaches and supper at the Rokis'. To Highball it sounded as though some real thought and effort was going into things, and if it seemed a world away from the cheerfully amateur set-up of the St Radegund's first visit then this was, all in all, no bad thing. It was encouraging.

Hoste's game against Zagreb, by contrast, wasn't. Asked to bat for thirty overs, the islanders were all out for 47 in a shade over 24. Zagreb, a team with its fair share of Australo-Croatians and a couple of Indians thrown in for good measure, scored 48 without loss in reply. It was an easy victory. Even Antonio Lipanović, usually so reliable, was out of sorts and later confided that he was going through a spell of particularly wretched form with the bat. Only Rob Dumančić managed any degree of fluency, scoring ten with the tail against a bowling attack that didn't want for accuracy and would probably have given the St Radegund team a damned good hiding.

In order to leave enough time for the journey back to Split to make the evening catamaran to Vis, Sunday's game was scheduled to start at nine in the morning. There was bad news for Hoste at the ground: Siniša had hurt his back the day before and was unable to bowl or field, and another of the team's number had dropped out of the Sunday game, so Rob asked Ben and Highball if they would step in to field. They jumped at the chance to help out.

The first time Hoste had played their mainland neighbours from Split they had put on a commendable score of 78, a competitive total Oliver had thought would be enough to give their novice neighbours a chance. Lipanović had chipped in with three wickets and the visitors were dismissed for a score of 30. The match in the Hrvatski Kriket Kup promised to be a different affair, the winning of which depended largely on the form of one Ivan Bilić, a massive Australo-Croatian and very accomplished cricketer who, along with his brother, was a regular in the Croatian national side.

Siniša's enforced absence had also left a hole in the bowling attack, so Ben and Highball shared his allocation between them, trying, increasingly desperately, for a breakthrough against Bilić's big hitting. Out of Split's total of 161, Ivan contributed 96 runs, including several fours Highball gifted to him by bowling full tosses. The pick of Hoste's bowling was Antonio Nad with three for 31 from six overs, including the prized wicket of Bilić. Lenko was not far behind with a very tidy two for 14, but all the other bowlers chipped in with wickets here and there, Highball excepted.

Chasing a total of 161 was going to require composure, but Hoste's reply was troubled from the outset. As had been the case with the game the day before, it was a degree of impetuousness that was the team's undoing. Siniša was run out for seven after failing to ground his bat, which he subsequently used to vent his frustrations on his batting helmet. Tom and Lipanović were out cheaply, and though Oliver Roki managed to score ten he soon skyed a chance that was pocketed comfortably. With half the overs gone and the score barely past 30 Highball entered the fray, and after Lenko had the misfortune to hit his wicket trying to turn a legside ball around the corner he was joined at the crease by Ben. For the scorer's benefit (or was it to disguise the fact that the two Brits were ringers?) Oliver had Croatised their names into "Stipe" and "Branko", and made a great play of shouting their new monikers encouragingly from the sidelines.

The Brits started briskly, running as many byes as possible to get the scoring rate up to somewhere it should be. With the sun blazing down, Highball soon realised that he would rather not spend the entire morning running around, so the first long hop he received he tried to pull through mid-wicket, where he was dropped. This forced him to re-evaluate his tactics. No more silly stuff, just work the bad balls and occupy the crease. Ben's approach was the opposite. He decided to cut loose from the off and hit Hoste's first fours and six of the innings. As Highball nudged and nurdled, Ben filled his boots and between them they pushed the score into respectability until Ben was bowled on 25. Highball fell shortly afterwards, after the redoubtable Bilić was brought on to end any thoughts Hoste might have had of getting within sight of Split's total. This the Australo-Croatian did with aplomb, removing first Highball caught behind off the glove from a lifter on that bouncy, just-short-of-a-length spot on the strip, and then Rob for a duck, caught at first slip, again off a glove. The innings subsided to what was (in its context) a fairly respectable 84 all out, but before the team could rue a disappointing couple of games it was time to board the van for the trip back to Split, leaving that city's cricketing representatives to contest the final against Zagreb on the Monday. This match Zagreb won comfortably.

The following afternoon, back on Vis, members of the team met by the Tamaris for an impromptu photo shoot with the under-13 side. Ben had decided that a good angle for his *Spin* piece would be Vis' development plan, but he needed photographs of a specific quality of resolution for the magazine, so asked if Highball would be prepared to come and take some shots. How could he refuse?

Highball snapped away as Ben and Rob staged photographs with the youngsters in the back streets of Vis town, before moving round to Prirovo where the under-13s conducted a short practice session. It soon became clear that there were some promising junior cricketers in their ranks. Rob was particularly proud of the fact that he progress made with the under-13s on Vis was way in advance of anything achieved by any of the other cricketing centres in the country, and it was a hope that the island would soon be able to host the European Cricket Council's under-13 tournament. Given Vis' pre-eminence, Rob expected the younger members of the Hoste team to form the backbone of Croatia's team. The question was, where would they play?

On their last night on Vis, the Memsahib and Highball went for dinner at Konoba Roki's. Oliver showed them a part of the old wartime airfield that he and Rob had started to turn into a cricket pitch. A permanent place to play was needed: the helipad at Samogor was not a practical long-term option and Hoste's portable artificial pitch was showing signs of wear and tear. As Highball looked at a field of freshly-turned red earth, he realised he had seen something similar in one of Bunter's photographs from his first visit there years before. Was this, Highball asked Oliver, the same spot he had showed Bunter? It was indeed.

Highball returned to Cambridge, and began to sow the idea of a return to Vis through the pages of that year's *Witless*. Bunter was even more enthusiastic than he had been the first time round, having come to believe that the long-cherished dream of a cricket pitch at the Rokis' was finally taking shape. Where Bunter's original *Witless* article had extolled the virtues of Vis as a location, Highball now sold the tour on the notion of renewing friendships: "It would be good to re-forge links with a special bunch of people whose hospitality and generosity – both material and spiritual – still staggers. Those things we had in common: an interest in cricket, a bond of friendship, and shared memories of a tour that is still talked of fondly on the island, seem to have grown stronger in our absence."[iv]

This time there was no difficulty in getting a team together, and some who had been on the original trip – JD and Frannie, Jugs, Crabbo Junior and Beard – were keen to go back. On a warm Friday afternoon in early May 2008, the St Radegund cricket team – older, but not necessarily wiser – gathered again under the bamboo thatch of Bejbi to meet Oliver, Rob and Tom, and started the serious business of acclimatisation training in preparation for the next day's game on the new pitch at Plisko Polje. In practice this amounted to little more than the side reacquainting itself with the world of Karlovačko beer.

In true St Radegund fashion, the team from Cambridge was not the first overseas opposition to grace the brand new pitch at Plisko Polje. That particular distinction went to the home team of one of the St Radegund's more recent players, who turned up en masse in April only to find the weather dominated by heavy showers, and themselves lucky to even get a game in. Whichever member of Kriket Klub Sir William Hoste had been given the task of praying for rain to help the new grass on the outfield had clearly made far too successful an appeal to the great umpire in the sky.

Another recent addition to the Hoste team appeared in Bejbi to meet the opposition. This was Craig Wear, another expat Yorkshireman who, with his wife, had started an activity holiday business based at their home in Rukavac on the south coast of the island. Here they offered chalet-style accommodation and a week's worth of activities from walking and cycling to sea kayaking. They had actually been on the island back when the St Radegund had first played there, and though Craig had been aware of the existence of Kriket Klub Sir William Hoste it had taken him a while to work out who to contact.

In the eight months that he had been playing cricket on Vis, he had established himself as one of the Hoste team's best players, particularly with the bat with which he was – until very recently – averaging over 100. This intelligence was enough to have the master strategists of the St Radegund working on ways to ensure Craig was in no fit state to play cricket the following day. It didn't work. Craig wasn't much of a drinker and well knew his limit.

He was, though, good company and had been involved in the preparation of the new pitch at Plisko Polje, the main work on which was done over four days in late February, when he, Rob, Tom and Oliver – none of them actually born in Croatia, and none of them with any experience of the job in hand – set to work digging the trench in the middle of the new pitch. At first there was a lot of standing around discussing what to do, and when the time came for the actual groundbreaking, the Rokis gave Craig an ancient English shovel that broke after less than five minutes' use.

The trench they dug was a hundred by eight feet and six inches deep. After two hours of hard work, during a well-earned beer break, Niko Roki appeared and cheerfully told the workers they had not dug deep enough. It was back to work, and by lunchtime Niko was ready for a second inspection. This time, he told them, they had dug far too deep. Eventually, after a lot of graft, they had dug out and re-filled the trench a couple of times. Fortunately, the farmhouse lunch provided by Niko and Valerie more than compensated for the effort. The afternoon's work was, predictably, not very productive.

The next day's job was that of filling in the trench with rubble. Craig and Tom were all for collecting every stone that had been turned up after ploughing the outfield. Rob, as site foreman, was having nothing to do with this. It was left to club president Oliver Roki to find a solution.

The main road between Plisko Poje and Podstražje was at that time being resurfaced, so Oliver went to ask the road crew if they would be happy to help. In exchange for a couple of bottles of Roki's wine they allowed Oliver to tow a trailer full of as much stone as they needed up to the pitch. The trailer was towed by tractor, not the fastest form of transport. It was calculated that filling in using the tractor-trailer method would take aeons. On the third day a solution was found. More wine was offered to the road crew and a dump truck promptly appeared on the pitch and emptied its load of rubble into the trench.

After all this, the concreting of the trench was pretty straightforward, particularly as the original four workers were joined by other members of the Hoste team. The work completed, the team celebrated with a large meal at the farmhouse. The principle of payment in kind came into its own again when the road crew returned to steamroller flat the outfield, and the island's de-land-mining team, equipped with high-powered hedge trimmers, removed a huge area of bushes at one end of the field in double quick time.

The day after their arrival, the members of the St Radegund got to witness the fruits of Craig's and the rest of the Hoste team's hard labour. The pitch at Plisko Polje was a thing of wonder. The outfield was even and well-grassed, save for a few patchy areas that would doubtless grow in time. The artificial batting strip, built on solid foundations, seemed to play true, with little in the way of uneven bounce.

There was no toss. Rob, captain of the home side, merely invited the visitors to bat first. As JD and Crabbo Junior strode out to open the St Radegund innings the other players, partners and a large group of local spectators – among them Goran Pečarević, Toni Luksić and Neo Poduje – sat in chairs under the welcome shade of a mulberry tree on the boundary. A couple of crates of Karlovačko were to hand, and Valerie had promised a Vis-style cricket tea at the change of innings. Later the two teams were to sit down and eat dinner together in the shaded courtyard of the farmhouse

Bunter, now 71 years old, turned towards Niko Roki and lit up a Rothmans.

"Well, Niko. Who would have thought six years ago we'd be sitting here today in your vineyards watching a game of cricket?"

"I said it would take time. What do you think?"

"I'm impressed. Everything you said you'd do, you've done. It's amazing."

"Well, there's still work to be done." Niko smiled. "There's always work to be done." Bunter took a drag on his cigarette and looked up at the game, where Crabbo Junior was preparing to face Siniša's first ball. The sun shone fiercely. Cars sounded their horns as they passed along the road that ran through Plisko Polje, high above the pitch. Bunter didn't think it likely he would ever come back to Vis again, so was happy just to savour the setting among the vineyards and in the shadow of the marker poles of the former airfield. He contemplated all that had been achieved.

"It's a miracle," he said.

NOTES:

i   'A Dalmatian Odyssey', in *Witless Cricketers' Almanack*, 3rd edition, 2003. St Radegund Public House, Cambridge
ii   Pocock, Tom. *Remember Nelson – The Life of Captain Sir William Hoste*, p. 179
iii   Kirby, Alex. 'King Willow's Adriatic Conquest', *From Our Own Correspondent*, BBC Radio 4, 25 May 2004
iv   'Dalmatia Revisited', in *Witless Cricketers' Almanack*, 7th edition, 2007-8. St Radegund Public House, Cambridge

Acknowledgments

This book's gestation was long and its completion longer, and suffered a number of false starts and dead ends. It is unlikely I could have finished it without the help of my fine travelling companions at the St Radegund and Champion of the Thames pubs in Cambridge. They generously provided valuable insights and reminiscences over a number of late nights as we mulled over a bottle or two. I therefore thank them – Ron Taylor, Jon Dawson, Frances Jones, Chris Metcalfe, Richard Naisby, Caroline Saywell, Lawrence Dixon, Pete Twitchett and Mike Wilson – even as I blow their cover. Although I may have broken one of the golden rules of touring in the writing of this book, namely "what goes on tour stays on tour," nothing I have included should be taken in other than a friendly and light-hearted way.

A number of the tourists, including some who have moved on from Cambridge, gave me access to diaries, logs, and accounts of their time on Vis. The book would have been considerably poorer without them, so I am indebted to Oliver Crabb, David and Nick King, John Whitney and, last but not least, Terry Kavanagh. Among the islanders of Vis, I am particularly grateful to Oliver Roki, Antonio Lipanović, Rob Dumančić, Tom Howard and Craig Wear.

David King read an early draft and encouraged me to see it through, and Lisa Dawson checked the typescript as it entered its later stages. Polly Patullo, my editor, enabled me to focus on the essential elements of the story when I was in danger of getting carried away. My wife Liz bore my enthusiasms and frustrations with patience.

One of my intentions for the book was that it help put Vis on the map as a destination for British cricket teams. Ben Heywood and Siniša Vodopija run a website for Kriket Klub Sir William Hoste (http://www.vis-cricket.com) that should provide anyone interested in touring with all the information they need.